M000215583

Hindi Is Our Ground, English Is Our Sky

Figure 1. Students in line at Saraswati Puja with the goddess in the background.

Hindi Is Our Ground, English Is Our Sky

Education, Language, and Social Class in Contemporary India

Chaise LaDousa

berghahn
NEW YORK • OXFORD
www.berghahnbooks.com

Published in 2014 by

Berghahn Books

www.berghahnbooks.com

First paperback edition published in 2016

Library of Congress Cataloging-in-Publication Data

LaDousa, Chaise.
Hindi is our ground, English is our sky : education, language, and social class in contemporary India / Chaise LaDousa.
pages cm
Includes bibliographical references and index.
ISBN 978-1-78238-232-4 (hardback) — ISBN 978-1-78533-211-1 (paperback) — ISBN 978-1-78238-233-1 (ebook)
1. Education—Social aspects—India. 2. Language and education—India. 3. Language policy—India. 4. English language—Study and teaching—India. 5. Social classes—India. I. Title.
LC315.I4L33 2014
306.43'20954—dc23

2013022442

British Library Cataloguing in Publication Data

A catalogue record for this book is available from the British Library

ISBN: 978-1-78238-232-4 hardback
ISBN: 978-1-78533-211-1 paperback
ISBN: 978-1-78238-233-1 ebook

For Dickie

One advertisement had become especially well known in Shivpalganj. It showed a healthy farmer with a turban wrapped around his head, earrings and a quilted jacket, cutting a top crop of wheat with a sickle. A woman was standing behind him, very pleased with herself; she was laughing like an official from the Department of Agriculture.

Below and above the picture was written in Hindi and English—"Grow More Grain." Farmers with earrings and quilted jackets who were also scholars of English were expected to be won over by the English slogan, and those who were scholars of Hindi, by the Hindi version. And those who didn't know how to read either language could at least recognize the figures of the man and the laughing woman.

—Shrilal Shukla, *Raag Darbari*

Mala Srivastava's mother lived in a two-room flat above a tiny kindergarten institution that called itself Harward Public School.

—Amitava Kumar, *Home Products*

Contents

Illustrations

Figures

Tables

Foreword

As a teacher in an Indian university, my life has significantly changed over the recent years. Usually a third, but quite often half, of my teaching time goes into translating. I say something in either Hindi or English, then translate it into the other language. The wasteful chore involves reconciling myself to a relatively new social reality. Hindi and English form two intellectual orbits comprising my class; they cohabit, and casually overlap, but unmistakably signify two distinct sections of society. The students who represent these two sections have been socialized differently, in two types of schools. Their future trajectories differ as much as their pasts. It is not just the languages in which they comprehend what I say that differ; the examples capable of conveying my point must also differ.

Is it surprising that the apartheid I witness daily in my class has received no recognition in the growing body of India studies? Chaise LaDousa's work shows why scholars, even sociolinguists, avoid mapping the boundary that divides the worlds that Hindi and English cohabit separately. The reason is that the boundary is fluid. Surveying it implies measuring aspirations and constraints, recognizing ideologies and symbols that characterize a moving social panorama. This is what LaDousa has accomplished in this volume.

He has studied India's vertical language divide in the North Indian city of Varanasi. The study takes us well beyond the shibboleths proffered about India's linguistic plurality. The key word that enables LaDousa to enter the separate yet interwoven milieus of Varanasi is "medium." The term is so omnipresent in the Indian urban environment that no one marvels at the versatile service it renders to India's society and state. It resides securely in the phrase "medium of instruction" that is used across India as a public code to identify two types of schools and the opportunity markets to which they promise access. LaDousa helps us delve into "medium" as code by taking us along into school offices, classrooms, and homes, and by helping us decipher billboards that schools use to sell the experience they offer. He shows us how to listen to voices buried alive in personal and national histories. We learn how important cultural archeology is for making sense of education, both as a system and as an everyday experience.

The painstaking, thorough study presented in this volume comfortably straddles disciplinary boundaries. Judicious and imaginative selection of material and methods drawn from social anthropology and linguistics enables LaDousa to take us to the intersection of ideology, status, and education. We stay long enough at this intersection to get over the emotive illusion of the term "mother tongue." This is undoubtedly the loudest refrain used in the tomes of educational policy since India's independence from British colonial rule. As far as the state—both the nation-state and the state of Uttar Pradesh where Varanasi is situated—is concerned, Hindi is the "mother tongue" of the children growing up in the city. Beneath that official truth lies the world of Bhojpuri, the language affectionately spoken in Varanasi's homes but denied the status that Hindi has in educational policy and the public sphere. The chapter LaDousa devotes to the denial of Bhojpuri reminds us that the construction of Indian modernity involves, apart from an ineluctable engagement with the West, an unspoken negotiation with India's own vernacular core. It is a major academic achievement to capture and delineate these vast cultural consultations in a book that could equally well be described as a nuanced and insightful treatise on India's system—or rather, systems—of school education.

Krishna Kumar
University of Delhi

Preface

Schooling in most of the world entails an engagement with multiple languages. Histories of colonial situations of control, nationalist efforts toward self-representation, and transnational modes of exchange have become embedded in languages—especially as they find, or fail to find, institutional homes in school systems. Schools often represent the dividing line between inclusion and exclusion, standardization and its lack, and official recognition and relative illegitimacy. Often people struggle to have languages recognized for use in schools or struggle to have languages included in the curriculum. These efforts show that the school as institutional locus and language as emblem of inclusion have become means of imagining the nation and who belongs.

Yet, in postcolonial nations involved in an international situation of advanced capitalism, language dilemmas do not end with efforts aimed at the inclusion and exclusion of languages in schools. Official efforts of language engineering operate in the wake of colonial language policies and habits, and languages are tied up with changing communicative practices and contexts that operate in ways hardly corresponding to the logics of language engineering efforts. Furthermore, the uses of language meet people in their particular situations, and many people struggle and cope with the contradictions and discrepancies between what they hope to do with school, what they find there, and how what happens at school resonates or fails to resonate in the contexts of their lives.

In many nations' school systems, languages are not just options or possibilities in school. They also define schools. One might say that schools and languages are mutually constitutive: schools are places where languages gain a certain type of recognition, and languages are used to identify, talk about, and compare schools. When one type of school corresponds to a former colonial language that has gained a reputation for international communication and commerce, reflections on the educational pursuits of the self and others can become especially complicated—and often contradictory. The language that has come to represent the nation and for which one might have a great deal of reverence can exclude language varieties that one uses regularly. At the same time, the language that is so tied up in pride for the nation meets a grim fate as one progresses in the educational system. Another language presents possibilities in such higher educational pursuits; its salience has spurred on the proliferation of associated schools but has also fractured the promise of educational advancement.

The aim of this book is to illustrate some of the institutional and communicative structures that people in a small city in India struggled with as they engaged with schools and made sense of their school experiences. Especially important is that when people made sense of their school experiences, the intricacies of language difference were always relevant. Schools rested on and helped people to re-create language difference. In the same way, they entangled people in the contradictions of living in a postcolonial polity in which political-economic forces had offered a certain kind of education in a certain kind of language as an avenue for a livelihood marking something new. Indeed, language difference and inequality inform the very possibilities of schooling in a postcolonial polity, and people's use of school to make sense of their past, present, and future implicates those people in cultural production.

Acknowledgments

I have accrued many debts as I have written this book. Some of the people to whom I am most grateful cannot be mentioned herein because I promised them anonymity. Students, parents, teachers, principals, and other school employees gave much of their time accommodating me, and this book would not exist without their generosity and efforts. I will never forget the patience and kindness of the people with whom I have worked in Varanasi. I can mention three people by name because they have passed away: Beena Burman, Madhu Tandon, and Manorama Yadav.

In Varanasi the American Institute of Indian Studies and its Hindi language program was a wonderful resource in language instruction and during fieldwork. Special thanks go to Neelam Bohra, Raju Kumar, Rakesh Ranjan, and Achutya Nand Singh. During recent trips to Varanasi, I have found a warm home at NIRMAN. Priya Iyer, Nita Kumar, Irfana Majumdar, Nandini Majumdar, and Arshad Mirza deserve special thanks. In Delhi, Kolkata, and Varanasi, discussions with Ravinder Gargesh, Krishna Kumar, Ravi Kumar, Manabi Majumdar, and Chandrakala Padia have been most stimulating, and I was honored and thrilled when Krishna Kumar agreed to write the foreword to the book.

Susan Wadley has been a mentor and friend, and no amount of thanks would be enough. Her advice and support mean a great deal to me and she has served as a model of how to be with students. Ann Gold has had a profound influence on me as well. Her disposition to the world is one that I have come to treasure. Others responsible for the education I received include John Burdick, Deborah Pellow, and Robert Rubinstein. Tej Bhatia fostered a love for Hindi and its linguistic exploration. I am lucky to have friends like Alicia DeNicola, Eric Estes, Francesca Gaiba, Joanna Giansanti, Mai Lan Gustafsson, Kwame Harrison, Mark Hauser, Lisa Knight, Kalyani Menon, Haripriya Narasimhan, Keri Olsen, Kathleen Skoczen, and Ginger Weigand. My undergraduate advisor, McKim Marriott, fostered an abiding interest in anthropology. I am sorry that Thom Swift will not see the book. May rest bring peace for him.

Many colleagues have offered excellent advice and feedback. They include Asif Agha, Jim Collins, Sonia Das, Virginia Dominguez, Kira Hall, Jane Hill, Erika Hoffman-Dilloway, Nita Kumar, Sarah Lamb, and James Wilce. Charlotte Beck, Haeng-ja Chung, Nathan Goodale, Tom Jones, and Chris Vasantkumar have been wonderful colleagues in the Department of Anthropology at Hamilton College. Bonnie Urciuoli deserves special thanks as many insights in the book were born out of discussions with her. I am so fortunate to have Bonnie as a colleague and a friend. I am also grateful to Joyce Barry, John Bartle, Donald Carter, Steven Ellingson, Dennis Gilbert, Jenny Irons, Anne Lacsamana, Elizabeth Lee, and Heather Merrill for stimulating discussions. Patrick Hodgens traveled with me to Varanasi in 2007, and provided much conversation about many of the ideas herein. Students at Hamilton who read parts of the manuscript include Paige Cross, Trevor Howe, Madison Kircher, Grace Parker-Zielinski, Melissa Segura, Kara Vetrano, and Anna Zahm. Robin Vanderwall has been a source of support and a friend in many ways. I am also thankful to Abhishek Amar, Rakesh Ranjan, and Jishnu Shankar for help with some of the translations.

Initial field research was supported by the National Science Foundation and subsequent trips were supported by various grants from Southern Connecticut State University and Hamilton College.

Erol Balkan and Henry Rutz first suggested Berghahn Books as a publisher. Marion Berghahn provided initial advice and encouragement. Ann DeVita expertly guided the manuscript through submission and review. She is a gem. Adam Capitanio and Elizabeth Berg were also very helpful. Anna Skiba-Crafts made excellent suggestions, polishing the book's prose. Peter Demerath, Kathy Hall, and Kira Hall revealed that they reviewed the book. They provided detailed suggestions for tightening the book's arguments and I am grateful to all of them.

I would like to express my appreciation for Kim, Travis, Porter, and Ella; Edie and Grayson; Tom; Bob; Charlie and Marilin; and Mike, Ann, Maggie, Stephen, Cory, and Gus. Thanks to Michael for our daily adventures and for so much else, and thanks to my mother, Dickie, to whom this book is dedicated.

The book incorporates some material that has been published previously. I would like to thank the American Anthropological Association for the use of "The Discursive Malleability of an Identity: A Dialogic Approach to Language 'Medium' Schooling in North India," *Journal of Linguistic Anthropology* 16: 36–57 and "Disparate Markets: Language, Nation, and Education in North India," *American Ethnologist* 32: 460–478; Cambridge University Press for the use of "Advertising in the Periphery: Languages and Schools in a North Indian City," *Language in Society* 31: 213–242; Elsevier for the use of "On Mother and Other Tongues: Sociolinguistics, Schools, and Language Ideology in Northern India," *Language Sciences* 32: 602–614; and the George Washington University Institute for Ethnographic Research for "Of Nation and State: Language, School, and the Reproduction of Disparity in a Northern Indian City," *Anthropological Quarterly* 80: 925–959.

Abbreviations

CBSE	Central Board of Secondary Education
DPEP	District Primary Education Program
EGS	Education Guarantee Scheme
ICSE	Indian Council of School Education
JEE	Joint Entrance Examination
NCERT	National Council of Educational Research and Training
NEP	New Economic Policy
NFE	Non-formal Education
NGO	Non-governmental Organization
OBC	Other Backward Caste
RSKV	Rajkiya Sarvodaya Kanya Vidyalaya
RSS	Rashtriya Swayamsevak Sangh
SCT	Scheduled Castes and Tribes
SP	Superintendent of Police
VA	Volunteer Agency

Transliteration Conventions

The transliteration conventions used throughout the book appear below with their Devanagari and International Phonetic Alphabet (IPA) equivalents. At some points in the text, I transliterate apparently English lexical items with the system for Hindi and Urdu to indicate that the lexical item might not be recognized as English. I use Devanagari script when it is important to represent the way in which something was written and appears publicly.

roman	Dev	IPA	roman	Dev	IPA
Vowels					
a	अ	[ə]	ā	आ	[aː]
i	इ	[I]	ī	ई	[iː]
u	उ	[ʊ]	ū	ऊ	[uː]
e	ए	[eː]	ai	ऐ	[æː]
o	ओ	[oː]	au	औ	[ɔː]
nasalized with tilde			(with any above)		
ã	अँ	[ə̃]			
Consonants					
k	क	[k]	kh	ख	[k^{h}]
g	ग	[g]	gh	घ	[g^{h}]

c	च	[cʃ]	ch	छ	[cʃʰ]
j	ज	[ʤ]	jh	झ	[ʤʰ]
ṭ	ट	[ʈ]	ṭh	ठ	[ʈʰ]
ḍ	ड	[ɖ]	ḍh	ढ	[ɖʰ]
t	त	[t̪]	th	थ	[t̪ʰ]
d	द	[d̪]	dh	ध	[d̪ʰ]
p	प	[p]	ph	फ	[pʰ]
b	ब	[b]	bh	भ	[bʰ]
ṇ	ण	[ɳ]	n	न	[n]
m	म	[m]			
y	य	[j]	r	र	[r]
l	ल	[l]	v	व	[ʋ]
ś	श	[ʃ]	ṣ	ष	[ʂ]
s	स	[s]	h	ह	[ɦ]
ṛ	ड़	[ɽ]	ṛh	ढ़	[ɽʰ]
ḳ	क़	[q]	ḳh	ख़	[χ]
j	ज़	[z]	p̣h	फ़	[f]

Transcription Conventions

,	short pause (less than one second)
.	long pause (one second or more)
(2)	pause of indicated number of seconds
. . .	speech slowing, followed by a new start
....	speech with quickened tempo (underlined)
~~	carefully enunciated speech with slowed tempo (underlined)
?	indicates question (sometimes with rise in pitch and volume)
" "	quoted or modeled speech
[ ]	author's commentary

Introduction

I sat waiting on a humid October morning in the entranceway to a house in which I had recently become a paying guest. The year was 1996 and the place was Varanasi, a city in northern India. The clatter of the gate latch meant that it was time to go to school—and to work. Mr. Sahni, my former Hindi teacher, had offered to introduce me to the principal of his daughter's school, which was called Saraswati Balika Vidyalaya. Saraswati is the goddess of music, culture, and learning; Balika means young girl; and Vidyalaya means school. Children dressed in maroon and white ran past or smiled from the backs of passing rickshaws as Mr. Sahni, his daughter Puja, and I approached the school's front gates. The cheerful noise grew deafening. Once we stepped through the entranceway of the school, drawing a stiff salute from the guard, Puja ran to join the line-up for the morning assembly. Mr. Sahni led me down a covered walkway and away from the action. On seeing us, another guard drew back the curtain from the doorway at the end of the walkway and entered the room. He reappeared after a few seconds to offer *praṇām,* placing his hands together, and said in polite Hindi, "come" (*āie*).

The principal sat behind a massive desk. Mr. Sahni did not sit, but stood behind me, and mentioned that I would like to talk to her, students, and teachers during the year. She cracked a smile when I began to explain that I was interested in education in India and that I would like to visit her school. I knew that my nervous and halting Hindi prompted her expression. I had anticipated the need for proof of who I was, and offered to provide a copy of my affiliation with an Indian university and my registration papers from the Superintendent of Police (SP).[1] The principal said that there would be no need—that I could do my work, and that she would see to it that I would not misbehave in her school. She then said something that would help to set the stage for my project. She explained that it was good that I was to spend time at the school to learn Hindi because this is India's "national language" (*rāṣṭrabhāṣā*). "This is a Hindi-medium school" (*yaha skūl to hindī mīḍiam hai*), she said, adding in English, "This school, its medium is Hindi." But, she added, I should spend time at an English-medium school so that I would be comfortable in my "mother tongue" (*mātrabhāṣā*). She concluded with a surprise. She explained that her school was for girls in the ninth- and tenth-grade levels, and the intercollege levels eleventh and twelfth. She suggested that I visit the school upstairs too.

As we walked back down the hallway toward the staircase, Mr. Sahni explained that he had no connection with the principal upstairs and that I should be fine alone. I knew that he had to get to work and would not say so. I wandered toward the curtained room with the sign *adhyāpikā* (female principal). I knocked on the doorframe and heard "who is it?" (*kaun hai*). I showed my face and the principal, sitting behind a desk identical to the one downstairs, motioned for me to sit. She pressed a buzzer on her desk that brought a young man, and ordered two cups of tea. I introduced myself and asked whether I might visit the school over the next year. The principal talked for nearly half an hour about the school's mission to love children, to serve in this role in support of parents and goddess, and to instill discipline with love, not corporal punishment. In an abrupt shift, the principal then told me that I would need to bring a copy of my passport, visa, letter of permission from the Government of India, and registration with the SP. When I explained that I had already met with the principal downstairs, the principal concluded our meeting by explaining that it was good that I should come to her school too because the Hindi in lower grade levels would be better for me since Hindi is not my "mother tongue."

The next day, I made my own way to the gate of a school whose principal was the sister of a friend of mine from previous visits to Varanasi. On my way, I noted that the school announced itself with a giant sign painted on the side of the four-story building, "Seacrest School." Cars vied for space at the front gate in numbers rivaling rickshaws. The guard gave a salute and another man in uniform ran from the front of the school to greet me. He took me across the courtyard and sat me in a waiting area in front of the principal's office. Another man entered from an adjacent room, motioned for me to remain seated, and knocked on the principal's door. This time the principal began the conversation, in English, about her sister. Yet another man brought us two bottles of Pepsi and substantial snacks. The principal and I chatted about her sister for half an hour or so. Finally, she asked what she could do for me. I explained that I was interested in education in India and that I would like to visit her school. She responded with "no problem," and proceeded to anticipate my research practices, giving her consent to each in turn. She received several telephone calls and messages relayed by employees while we chatted, and I took yet another interruption as an excuse to go. As I prepared to say goodbye, she explained that I would be comfortable working in her school because English is my "mother tongue," but that in order to hear "the real Hindi," I should also visit a Hindi-medium school. "Hindi is our national language, *rāṣṭrabhāṣā* as we say."

Tea versus Pepsi, rickshaws versus cars, one assistant versus several, mother tongues versus national languages, Hindi- versus English-medium: I sensed that differences between the schools aligned across a set of domains even though I had little knowledge of the domains themselves. During the next year and shorter visits over the next ten, I would find that the issue of a school's language medium involves further distinctions. Whether a school teaches in Hindi or English resonated through conversations in Varanasi about what is native versus foreign, national versus international, government versus private, cheap versus expensive, mobile versus stationary, and rural versus urban. I came to learn that people's reflections on schools in India often entail reflections on languages, and reflections become meaningful and recognizable because, among types of schools, what is considered to be Hindi contrasts with what is considered to be English. Indeed, the contrast has become more significant for those who have grabbed so much media and scholarly attention in contemporary India: the new middle classes. This book considers the ways in which language-medium schooling in India has structured the emergence of social class distinctions amid political-economic shifts in the wake of India's New Economic Policy (NEP) of the early 1990s.

Many scholars have shown that nationalist activity often includes the engineering of a national language. Such activity often sets its sights on schools and other institutions as places where the national language will be used and through which it will be spread. A predicament in many nations is that the languages that have been engineered as these nations' own have not been the languages that figure in images of participation in economic relationships involving the largest capital transactions or the most distant places. One cannot, however, use a nation's success or failure to inculcate a language of international salience to understand that nation's educational system. In order to understand better the educational practices of people in most of the world, one must consider that languages of participation in a world beyond the nation or the local emerge as meaningful in multiple ways. Often, the same language will be tied up with types of people, institutions, and nations in different ways in a single community. In this account, what English is and why it matters depends to a great degree on what Hindi is and why it matters. The same can be said for types of schools: English-medium schooling draws its significance from Hindi-medium schooling, and vice versa. The self and images of the nation figure centrally in the differences between language-medium schools. Hindi-medium schooling, for example, can evoke pride or prompt derision.

Schooling in India is not just a matter of projecting different images of the self and nation. The picture that emerges depends on the speaker and her own educational history. Sometimes what attendance at a Hindi-medium school can mean depends on whether someone is involved in talk or in another activity, such as reading advertisements for schools around town or in the newspaper. People engage in practices and pursuits that are always already entangled in meanings and uses of languages, institutions, and places. The ways in which practices and pursuits emerge as meaningful in the world often provide evidence that both languages and institutions are useful in different ways and often are unequal. Institutions, the practices they entail, and the places with which they are associated can resonate closer to or further from the center of what is understood to constitute the nation. Language-medium schooling in India can be used to reveal that places are not simply locations within the nation, but are rather loci in which different possibilities of national belonging exist. The book considers the ways in which language-medium schooling provides organization to middle-class life in the city of Varanasi, but also considers the ways in which schooling reveals its unequal and often contradictory qualities. The central conundrum is that the notion of a national language resonates with the city of Varanasi and, in so doing, can relegate the city to the periphery.

The Political-Economic Context of Education in Contemporary India

This study emerges from a period of political-economic shift in India that has seen an increasingly complex relationship develop between schooling and social class. The changing policy of the central government has fueled the rise of what many pundits, journalists, and laypeople call India's new middle classes. It is difficult to pin down who belongs to the new middle classes and how the groups have come to exist. William Mazzarella, for example, argues that it is more fruitful to approach the middle class in India as an emerging discursive space oriented to concerns such as "Hindu nationalism, consumerist liberalization, and the pluralization/fragmentation of national politics" rather than as a group to be defined by a single criterion and then counted (2005: 1). Mazzarella is following Partha Chatterjee (1997) in noting that the middle class in India has never attained majority status, much less hegemony. What is certain is that a sea change in discourses of class in India has occurred; what is less certain is how to describe the importance of such changes in people's lives.

A sure sign of the complexity of class transitions in India is the fact that different scholars as well as indigenous and international media have pointed to different policy measures of the Government of India as origins. Among these measures are Prime Minister Indira Gandhi's 1973 Pay Commission, Prime Minister Rajiv Gandhi's 1986 efforts to loosen investment and licensing restrictions, and Prime Minister Narasimha Rao's 1991 moves toward liberalizing the economy and privatizing some areas of the government sector. Rajiv Gandhi, some have argued, turned toward consumption as a theme that would resonate with changes in economic policy during the 1980s: "If the tenets of Nehruvian development could be captured by symbols of dams and mass-based factories, the markers of Rajiv Gandhi's shifted to the possibility of commodities that would tap into the tastes and consumption practices of the urban middle classes" (Fernandes 2001: 152). With the middle classes in mind, Rajiv Gandhi's policies sought to dismantle some of the barriers to consumerism from the earlier era: "Rajiv Gandhi's vision substantially rested on the role of the middle classes. His vision was encapsulated in concrete economic policies that began to loosen up import regulations in order to allow an expansion of consumer goods (such as automobiles and washing machines), that could cater to middle- and upper-middle-class tastes; even his vision for village development included the slogan 'A computer for every village'" (Fernandes 2000a: 613).

Such policies initiated a departure from Nehruvian concerns with development focused on the poor: "During the late 1980s the government's economic policies promoted the growth of the private sector, industrialization geared to urban middle-class consumers, and the reduction of transfer payments from rich to poor organized by the state" (McKean 1996: 11). The promotion of consumerism and the withdrawal of the state from a redistributive role were general characteristics of Prime Minister Rajiv Gandhi's government. Prime Minister Narasimha Rao's government's acceptance of the International Monetary Fund loan in 1991 fixed such trajectories. A stipulation of the loan included the further dismantling of protectionist economic policies, internal licensing, and redistribution schemes.

The emerging middle classes were and are anything but homogenous, and the label links multiple, disparate groups in its modes of membership and display (K. Kumar 1998: 1394). The disparate quality of middle-class membership is often lost when the focus is on a particular employment niche. For example, call centers are the focus of much of the international news about new economic opportunities in India.[2] While some reports focus on the importance of English among the middle classes for such work, others foreground the declining fortunes in the country from which jobs are—ostensibly—being taken: "Images of middle class Indians working at computers now routinely flash on American television as the symbol of white-collar and service-sector job losses in the United States" (Fernandes 2006: xxvii). When reports of economic change in India do not focus on such new employment niches, however, they are largely celebratory. The current frenetic pace of growth contrasts with the economic situation of the four decades or so following independence. The earlier period is often described as an isolated slumber and the present as an awakening.[3] Yet, the new middle classes include people in a wide range of occupations and types of positions such as "urban professionals and managerial groups, commercial and entrepreneurial classes, white- and blue-collar employees as well as substantial rural landowners and farmers" (Chakravarty and Gooptu 2000: 91).

Education has increasingly involved the child in the family's struggle for class mobility, raising the stakes for performance in school, especially on exams. Purnima Mankekar notes such tension in the precarious position of those whose desires and aspirations have been fueled by liberalization: "All it would take is a layoff, a bad debt, or a failed examination on the part of one of their children, and many of them would slide right back into poverty" (1999: 9). Mankekar pays special attention to the double bind in which middle-class girls find themselves wherein education is oriented to the satisfaction of spouse and family.[4] Whereas the education of girls is increasingly seen as important, many people told Mankekar that a girl should be educated to provide a suitably interesting companion for her husband. In those cases in which a girl's education made work outside of the home possible, Mankekar notes the gendered dual burden of domestic and professional labor. I can confirm Mankekar's insights. While I did know a handful of girls whose families supported their pursuit of higher education, most girls were being educated to the tenth- or twelfth-grade level in order to be suitably married and to be able to run a well-ordered household via "home science" courses in which hygiene, food procurement and preparation, and the management of household funds are taught.

Though she does not focus on them, Fernandes argues that schools take their place among the profusion of consumerist practices characteristic of the new middle classes by virtue of being "diploma-granting institutions which provide skills and credentials" (2000b: 90). Nita Kumar underlines the importance of education to the discursive space of the new middle classes in Varanasi: "The community and class background of these children, as befits a 'mainstream' group, has not been discussed at any length. They are from a class that forms the 'backbone of the nation,' that wants liberal education and secure 'service' jobs for its sons, marriages into service families for its daughters and now maybe careers as well, if in proper establishments" (2001: 270). Kumar's invocation of "service" (*sarvis*) and its presumption of educational attainment provide an excellent illustration of the emergence of the discursive space of the new middle classes and the maneuverability it brings into focus. In the Nehruvian era, "service," more marked than the more encompassing "job" (*naukarī*), or the yet more encompassing "work" (*kām*), often denoted an employment niche in the government sector, the apex of which is a position in the Indian Administrative Service (IAS).[5] It is this sense of service that D.P. Pattanayak addresses when he writes that "developing third world languages" are "passports to governmental positions which control the economy" (1981: xvii). Entrance to the IAS is controlled by an exam that is administered by the central government and presupposes higher educational achievements in a standardized language, and employees are sent to their posts at the district level. Such posts, as well as lesser ones, are extremely desirable for their prestige, but also for their well-known perks and pensions.

In the post-Nehruvian era, however, "service" denotes a broader set of desirable jobs and the term is no longer used primarily to refer to a government post. A vignette illustrates the change. Sharma Dry Cleaners sits next to the small convenience store owned by the man who was my landlord during the first year of my field research. Mr. Sharma has three sons, from eldest to youngest, Raju, Ramesh, and Guddu. Raju opened a branch in Sigra, a neighborhood five kilometers away from his father's store, and Ramesh uses a motorcycle to run orders between the stores as well as from and to customers' homes. Guddu was already known as an especially gifted student at the fourth-grade level (in 1997).

During a visit in 2005, I asked Mr. Sharma whether Guddu would join his brothers in the family business. His reply was cryptic: "We are waiting" (*ham intazār kar rahe hãi*). Guddu approached and explained that he had been working extremely hard studying for his twelfth-level exams. I asked about what he planned to do after school. He replied that everything depended on his exam results. If he did well, he would apply for admission to Banaras Hindu University in order to study accounting. He had developed an interest in computers, he remarked, and gently teased that he had tried, without success, to convince his father to generate receipts and keep records electronically. His father used the word "service" in order to explain, "accounting is good work" (*akaunṭing kī sarvis acchā kām hai*), but, waving his receipt book overhead, said that he would never entrust his business to computers because the electrical power in Varanasi comes and goes. When I expressed confusion, asking, "service is a government matter, no?" (*sarvis sarkār kī bāt hai, na*), Mr. Sharma replied vehemently that he lacked the connections necessary to acquire such a job for his sons, and that reservations for disadvantaged groups had made the prospects for getting such a job that much more difficult. Guddu reassured me that were he not able to gain entrance to the university, he could always join his brothers in the family business. With a sweep of his hand over the shop's linoleum counter, he concluded, "this is good service too" (*yaha bhī achhī sarvis hai*). This vignette shows the ways in which education has become linked to new careers such as digital accounting, but also the ways in which such educational possibilities themselves rest on the class status of those people supporting the student.

Schooling, Language, and the Reproduction of Class

In social reproduction, "Up for grabs are what constitutes being skilled, what kinds of knowledge are permissible and useful, what work attitudes are acceptable, and by whose authority these are determined" (Katz 2004: x). The school is such an interesting site for the study of social reproduction because "School produces categories, assigns students to these categories, and directs their actions accordingly" (Doerr 2009: 1). The categories produced by school, in turn, exhibit "specific forms of difference and inequality" (Pollock and

Levinson 2011: 6). Some scholars have investigated individual educational institutions as sites for social and cultural reproduction because the school provides an arena in which differences in dress, talk, and other behaviors emerge in patterns to produce types of students. The behaviors of types of students, in turn, articulate with school policy in different and unequal ways. In classic cases, working-class Lads at Hammertown Boys enjoy "having a laff," rejecting what they see as the conformity of the middle-class Ear'oles (Willis 1977); Burnouts at Belten High School eschew the corporate logic of class rank and individual success of the Jocks (Eckert 1989); and working-class Vatos at North Town High attract white youth marginalized from the "most popular, attractive standard-bearers for the school" (Foley 2010: 84). In all of these cases, the school works to reproduce large-scale social class membership with symbolic elements not easily related to class formation.

In order to explain the relationship between symbolic structures and the formation of groups, scholars of education have often utilized Pierre Bourdieu's extension of the notion of capital from the economic to the social and symbolic. Bourdieu famously argued that education, like all human practice, involves the investment of time and body that requires and anticipates the transfer of the economic, in the form of wages and investments; the social, in the form of occupations, memberships, and contacts; and the symbolic, in the form of behaviors and dispositions betraying prestige and cultivation (1986).[6] Schools foreground intergenerational concerns in such investments and transfers: "Person, family, and class are mutually constituted through multiple capital conversions and the practices associated with them" (Rutz and Balkan 2009: 16). School entails an investment beyond the student, and the enormous resources expended on schools provide evidence that schools participate in the ways individuals, families, and governments anticipate the future and their place in it.

Bourdieu also points out that schools participate in the production of a special type of capital, educational capital. Educational capital is so valuable because it is underpinned by state sanction "with the academic qualification, a certificate of cultural competence which confers on its holder a conventional, constant, legally guaranteed value with respect to culture, social alchemy which has a relative autonomy vis-à-vis its bearer and even vis-à-vis the cultural capital he effectively possesses at a given moment in time" (1986: 248). In contemporary India, the production of educational capital is made especially complex by the selective participation of the state in schooling as well as by the ways in which educational bureaucracies become meaningful to people in moments of reflection. This study focuses on multiple schools because among the schools themselves there is the production of different forms of educational capital depending on whether a school is Hindi- or English-medium. The language in which classroom activity predominantly occurs, among other differences, produces different images of students, different dispositions toward further schooling, and different notions of the difficulties faced by students. Whereas many studies focus on students' dispositions in a single school, this one draws attention to multiple schools because they help to constitute one another as recognizable institutions.

Bourdieu's notion of educational capital focuses attention on the fact that the school system in India entails a distinction between those institutions able and unable to provide the "legally guaranteed value" of educational credentials. On the one hand, there are highly selective schools far from Varanasi, some nationally and even internationally known, that have, since the colonial period, fostered the cosmopolitanism of elites. Sanjay Srivastava writes that the Doon School located in Dehradun, several hundred kilometers from Varanasi, has cultivated its own sense of being modern through the notion that "'uncivilized' existence is *elsewhere*" (1998: 198). He describes the practices of the civilized at the school: "the 'secular' morning assembly, student interaction which emulates life in the contractual space of the metropolis which does not inquire after the caste of its citizens, and the constant effort to establish the 'scientific temper' as the defining ethic of the post-colonized nation state" (1998: 198). Founded in 1935, the Doon School has produced many members of India's "postcolonial intelligentsia—journalists, editors, novelists, social scientists, [and] cultural functionaries of the state" (S. Srivastava 2003: 1016). No school of national (much less international) stature exists in Varanasi. Furthermore, many residents of the city told me that a student who had attended schools in Varanasi for any length of time would have little chance of ever being admitted to the Doon School. While such claims might have been apocryphal, they give the correct impression that Varanasi's own residents do not feel like they have access to a local institution that could confer a cosmopolitan and elite status.

On the other hand, there are many schools in Varanasi that do not play a part in fantasies of class mobility. Nita Kumar (2001), for example, reflects on her conversations with students from the Muslim weaver community in Varanasi attending Jamia Hamidia Rizvia, a school organized around sectarian divisions in Islam.[7] Students there hold dear the craft of weaving, an ideology of freedom, and an identification with local neighborhoods. Left out of their pedagogy is the officially sanctioned history of the nation, a subject of school board–administered exams. Indeed, few schools with overt religious ties have managed to have their syllabus approved by a school board. A glaring exception is the "convent" school in Varanasi that holds a prominent role in the group of schools that can offer the "legally guaranteed value" of an education sanctioned by the state, and thus can provide a vehicle for fantasies of class advancement or reproduction.

Also excluded from pedagogy that enables students to compete for educational credentials are schools that belong to what was called for a time the non-formal education (NFE) sector.[8] The NFE sector was established in 1979–1980 by a mandate of the Education Commission of 1964–1966 to accommodate non-enrolled children in ten educationally backward states (including Uttar Pradesh, the state in which Varanasi is located). The National Policy on Education of 1986 revised the NFE sector to accommodate volunteer agencies (VAs) and non-governmental organizations (NGOs) in order to address the sector's limited successes (Ghosh 2004).[9] As part of the World Bank loan taken by Prime Minister Rao's government in 1991, the District Primary Education Program (DPEP) was launched in 1994 to address perceived failures of the NFE schemes, including a greater focus on the education of girls and members of Scheduled Castes and Tribes (SCTs) in rural areas deemed educationally backward. The nomenclature of the educational sector thus grew in complexity with the addition of alternative schools (ASs) and education guarantee schemes (EGSs) to address the needs of groups not well served by the NFE sector (Ramachandran 2004).

Article 21A, amended to the Constitution of India in 2002, declared that the state will provide free and compulsory education to those between six and fourteen years of age.[10] The Indian parliament passed the Right of Children to Free and Compulsory Education Act in 2009 and it took effect in 2010.[11] Appropriate governments will have to be in compliance by 2013 (De et al.: 2011). This should not imply that schooling in India is heading toward some sort of equality, however. Surabhi Chopra argues that "lower-tier private schools" will be negatively affected by new norms and penalties for violations (2011: 18). If a private school is not already affiliated with a board, the regulations of the act will present a new burden. During fieldwork in 2010, none of the three principals of the schools introduced at the beginning of the book expressed any concern about the act. They saw the act as affecting schools "at a lower standard" with students with poorer families or in rural places where private schools might be the only ones available.

Regardless of particular organizational affiliation, NGO and volunteer schools can be considered to comprise a group because they generally aim to reach the population excluded from board-certified educational institutions. Strategies include charging extremely low or no fees, allowing students to forego uniforms or wear relatively simple ones, providing materials, and accommodating students, sometimes adults, with flexible hours. During an interview conducted in August 2004, Krishna Kumar, longtime scholar of education and newly appointed director of the National Council of Educational Research and Training (NCERT), one of the Government of India's highest posts in secondary education, told me: "It's very difficult today to clearly distinguish philanthropic private activity in education from NGO activity. And purely commercial activity in education is also widely rampant. The situation is far more complex than one could have seen in the early eighties when the state was definitely the main player in education, certainly in school education, and even in higher education" (LaDousa 2007: 139–140). Today, the sponsorship of a school by an NGO can expose the school to the charge that entrepreneurial activity—and not education—is the primary reason for the school's existence.[12]

One NGO school in Varanasi in which I conducted some fieldwork considered itself a laudable alternative to board-certified schools as well as other schools run by NGOs for its incorporation of student creativity in the curriculum, flexible approaches to discipline, and involvement of parents in learning and communication with teachers. The principal told me that board certification would lend the school legitimacy and assuage fears of corruption. She explained that such a move would also resolve the school's enrollment problems connected to the fact that some parents remove their children from the school and place them in a board-certified institution in the years just preceding their board examinations. But, the principal explained, the prospect of the school becoming a "diploma factory" helped staff members to reconcile the school's administrative disadvantages. Accordingly, the school will remain under the purview of an NGO and will not seek board affiliation.

The remaining schools in Varanasi and across Hindi-speaking North India are affiliated with school boards. School boards provide curricular guidelines and administer examinations in which hundreds of thousands of students participate annually. Exams at the end of the tenth and twelfth levels partly determine one's future academic possibilities. Thus, boards play a key role in bestowing the academic qualifications that Bourdieu notes are key in the production of educational capital (1986).

School boards in India are massive organizations with thousands of affiliated schools (Guichard 2010: 43–44). In Varanasi, two boards were on people's lips: the Central Board of Secondary Education (CBSE) and the Uttar Pradesh Board (UP Board). People took the boards to be contrasting, not simply different. They understood the CBSE to be private and took for granted that a school affiliated with the CBSE charges fees. Most people with whom I worked knew that the CBSE was administered in Delhi, the national capital. There are school boards that are more prominent than the CBSE in other regions of India, and some schools in Varanasi are affiliated with them. One of the most prominent examples is the convent school that was founded by Christian missionaries. Whereas the school once represented one of the only avenues to an English-medium education in the city, now hundreds of schools offer it. Furthermore, several other English-medium schools have surpassed the size and cost of the convent school. People in Varanasi consider the CBSE to be the most prominent school board most likely because the largest private school in town has long been affiliated with it.

The UP Board is administered by officials of the state in which Varanasi and its district are located, Uttar Pradesh. A school's affiliation with the UP Board brings subsidies such that people describe such schools as relatively cheap or even free. People call UP Board–affiliated schools "government schools" (*gavaṛnment skūls* or *sarkārī skūls*) and understand them to be different from "private schools" (*prāyvaṭ skūls* or *fīs lenewāle skūls*).

Table 1. School types, class distinctions, language medium, and board affiliation.

Prestigious schools outside of Varanasi (English-medium)

- Doon School (Dehradun)
- Modern School (Delhi)
- Woodstock School (Mussoorie)

Schools in Varanasi whose board certification serves as a vehicle for class maintenance or mobility (Hindi- versus English-medium schools affiliated with the Uttar Pradesh Board, the Central Board of Secondary Education, and the Indian Certificate of Secondary Education)

- Saraswati School (Hindi-medium)
- Seacrest School (English-medium)

Schools in Varanasi unaffiliated with boards

- most Madrassas
- volunteer schools
- Non-formal Education (NFE) schools

Language plays a dual role in school distinctions. First, people assume that an expensive private school (often affiliated with the CBSE) is English-medium and assume that a government school (often affiliated with the UP Board) is Hindi-medium. "Medium" is a commonly used word in both Hindi (*mīḍiam*) and English that refers to a school's primary language of pedagogy. It is not always the case that private schools are English-medium or that government schools are Hindi-medium, but through a complexly arranged set of contrasts presented later in the book, people often refer to schools based on their language medium and understand the reference to be tied to a number of differences among students, their families, and teachers. In sum, by mentioning the medium of a school, Hindi or English, one is necessarily talking about a kind of school that produces educational value underpinned by the state's recognition of certain school boards and bureaucracies. That value, however, is highly unstable as it emerges in the particular reflections of particular people with particular histories of schooling.

Language also plays a part in school distinctions because it is only among board-certified schools that language-medium distinctions matter. Nationally and internationally known schools such as the Doon School—far from Varanasi—are assumed by all to be English medium. Local schools lacking board affiliation are not discussed as Hindi-medium or English-medium because any claim to be English-medium would ring false. A board affiliation allows a school to offer a seat at tenth- and twelfth-level examinations, and it is among such schools that language-medium distinctions matter. Thus, language plays a major role in schooling that does feature in practices underpinned by class differentiation and fueled by fantasies of class mobility. Indeed, the question of a school's language medium is tied up with the question of its board affiliation, and many other attributes too.

The notion of educational capital helps to explain how it is that people invest in the school system in a manner not predicted by their current attainment of economic or cultural capital. In other words, expensive schools do not preclude the attendance of those with class aspirations. Schools thus participate in the "inevitable incompleteness of the project of being middle-class" (Baviskar and Ray 2011: 19). Indeed, most of the people who can be considered to be in the new middle classes lack the luxury enjoyed by Guddu Sharma in the vignette above, a guaranteed job opening in the event of academic failure. I met many students whose families struggled to put their child or children through schools without the possibility of security in the face of failure. Indeed, they were aspiring to become part of the new middle classes.

The Multidimensional Significance of English in Indian Education

A number of ethnographic accounts share the awareness that education has become crucial for the understanding of class in liberalizing India, but focus largely on English. English resonates with many ideas about change in Indian society: "A combination of various forces—economic, political, intellectual and social—has propelled the craze for English, successfully marketed as the language of development, modernity, and scientific and technological advancement" (Rubdy 2008: 136). Leela Fernandes chronicles the rise of the new middle class in the city of Mumbai and the importance of the class in nationally distributed advertising images. An education in English has emerged as a defining feature of a new Indian middle class: "this group largely encompasses English-speaking urban white-collar segments of the middle class who are benefitting from new employment opportunities" (2006: xviii).

Fernandes is very careful to differentiate those people who were already fluent in English at the onset of liberalization from those people whose economic aspirations have led them to seek fluency in English since the onset of liberalization. Fluency was required for jobs in finance and in the upper echelons of the corporate world, and cities like Mumbai have become associated with the availability of such jobs to the exclusion of the hinterland. Others lump these gradations together and talk about the middle classes as a group emergent in the wake of liberalization. People who seek fluency, Fernandes explains, are served by a massive proliferation of English-medium schools and coaching centers, but good training is uneven. People often show evidence of lower-class origins by the ways in which they speak English and are denied access to the employment opportunities they seek. Schooling, particularly relatively expensive English-medium schooling, has become an increasingly attractive activity of consumption for people who aspire to join the new middle class, but there is no guarantee of success in the massive proliferation of schools.[13]

In their work on the consequences of neoliberal reform among Kolkata's middle class, Ruchira Ganguly-Scrase and Timothy Scrase point out that: "English has ... increased dramatically in popularity in India from the early 1980s. Apart from the class position of the speakers (largely upper and middle classes) and their consequent social and political influence, there was the continued proliferation of the teaching of English in various schools and colleges, and the mushrooming of spoken-English institutes and private English-medium schools (many of dubious quality) continued at a rapid pace, particularly in urban areas" (2009: 136–137). They concur with Fernandes that "English proficiency is a virtual prerequisite for those wishing to work in new 'smart' industries like call centre work and in the business process outsourcing (BPO) sectors" (Ganguly-Scrase and Scrase 2009: 149).

Working in Bijnor district, in the western part of Uttar Pradesh, the state in which Varanasi is located, Craig Jeffrey, Patricia Jeffery, and Roger Jeffery found that "The prominence of English-medium institutions reflects an increased desire for English proficiency among large sections of the urban and rural population" (2008: 46). While none of the people with whom the anthropologists worked had ready access to the employment possibilities typical of the new middle class in Mumbai or Kolkata, one caste group in particular, Jats, had begun to invest in secondary education, primarily for sons, to "diversify economic risk" from a sole reliance on agriculture (2008: 53). Jats living in rural areas were often able to draw on urban kin networks to have their sons educated in better or higher-level schools. The best education is English-medium, costly, and outside of Bijnor district: "in the early 1990s parents in the three richest Jat households had sent their sons to the regional educational center of Dehradun for prestigious English-medium education within private boarding schools" (2008: 55).

An important exception to the focus on English in work on education in India and its association with class mobility is Viniti Vaish's study of the Rajkiya Sarvodaya Kanya Vidyalaya (RSKV) or State Sarvodaya Girls' School of East Vinod Nagar in Delhi, the capital, run by the Delhi Administration. The students who attend the school are from families of modest means: "At best they [the parents] have jobs in government offices where they could be peons, clerks or security personnel" (2008: 4). Indeed, the Sarvodaya School scheme was initiated to "service some of the poorest in urban India and give them access to the linguistic capital of English, which, before the 1990s, was the fiefdom of the upper middle classes" (2008: 93). Vaish explains that "until 1999 the whole school was English medium, but the principal felt the children could not cope up with the English medium so she made one section Hindi medium for the weaker students" (2008: 3).

Vaish finds resonance between the English that students learn at school and the English that call center workers must use on the job, and describes the identity of call center workers as "a hybrid pastiche" (2008: 100). While the school does not provide the ability to use English in such a way that one could work in a call center, Vaish stresses the positive aspects of the employment possibilities that are initiated by the "'emergent competencies' provided by such schools"

(2008: 90). This book presents an argument that does not share Vaish's optimism about the intersection of languages, schools, and social class in India. Vaish's study focuses on a Sarvodaya School committed to bringing English to the disadvantaged. This book focuses on the way that Hindi and English provide a way of differentiating many types of schools in a city where call center work is not locally available. Vaish's optimism is aimed partly at countering an overly pessimistic view of globalization. That the mention of globalization indexes a concern with English should not come as a surprise. I found that people in Varanasi use the connection between English and the global to describe one kind of school and to contrast it with another associated with Hindi.

The focus on English in studies of schooling in contemporary India is understandable and even expected for two reasons. First, colonial education policies set English in a superior position to Hindi and other indigenous languages, and second, globalization has further enhanced English-medium schooling's part in strategies of class mobility. Many scholars have traced the unequal avenues to social and economic power that colonial dispositions toward languages helped to construct in India. Washbrook (1991) argues that the colonial encounter involved not only disparate languages, but also disparate ways of reckoning languages' relationships to the social world. British ideas about standards (whose artifacts are grammars and dictionaries) and language populations (whose artifact is the language census) were simply not amenable to indigenous notions about language, based as they were in ideas about substance, contextual variability, and relative plurilingualism. Plurilingualism, Washbrook argues, established South Asia in the eyes of the British as a "land of Babel brought to perpetual chaos by the sheer perversity of its natives" (1991: 187).

Trautmann (1997), however, charts a shift in British attitudes toward South Asian languages. The first period that Trautmann calls "Indomania" was characterized by keen British interest, if only in South Asian languages' ability to provide grist for hypotheses rooted in Biblical scholarship or the reinvigoration of British aesthetics. This period lasted from the conquest of Bengal after 1760 to the early years of the nineteenth century. "Indophobia" followed. The period was characterized by British denigration of indigenous languages and ideas, a consequence of a larger project to uplift the morality of natives by distancing them from their own lack of reason.

During the period Trautmann calls Indophobia, debates raged and shifted within the colonial regime about the place of English and indigenous languages in government institutions, including schools, as well as the appropriateness and potential effects of natives engaging with English literature.[14] Pitted against one another were the rationales of Christian moralists and utilitarians. Moralists claimed that "the study of English literature had merely succeeded in creating a class of Babus ... who were intellectually hollow and insufficiently equipped with the desirable amount of knowledge and culture" (Viswanathan 1989: 159). Utilitarians "found that the humanizing motive [of the moralists] was in fact an evasion of responsibility toward equipping the Indian with the knowledge required for making him useful to society" (Viswanathan 1989: 158). Viswanathan points out that moralists and utilitarians engaged in the critique of policy only insofar as the Indian was deemed insufficient in the mirror of the competing colonizing project. Out of these tangled debates emerged a new force in Indian society, an elite whose identity was partly constructed by the English language and whose access to the language was mediated by education.

There were many who advocated for and worked toward the provision of education in indigenous languages during the colonial period. Writing about colonial Bengal, Sengupta illustrates the great interest *bhadralok* or upper-caste people had in vernacular education: "The education of students in Bengali, in addition to English, would ensure that education would not merely be a form of 'Westernization' but rather a form of 'modernization.' The cultural anxiety over retaining one's own culture, however reconfigured, in the face of colonial culture was one that marked all colonial societies, and the Anglo-vernacular school provided the *bhadra* classes with one solution" (2011: 35). The crafting of school textbooks played a major part in the standardization of modern Hindi (Orsini 2002). These schools, however, did not generally attain the prestige of English-medium institutions, because English-medium institutions provided the gateway to higher education and employment. Writing about colonial Bengal, Sanjay Seth explains: "A middle school certificate usually meant education to a certain standard in the vernacular. However, it was reported, such learning was not valued, and it became progressively devalued once the acquisition of a government job of even lowly rank began to require more advanced qualifications, and hence education in English" (Seth 2007: 19). With higher-level education and with government employment came the necessity of schooling in English.

The two-tiered relationship between English- and Hindi-medium schools has been largely preserved in independent India: "The standard arguments in favour of English as the medium of instruction are: equality of education, poverty of the regional language and their inability to meet the demands of the role of a medium of instruction, paucity of books in the regional languages, the near-impossible task of large-scale translation, and the contact and mobility of scholars" (Verma 1994: 119). A direct link between competence in English and a middle-class disposition thus continued beyond India's independence. The link is embodied in the form of the private school (K. Kumar 1996: 61). In a state-of-the-art volume on the sociolinguistics of English in India, scholars include such comments as "English still continues to be the only sure key to good jobs and careers in the country today" (Nadkarni 1994: 131), and "In short, it [English] is regarded as an essential part of the 'middle class' baggage" (Khubchandani 1994: 78). Needless to say, by "baggage," Khubchandani means something like "luggage" and not something like the popular psychology–infused "issues." And, as Fernandes and Jeffrey, Jeffery, and Jeffery rightly report, English-medium schooling has taken an increasingly prominent place in people's class aspirations. It has enabled the already knowledgeable to make good use of the new possibilities of liberalization, and others to attempt to engage with English, largely through schooling. The prominence of English in discourse about social class in India is reflected in the 2005 National Curriculum Framework developed by the National Council of Educational Research and Training: "it is necessary to address the question of developing effective competence in a language [English] that is now an essential part of aspirations and access to opportunities of livelihood, knowledge and power" (NCERT 2005: 37, quoted in Advani 2009: 50).

Many of the same words were used in both Hindi-medium and English-medium schools as well as in official discourse emanating from the many bureaucratic organizations that oversee the curricula of Hindi-medium and English-medium schools. One of the most obvious ways in which contemporary education in India bears colonial traces emerges from the words used for common objects, practices, and ideas. Indeed, words such as "complex" (*kāmpleks*), "fees" (*fīs*), "tuition" (*ṭūiśan*), and "board" (*borḍ*) take their place in both English and Hindi and are thus "bivalent" in the parlance of Woolard (1999).[15] I heard and used such words in conversations that were conducted almost entirely in Hindi. Indeed, some people in Varanasi claimed that some of the terms are Hindi. Such words question "the naturalness of rigid boundaries between languages" (Woolard 1999: 23). Yet, in the relatively elite context of the most expensive English-medium schools, no word that would likely be identified as Hindi was used to refer to objects, practices, or ideas. While such terms as *kāgaj* (paper) and *kalam* (pen) were used in Hindi-medium schools, no such term was used in the more expensive English-medium schools. Terms that might be identified as English—but are often thought to be Hindi—are pervasive in reflections on schools of either medium in northern India, while terms that might be identified as Hindi—and are not thought to be English—are used in Hindi-medium schools and not in the most expensive English-medium schools. There is little doubt that this selective phenomenon points to the colonial origins of the institutional differentiation of language medium maintained in contemporary schooling (K. Kumar 1991b).

Globalization has enhanced the salience of English for its seeming omnipresence and the connection to distant others it might provide. This has taken on particular significance in India. Sometimes, English's association with the global has served certain politicians in India in their nationalist rhetoric of defense. Sometimes, specific groups such as Muslims or Christians are targeted as alien transgressors through an association with language: Muslims with Urdu and Christians with English. Most often it is Hindi that is invoked in opposition as a language that is national. Sanskrit often emerges as an ancient language of an essentially Hindu collective with Hindi as its contemporary manifestation.

Globalization, of course, is an idea that circulates beyond the borders of India. Yet, there are aspects of the concept that generally resemble its specific uses by right-wing Hindu-fundamentalist politicians. Globalization often entails bifurcation. On the one hand are those who argue with a "euphoric, utopian thrust" for the "complex connectivity and circulation of all global processes" (Jacquemet 2005: 258–259). On the other hand are those who engage in a "dystopic, neo- or post-Marxist, political economic critique" and tend to see global relations as "antagonistic and asymmetrical" (Jacquemet 2005: 259). While this book can be placed in the latter camp, it does not join the linguists who have seen in the processes of globalization "linguistic imperialism, endangered languages, language loss, and language death" (Jacquemet 2005: 260). There are several reasons for this. Hindi participates (even if often in a subordinate position) in the schooling system, and what gives English meaning in Varanasi depends on Hindi. In conversations with people about schooling, I found that talking about English medium always prompted talk about Hindi medium and vice versa. Hindi and English are relational and mutually constructive. This is true of the languages as well as the institutions that are identified by them.

Furthermore, while people's reflections on the division between Hindi and English mirrors euphoric and pessimistic visions of the effects of globalization in some respects, there are multiple realms of value through which Hindi- and English-medium schooling can emerge as meaningful. A move from one realm of value to another—from the local to the national, for example—can transform the relationship between the language mediums. Finally, the mode of communication matters a great deal in what relationships between Hindi and English emerge in different situations. When people are talking about Hindi- and English-medium schools, for example, the possibility exists that Hindi- and English-medium schools in Varanasi might be seen as valuable. Such is not true of advertising for schools in locally distributed newspapers.

In short, "people manage or fail to make sense across contexts; their linguistic and communicative resources are mobile or lack such semiotic mobility, and this is a problem not just of difference, but of inequality" (Blommaert 2010: 3). At times, manifestations of Hindi- and English-medium schooling do seem to divide the world or seem to rest on totalizing visions of it. I strive to show that such manifestations and visions are never actually total, but rather are partial, and beg for placement.

Language Ideology, Educational Institutions, and Language-Medium Schooling

A theoretical notion that has enabled me to appreciate the interplay of Hindi and English in concerns about schooling in North India is that of language ideology: "ideas with which participants [in discourse] frame their understandings of linguistic varieties and the differences among them, and map those understandings onto people, events, and activities" (Gal and Irvine 1995: 970).[16] When speakers are talking about languages, they often focus on people, events, and activities—and, I would add, institutions. Educational institutions are key sites for the production of language ideology: "A society's beliefs about language—as a symbol of nationalism, a marker of difference, or a tool of assimilation—are often reproduced and challenged through educational institutions" (Wortham 2003b: 2).

An aspect of discourse that is productive of language ideology is what Michael Silverstein (1992) has called "overt metapragmatic discourse." This refers to the practice of overtly describing the relationship between language phenomena and their contexts of use. Discourse that explicitly names or describes a language is important and deserves special attention because it so often includes commentary about its linguistic form, appropriate or inappropriate uses, characteristic or uncharacteristic users, and relationships to other languages (Mertz 1998). This book will represent such discourse because it provides clues as to what possibilities exist for tying institutions to each other and to social groups, often in complex relationships to different time periods brought into view in a conversation or interview. Indeed, people in Varanasi had much to say about Hindi- and English-medium schooling, and tracing the different versions can reveal much about how different people use schooling to comment on their worlds differently.

Institutions of whatever type, however, have largely been overlooked in studies of language ideology. One reason, Patrick Eisenlohr (2004) argues, is that scholars have tended to focus on overt discourse and ignore other sorts of semiotic relationships between participants, their linguistic production, and the non-referential aspects of what is happening. Eisenlohr argues that a sole focus on overt discourse within and about institutions risks the erasure of "less overt institutional and linguistic practices": "The conceptual tools and mechanisms of linguistic ideologies have become increasingly well understood, but an understanding of how such politically charged interpretive schemata are mapped onto people, events, and situations also needs to be grounded in an analysis of how institutional and everyday practices form a constitutive part of such ideologies" (2004: 63). Eisenlohr's insights are salient to the ethnographic account presented herein because I have derived some aspects of Hindi- and English-medium schools from overt descriptions that people offered in conversations and interviews (such as "It is good that one goes to a Hindi-medium school because Hindi is our national language").

Yet, such descriptions do not exhaust the ways in which the distinction between Hindi- and English-medium schools shape the ways in which people can reflect on it or use it to make social commentary. Some possibilities in discourse—through which institutions become meaningful—are more ready-made than others. The ways in which cost and board affiliation, for example, do not actually predict the language-medium status of a school, but rather lead one to assume it, demonstrates the need to consider statements made by interlocutors in ethnographic fieldwork, but always alongside a consideration of institutional practices that underpin such statements. Some speakers will meet such ready-made discursive constructions of institutions differently. Not everyone in Varanasi, for example, finds the distinction between Hindi- and English-medium schooling relevant, and this is true for different reasons. By tracing language ideology through institutional practices and their circulation in discourse, this book seeks to appreciate "the situated, partial, and interested character of conceptions and uses of language" (Errington 1999: 115).

A conversation that provided the title for the book serves as a good example. In 2007, I sat talking to two professors at Banaras Hindu University (BHU), the largest university in Varanasi. While BHU is a central university, and thus officially on par with India's elite institutions of higher education, its prestige has waned in the last few decades. One of the ways in which many people reflected on its status was to explain that many courses offered there that should be taught in English are taught predominantly in Hindi. One of the professors, Professor Mishra, had been teaching in Varanasi for approximately ten years. The other, Professor Tiwari, had come from another smaller university, but had been teaching for thirty years and was the senior professor present. I had been explaining the research I had done on previous visits when the following ensued:

> Professor Mishra: You can really go in deep to understand the emotion behind this language [Hindi]. You will find something common here, nationalism being attached to Hindi. You can go deep in that. Sometimes you can find that it is not sincere nationalism because there are people who do not know Hindi, but they will be more nationalistic than me, from Hindi. Sometimes you can find a national crisis, a cultural crisis, in those people. Because, of course, they need English too.
>
> Professor Tiwari: But then the fact is there, English is a language of convenience for us. Because through Hindi you'll become national, not international. We Indians can be disconnected from the world, but like any other country we have this English. But despite this, as far as Hindi is concerned, I must say that as Professor Mishra was saying, the language for India, it can never be English. This nation wants to see itself in Hindi, feel itself in Hindi. So, the children, they know the power of English because they want to excel in the market, want to excel in the business, but they feel in Hindi. English has come to stay. Education will need English, benefits of English. So our ground ... maybe ... we are standing on firm ground, but English is our sky. So, Hindi is our ground, English is our sky.[17]

I was so taken with the metaphor offered by Professor Tiwari because, when considered in the shadow of the conversation in which it emerged—much less in the shadow of the larger context of schooling in the region—the metaphor exhibits so many features of language ideology. The poetic metaphor uses fundamental and universal aspects of the world to describe the relationship between two languages. Professor Tiwari utilizes Professor Mishra's linking of Hindi with emotion, but transforms the possibility of political manipulation into a stable connection to the world. She also transforms Professor Mishra's notion of political manipulation into a marker of national rather than international boundaries.

Struck by Professor Tiwari's image, I listened to the recording. Professor Mishra never returns to the political uses of Hindi, and Professor Tiwari excuses herself just after the offer of her metaphor. After she leaves, however, Professor Tiwari explains that he had been schooled in Hindi-medium schools until reaching the university level, while Professor Tiwari had been schooled in both Hindi- and English-medium schools. I noticed that neither Professor Mishra's nor Professor Tiwari's initial commentary was about schools, and yet I found that talk about language had invoked talk about schooling after Professor Tiwari's departure. I am unable to offer an explanation of why Professor Mishra began to talk about schools after Professor Tiwari left because he never offers an explanation. But from the short interchange, I can attest to the intertwined nature of Hindi and English, the multiplicity of ways in which the division can resonate in the lives of conversations and people, and the relevance of schooling in reflections on the world, the nation, and the self.

Fieldwork Contexts

I carried out the research on which this book is based over several trips of varying length to different locations in northern India. Long-term and multi-sited research has allowed me to claim that discourse about language medium explored herein is lasting, particular to certain types of schools and their students and families, and of widespread salience. From October 1996 until October 1997 I conducted my first field research on schools in Varanasi, a city of approximately two million. The city is famous within and outside of India for its Hindu holy sites, including the Viswanathan Temple, cremation grounds, and ghats, or steps, leading from the Ganges River up to the city. Lawrence Cohen describes a much-stereotyped view of the city from the point of view of a boat in the Ganges: "The scene—river, ghats, lanes, boats, and bathers—is clichéd. It has come to stand in for the city as a whole in a variety of registers: religious, touristic, sanitary, scholarly" (1998: 9). Unless they are scholars, less familiar to outsiders is the geography of pleasure that many of the city's residents describe as unique to Varanasi. Nita Kumar (1988) recounts residents' descriptions of the

Ganges as a space of recreation, the bank across the river from the city as a space of relative freedom, and the lanes of the city as spaces of carefree movement.

The leisure and pleasure associated with the city as well as the region in which Varanasi is located, eastern Uttar Pradesh, have been largely left behind in the growth in India's IT sector, including the call service industry, that depends on a large supply of English speakers. Nevertheless, the city affords an array of occupations that—while not typical of that portion of the new middle class singled out by Leela Fernandes (2006) for its already-established abilities in English—does offer the ability to pay school fees, sometimes of considerable amounts. Millions of people on pilgrimage and other tourists visit Varanasi annually, drawn by its sacred practices and sites. Research in schools largely kept me out of the orbit of pilgrims, tourists, and the vast array of people whose living depends on them. Few parents of students attending the schools in which I worked were involved in Varanasi's religious world, whether riverside or elsewhere. Some were petty shopkeepers, such as my landlord, who explained that pilgrimage was good for business for the city, but that he saw little of it in his shop's residential location. A few owned restaurants or were involved in Varanasi's main markets of Godowlia and Chowk where silk, toys, and other items associated with the city are available for purchase. Certainly, none of the children found near the river conversing with tourists during the day were those of parents with whom I usually visited (Huberman 2005, 2012). Indeed, such children, themselves engaged in business, were those targeted by a number of volunteer schools unaffiliated with school boards.

Parents' occupations varied considerably, whether they were sending children to Hindi- or English-medium schools. Some were professors, some were secretarial and janitorial staff, and some were groundskeepers at Banaras Hindu University. Some were engineers and some were secretarial and janitorial staff at Varanasi's massive Diesel and Locomotive Works. A handful of parents were physicians, and a handful of parents were rickshawallas. The difference in income between different sets of parents of students in the same school could be much greater than the income difference between some parents with low-paying jobs and the parents of students at volunteer schools. Thus, middle-class status does not exclude attendance at Hindi-medium schools, just as English-medium schooling has become a salient part of preparations for class mobility.

Caste, of course, is as complex a social reality as class. The two do tend to work in tandem, but this is not always true, and the relationship between class and caste has shifted in the period of liberalization. Well known is that many high-caste rural Brahmins and urban Brahmin priests can be found at the lower end of the class spectrum. Varanasi is famous for the fact that Dalit—or untouchable—Doms have risen to some of the highest class levels of the city for their participation in the city's rituals and industry surrounding death (Parry 1994). New reservations mandated by the Right of Children to Free and Compulsory Education Act of 2009 require private schools to reserve 25 percent of their seats for the needy (Chopra 2011: 18). Such children usually come from Dalit and lower-caste backgrounds, but there are exceptions. Rumors have run rampant that such schools will not care to have such children as students and will encourage only those with high marks to stay. Residential segregation of Dalits often leads to the formation of a volunteer or NGO school for neighborhood children because the children's families cannot afford the tuition and other costs of board-certified schools, even those subsidized by the state. At the university level, students of lower castes have begun to want English literature that resonates with them, but this seems to be emergent within graduate programs (Mukherjee 2009: 37).

From the vantage point of precollege schooling, Varanasi resembles the cities around it, including Allahabad, Gorakhpur, and Patna. Although rural areas surrounding these cities are agriculturally less efficient, more densely populated, and generally more impoverished than rural areas to the west—toward the cities of Agra and Delhi, and further west toward the states of Haryana and Punjab (A. Gupta 1998; Wadley 1994)—the cities themselves offer a wide array of school options. In Varanasi, and in other cities in northern India, people place individual schools into many categories: central (administered by the national government from Delhi), convent (administered either currently or previously by Christian organizations), government (administered by the government of the particular state in which the school is located), private (administered by an individual, family, or organization that owns the school), madrassa (in which students learn the Koran and tenets of Islam), Montessori, and so on.[18]

Initially, I focused my research activities on the Saraswati and Seacrest Schools. A combination of my personal relationships and the schools' administrative affiliations made the three suitable choices. My landlady's two daughters, one in the ninth-grade level and the other at the eleventh-, attended what I have called the Saraswati School with Mr. Sahni's daughter. In a pattern observed in many families across North India, Mr. Sahni's son (younger than his sister) attended the more expensive Seacrest School (De et al. 2011). The girls' grade levels meant that they were attending the school on the ground floor of the building because the school upstairs served grades one through eight. I would later find out that the schools were distinct even though people called both Saraswati School. The downstairs school enrolled a student body of girls who comprised roughly half of both schools' enrollment of approximately 1,600 students. The upstairs school was coeducational. The principal of the primary and middle school upstairs had explained that hers is a private school that charges students' families fees and whose school board affiliation differentiates it from the one downstairs. The downstairs school maintains affiliation with the Uttar Pradesh Board, making it a government school. The upstairs school is affiliated with one of the many private, multistate boards in northern India, but not the CBSE, to which Vanarasi's most prestigious schools are affiliated. In the coming argument, fee structures and board affiliations will play a major role in differentiating schools in terms of language medium.

Most of the students attending the two schools that made up what people called the Saraswati School lived in New Colony, the neighborhood in which the schools were located and in which I resided. New Colony had been planned decades before as a government scheme to offer decent two-story housing at subsidized cost to government employees. In the 1950s and 1960s, many people living in the neighborhood sold their houses and plots to move elsewhere in the city. The new owners built spacious mansions along the main boulevard of New Colony such that only a handful of the scores of original houses are left. For a time, it seemed that New Colony would become one of Varanasi's posh neighborhoods. Several circumstances thwarted its realization as such, including an influx of lower-middle-class residents—among them the family with whom I lived—who built more modest houses in the lanes behind the colony's boulevard, the growth of a large slum area on the very edge of the neighborhood, and flooding in the boulevard with the onset of each monsoon. The student body of the schools reflected the lower-middle-class status of most of the neighborhood. Most of the students came from families wherein the breadwinner, usually the father, was employed as a merchant, a secretarial worker, or a low-level civil servant.

The third school in which I started fieldwork, early on, I call the Seacrest School. During our initial interviews, the principal stressed that Seacrest maintains strict standards by virtue of its affiliation with the Central Board of Secondary Education and that this affiliation with the CBSE justifies the school's extremely high fees. The school, located approximately two kilometers (about 1.2 miles) west of sleepy New Colony, lies just off one of southern Varanasi's most heavily trafficked intersections. Indeed, most of the students take rickshaws or are driven to school from locations all over southern Varanasi. Seacrest students' transportation habits generally reflect their superior social class positions as well as their more widely dispersed residential origins vis-à-vis students attending either section of the Saraswati School. But it is important to remember that there are exceptions. Some Seacrest students came from modest backgrounds, and tuition and other costs stretched family budgets to the breaking point. A handful of children of doctors, professors, and engineers attended Saraswati's private and government schools.

The Seacrest School has grown to become the largest private school in eastern Uttar Pradesh. When I was conducting initial fieldwork in 1996, the school had a total of nearly 10,000 students with approximately 2,000 enrolled at the branch near New Colony. By 2010, my most recent field research in Varanasi, the school had six new branches, two in nearby cities, with a total enrollment of over 20,000 students. Whereas Seacrest had become a Varanasi-wide institution by 1996, it was branching out to become an institution associated with the larger region of eastern Uttar Pradesh by 2010.

I began my first fieldwork at the beginning of October. Thus, from roughly October to March, and, again, from June to October, I was able to visit schools when they were in session. During the first two months of fieldwork, I spent each day from Monday through Friday in one of the three schools. I attended classes, audiotaped classroom interaction after my presence had become less awkward, talked to the principals and teachers after their breaks, and talked to students between classes and during recess. After school, I accompanied students on their daily treks to buy cheap snacks at a local stall or store where we could linger and talk about school, life circumstances, and ambitions. Weekends and the summer break provided me with opportunities to visit principals, teachers, and students' families outside of school. These breaks also provided opportunities for me to travel to Delhi to visit schools and talk to officials employed by or retired from educational boards, usually the CBSE.

After a couple of months, I spent two days a week visiting other schools in Varanasi, trips sometimes requiring a rickshaw ride to distant parts of the city. Thus, from this point until the end of my first year of fieldwork, I spent one day a week in each of the three original schools. These visits gave me further exposure to the wide array of pedagogical goals, bureaucratic affiliations, and socioeconomic backgrounds of students represented in Varanasi's schools. Among the schools I visited was St. Joseph's School, located on the western outskirts of the city. St. Joseph's is a coeducational private convent school affiliated, like Seacrest, with the CBSE. I also visited several schools affiliated, like the downstairs level of the Saraswati School, with the UP Board. These schools vary in grade levels as well as in gender inclusion. Some are for girls, some are for boys, and some are coeducational. I visited many schools without board affiliations. These included two madrassas, differentiated by Islamic sectarian distinctions, as well as a school run by the Rashtriya Swayamsevak Sangh (RSS), an organization with complex ties to political groups that have called for the realization of an essentially Hindu India (Basu 1996). These schools, not affiliated with a board, also included several voluntary schools, most of them located in or near slum areas, that try to accommodate extremely poor students by offering flexible hours, school supplies, and pedagogical techniques in keeping with the needs of those who attend, such as the provision of basic math and literacy instruction.

I spent ten weeks in 2004 at the University of Delhi talking to graduate students in linguistics and English about their ideas about Hindi and English and language-medium schooling. At night, I used insomnia as an excuse to play cards and chat with a chaukidar, or guard, of the guesthouse in which I was staying. He was from Bhabua, a town in Bihar quite close to Varanasi. He spoke from a lower class position than those people with whom I had worked in Varanasi, at the Saraswati and Seacrest Schools, and his notions about Hindi and English were significantly different from those of people engaged with board certified schools. Sending two children to a Hindi-medium government school was a barely affordable option given his income of approximately 1,000 rupees (Rs) a month (approximately $25.00 (U.S.)) in one of India's most expensive cities. He stated that English is important for contemporary life and that Hindi is the mother tongue and should be respected and cherished. The examples he offered of ways in which English is valuable, however, differed significantly from the explanations of the people with whom I had worked in Varanasi. The value attributed to English by the guard will be a theme of chapter 6 because it throws into relief the notion of English emergent from discourse on language-medium schools.

I was able to spend a total of twenty-two weeks in North India, predominantly Varanasi, during the two trips I took in 2007 and 2010. On both occasions, I was a guest of NIRMAN, a school founded by Som Majumdar in 1988 to offer people with a wide variety of class backgrounds an education that the school sees as missing from other schools in Varanasi. In short, the school seeks to include families in the space of the school's activities, to provide small classes, and to teach in a way in which the student is supposed to come to discipline her- or himself.[19] I spent most of my time outside of this atypical school visiting the schools in which I had worked previously. I was able to interview students, teachers, and, of course, the principals, two of whom were new since 1997.

I encountered much of the same reflections on language that I had found in my initial fieldwork. People argued that English is an international language and allows people to plan to travel beyond Varanasi to attain jobs not available locally, usually in the information technology sector. People still defined English alongside Hindi, emphasizing the latter's status of mother tongue, and argued that to be an Indian one must have Hindi. A new development, however, was striking. Many individuals' commentary on the importance of English began to focus on coaching institutes offering lessons in conversational English, interviewing practice, and advice about comportment to those who have finished school, intercollege, or university. Nita Kumar quotes an administrator of a coaching institute in Varanasi: "See, in metros if students do professional degrees, they can get jobs. In [backward areas like] Purvanchal [eastern Uttar Pradesh] there are no career opportunities, except as labourers and in government service. By joining coaching centers, students try to qualify for national exams such as the JEE [Joint Entrance Examination]" (2011: 240). Kumar reports that many students of such institutes find the personalized instruction they receive superior to their experiences in school, where discipline, textbooks, and exams were paramount. I cannot comment other than to affirm that many teachers and students in board-certified schools recognize in coaching centers the ways in which English-medium education is oriented outward beyond Varanasi, in contrast to Hindi, the language of home. Although this book finds that such ideas "mask what are typically multiple and contradictory notions about the nature and basis of social order," the ideas have remained remarkably consistent during the period called liberalization (Ka. Hall 2002: 122).

Plan of the Book

Chapter 1 considers education in India through a particular ideological lens, the mother tongue (*mātrabhāṣā*). The chapter proposes that one reason that schools are largely absent in the large body of work on the sociolinguistics of India can be traced to notions of mother tongue. Scholars investigating social aspects of language difference in India considered schools to be modern institutions wherein standardized language varieties made people's engagement with their mother tongues impossible. In contrast, chapter 1 demonstrates that the notion of the mother tongue is a primary means through which many middle-class people in Varanasi recognize a language used in school, Hindi, and recognize a type of school, the Hindi-medium school. People in Varanasi imagine Hindi to be the language accessible to all because it is their mother tongue. Though many people in education understand that Hindi puts one in an increasingly inferior position as one advances in the educational system—a position, they claim, that can produce a "complex"—even they maintain that one should have pride in her mother tongue. In turn, people who have developed fluency in English explain that an exclusive claim to English rings pretentious and suspect. Indeed, what constitutes Hindi—even as a primordial identity understood to be essential to the self—depends to a large extent on English. The notion of mother tongue is so conflicted in the world of schooling because it is something in which one should have pride at the same time that it is something that is subordinate in schooling and problematic to embrace. Thus, chapter 1 argues that processes of economic liberalization and globalization hardly entail a uniform embrace of English, but rather entangle people in tacit and contradictory claims.

Whereas chapter 1 explores the ways in which the language-medium divide implicates the self through notions of mother tongue, chapter 2 moves to the arena of the national language (*rāṣṭrabhāṣā*) to show that Hindi- and English-medium schools offer different types of capital, in the parlance of Pierre Bourdieu. What is valuable about Hindi-medium schools and English-medium schools can shift radically depending on how they are understood to relate to local, regional, national, and international arenas. Furthermore, the relevance of Hindi- and English-medium education can disappear when people feel that no educational institution in the city is up to the task of educating their children. The realm of value creation that depends on a certain kind of English shows Varanasi (or India) to be a peripheral place. In India there are multiple arenas of linguistic value that depend on different symbolic manifestations of different languages, and schools in Varanasi cannot participate in all of them. Thus, just as ideas about the mother tongue can be sustained as valuable up to the point of comparison with English-medium schools and their ability to further one's educational goals, ideas about the variable values emanating from Hindi- and English-medium schools can be maintained up to the point of comparing Varanasi's schools in the national sphere of education. Processes of economic liberalization and globalization have interjected an unsettled quality to language-medium distinctions just as they have continued to relegate Varanasi to the periphery.

If some language markets show that Varanasi is a peripheral place in the nation via the ways in which its educational institutions fail to participate in the national realm of the production of value, advertising for schools is a practice that relegates Varanasi to the periphery in a particularly robust way. Chapter 3 explores the relationship between language and the script used in school advertising in terms of what kind of school is being advertised. An especially clear distinction between Hindi-medium and English-medium schools emerges. Advertising for tutorial services, ubiquitous in Varanasi and across North India, supports the maintenance of the distinction between Hindi- and English-medium schools. Chapter 3 compares advertising for schools found around town in Varanasi with advertising for schools found in national newspapers that are distributed locally. Out of the differences emerges further evidence that Varanasi is a peripheral place unable to offer the kind of schooling found in more cosmopolitan locales. The English-medium school is the only kind of school in the newspaper. Any indication of Hindi-medium schools as valuable in the national sphere disappears just as does evidence of the existence of prestigious or cosmopolitan English-medium education in Varanasi. Indeed, in school advertising in the newspaper, unlike in spoken interaction, there seems to be little possibility of maintaining that schools in Varanasi offer much value.

The differentiation between Hindi- and English-medium schools is an easily accomplished and seemingly inevitable aspect of schooling for those who describe schools or sit for their exams. Chapter 4 introduces someone who was an exception. A teacher at a Hindi-medium government school was able to reflect on her past and compare it to the present in a way that threw into question the inevitability of the stark division between Hindi- and English-medium schools. I came to cherish the teacher's words—however singular for me they may have been—because they were so disruptive of the commentary I was hearing constantly. The chapter invokes Mikhail Bakhtin's notion of voice to explore what made the teacher able to disrupt the inevitability of the divide between Hindi- and English-medium schools. While it is true that the teacher's perspective on schooling was unusual and, therefore, indicative of the pervasiveness of the language-medium discourse explored in the rest of the book, her narrative reminds us that seemingly inevitable divisions are never total or beyond the reconstructive touch of the narration of experience. She calls into question—albeit in an implicit way—the notions that make the "complex," introduced in chapter 1, so important, yet ultimately confounding.

Chapter 5 asks questions about the use of English by people whose desire for English is often ridiculed by reflections on language-medium schooling, including Hindi-medium students and people who are working-class with little or no experience of schooling. The chapter considers interaction in school classrooms and finds that in some there exists a routine typical of interaction in classrooms in many postcolonial societies wherein the former colonial language is beyond the capacity of teachers and students. Specifically, the ways in which Hindi-medium teachers and students interact when discussing texts written in English exhibit many of the features that Chick (1996) calls "safetalk." The notion refers to interactional routines engaged in by teachers and students to manage their lack of knowledge of and practice in the language in which they are mandated to engage, thus saving face. In English class in one of Varanasi's most prestigious (English-medium) schools, teachers and students frame talk about the English text in English, whereas in a Hindi-medium school, the English teacher frames talk about the text in English and Hindi, and uses Hindi to provide exegesis on the text. The interaction between teacher and student in both cases is minimal, and the students speak to the teacher largely in English. This is possible because the teacher of the English class in the Hindi-medium school uses Hindi as well as English, and what English she does use is primarily derived from the text. Chapter 5 of this book will use Chick's insights to question whether the notion of "safetalk" exhausts the uses of English for the kinds of students who attend Hindi-medium schools, or even the kinds of people who have not attended a board-certified school.

Notes

In sections, especially "The Political-Economic Context of Education in Contemporary India," the introduction incorporates material from the publications listed in the acknowledgments.

1. Increasingly, people in the city in which I conducted fieldwork are using the officially recognized name, Varanasi. In my initial fieldwork in 1996–1997, almost everyone used Banaras if talking about the city generally, and sometimes Kashi if talking about the city for its importance in a Hindu religious vein.
2. In her study of call centers, Reena Patel shows that they are quite discriminatory with regard to the English abilities of potential employees. Discrimination

is often based on distinctions between places judged more or less cosmopolitan. She reports, "Linda, the executive of TYJ Corporation in Mumbai ... stated during an interview, 'If an applicant is from Ahmedabad, we don't touch them. Their accents are untrainable. We tried before, but it just didn't work'" (2010: 46). The executive has come to understand Ahmedabad as a place of untrainable workers because of the way they speak English.

3. Some have sought to point out the rising inequalities during the period of growth (Deshpande 2003; D. Gupta 2010; Khilnani 1999).
4. For descriptions of gendered antagonism between education and marriage, especially as girls approach higher grade levels, see Gold (2002), Mukhopadyay and Seymour (1994), Seymour (1999, 2002), and Wadley (1994). See N. Kumar (1994) for a fascinating discussion of the role of women in the creation of several schools in Varanasi.
5. See Upamanyu Chatterjee (1988, 2000) for irreverent, hilarious depictions of a fictional civil servant's experiences. Chatterjee's lampoons brilliantly capture the hierarchical nature of relations among different posts.
6. Symbolic capital, Bourdieu explains, is particularly subject to a process he calls "misrecognition," the understanding of some practice in a particular domain of capital formation such that the larger social position of the person or group in question becomes hidden. Taking the examples of the Lads, Burnouts, and Vatos, Bourdieu might explain the ways in which teachers understand such students to be unintelligent based on their poor performance in school to be a kind of misrecognition of the larger process of their production as a kind of student in the school (and wider world).
7. These schools use literate materials written in Nastaliq script that marks them as schools in which Urdu is used. Thus, they are not part of a much larger category of schools called "Hindi-medium," in which Devanagari is used.
8. Rebecca Klenk (2003) describes women's memories of participation in Lakshmi Ashram, a Gandhian pedagogical institution in the Northern state of Uttaranchal, that has facilitated the realization of non-normative gendered subjectivities. In retrospect, some of the women regret not having received a board-certified diploma, believing that the lack of such credentials had barred them from opportunities.
9. Part of the 1986 National Educational Policy mandated that a Navadoya school would be built in each district of the nation. The rationale was that this would make competitive English-language institutions available at no cost to rural areas (K. Kumar 1991a). Both Krishna Kumar (1991a) and Gauri Viswanathan (1992) express skepticism about the schools' democratic goals by pointing out the Navadoya system's neoliberal emphasis on skill and merit at the expense of social equality.
10. This coincides with the definition of elementary education as levels one through eight.
11. The act defines the locus in which a school must exist as a "neighborhood," but S. Chopra (2011: 18) notes that a definition is not provided.
12. Aradhana Sharma (2006) notes that workers in Mahila Samakhya, a women's empowerment program launched in 1988 as part of the Government of India's New Education Policy of 1986, strategically project the professional dispositions of a government or NGO employee depending on perceived contextual advantages. Such maneuverability seems to be erased in discursive reflection on school boards.

13. The ideological reverberation of English in India is the subject of an immense body of scholarship. Selected examples include Aggarwal (1988), Annamalai (1991, 2001, 2004, 2005), Brass (1990), J. Das Gupta (1970), P. Dasgupta (1993), Dua (1994a), Faust and Nagar (2001), Joshi (1994), Krishnaswamy and Burde (1998), Kurzon (2004), Pattanayak (1981), Ramanathan (1999, 2005b), Rubdy (2008), and Sonntag (2000).
14. These debates were spun around a central tension in the colonial project: the promotion of an (inequality-producing) bureaucratic regime required for capitalist expansion versus the moral reform of a degenerate, hapless society with the dissemination of (equality-producing) Western knowledge.
15. Terms such as "complex" (*kāmpleks*) highlight the ways that representing language with the written word poses ethical dilemmas to any scholar of linguistic interaction, ranging from concerns about distinctions between standardized and non-standardized forms (Jaffe 2000) to often-related options for the transliteration of phonological features (Schieffelin and Doucet 1998).
16. See also Blommaert (2006), Friedrich (1989), Kroskrity (2004), Philips (1998), Rumsey (1990), and Silverstein (1979).
17. Krishna Kumar noted that "ground" resonates with *zamīn,* which can be translated as "earth." Thus, "ground and sky" might be rendered "earth and sky."
18. See N. Kumar (1998) for a longer list of school types in Varanasi, and N. Kumar (2000) for a history of education in Varanasi.
19. Unpublished transcript of interview with Nita Kumar by Chaise LaDousa, 2007.

Chapter 1

On Mother and Other Tongues

Language Ideology, Inequality, and Contradiction

School principals at the Saraswati Schools and the Seacrest School differentiated themselves from me by pointing out that we had different mother tongues, and they talked about their schools in the same breath. I was taken aback because the assertion that a school can be identified with a mother tongue (and vice versa) contradicted a large body of scholarship published on language in India beginning in the 1960s. The principals' comments prompted me to reread and rethink much of the sociolinguistic work on India that I had read in preparation for fieldwork. Some of the most prominent sociolinguists of India have argued that the school is a place of standardized language, and is therefore incompatible with the nature of language variation in India. They see India as a place of complementary language variation whereas they see the West as a place of alienating standardization. In such work, the school emerges as a metonym of the problems of standardization.

In contrast to the ways that sociolinguistic work on India has excluded schools from consideration, I found that schools are one of the primary institutions through which people in Varanasi and elsewhere in the Hindi Belt of northern India imagine their mother tongue to be located. They believe that all schools offer a class in Hindi, the mother tongue, and they also believe that one type of school, the Hindi-medium school, offers most of its classes in the mother tongue.

Discussions of schools and mother tongues were especially helpful in understanding the relationships between language, school, and self that seemed so ready-made. For example, the school principals in the opening vignettes of the book used language difference among school types to identify us as different. Hindi was their mother tongue and English was mine, and this, they argued, would make my experiences in Hindi- and English-medium schools different.

One of the reasons that the idea of the mother tongue is so salient when people talk about schools is that the possibilities of what the mother tongue can stand for outside of schools are drastically narrowed. Outside of schools, people claim a huge variety of languages as their mother tongue, sometimes using names of language varieties, sometimes naming languages according to where or with whom they are typically spoken, and sometimes simply by using the word "language" (*bhāṣā*). In schools, people speak of Hindi alone as the mother tongue, and do so in focused contrast with English. The notion of Hindi as mother tongue is salient at the level of language as well as educational institution. Thus, the notion of mother tongue is salient to people in a range of social class positions, as well as to people who are not attending a board-certified school. The notion of mother tongue, however, can be used to show that language-medium distinctions do matter significantly to people wishing to attain the kind of schooling thought to be necessary for class mobility.

People express pride in and love for the mother tongue whether they study in Hindi-medium or English-medium schools. Pride and love for the mother tongue begins to show cracks as people envision students progressing in grade levels toward university education. The Hindi-medium student entering an English-medium environment—that of the most prestigious universities and lines of study—prompts the mention of a "complex" (*kāmpleks*), a feeling of inferiority on the part of the Hindi-medium student vis-à-vis English-medium students and environments, or a feeling of superiority on the part of the English-medium student vis-à-vis Hindi-medium students and environments. One might call the complex a "cultural construct" in the parlance of Paul Willis (2003) because the notion is emergent neither from the qualities of the Hindi-medium school nor from the qualities of the English-medium school. Rather, people seem to use the notion to make sense of the contradiction between positive feeling for the mother tongue, on the one hand, and a larger educational system in which success subordinates the mother tongue, on the other hand.

Two people's extended reflections on schooling show what happens when the underpinnings of language-medium discourse start to give way because that discourse is inadequate for reflections on school experiences. In the first example, a university professor decries the pretension of students who have studied in English-medium schools prior to coming to university and reports telling her students to be proud of their mother tongue. At the same time, the professor reports having attended Hindi-medium schools herself, but having escaped the complex with high marks. In the second example, a secretary dramatizes the pretension of a high school student's claim not to know Hindi. She recounts how she unmasked the student's true origins by invoking a language variety, Bhojpuri, considered unacceptable in schools. The extended examples show the ways in which people wrestle with the contradictions of the mother tongue in schooling through the notion of complex, but also demonstrate that the notion of complex is ultimately inadequate to describe of their own experiences. Both professor and secretary are comfortably middle-class and are in occupations that require a good knowledge of English. Neither of these middle-class women, however, attended English-medium schools, at least not for most of their educations. And yet, most of the women's reflections on schooling are oriented toward the significance of English-medium education.

The Mother Tongue in Sociolinguistics in India: Present in the Census, Absent in the Schools

The term "mother tongue" can have many meanings, but always connects language and person through origin, essence, and authenticity. Thus, mother tongue is profoundly ideological at the same time that it is treated by people as an objective and unmediated aspect of the world. Scholars and laypeople alike have argued on various grounds for a mother tongue's existence. These include the notion that a language was learned first, that a language is known best, and that a language is used most (Skutnabb-Kangas and Phillipson 1989: 453). Developments such as the "insistence on the authenticity and moral significance of 'mother tongue' as the one first and therefore *real* language of a speaker, transparent to the true self" are not natural but historically and politically particular since they can be traced to the Herderian equation of a people and a language (Woolard 1998: 18). The uses of such arguments are legion and many political movements include the call for some public recognition of one's mother tongue, the call for the inclusion of one's mother tongue in institutions or public media, or the valorization of some practice or group associated with a mother tongue. Mitchell explains that "the defense of one's 'mother tongue,' whether in public or in private, is a learned behavior rather than a natural impulse. Yet, this does not mean that such a learned behavior is insignificant or should be dismissed" (2009: 23). Pattanayak writes that "'mother tongue' is both a sociolinguistic reality and a product of the mythic consciousness of a people" (1981: 54). The notion of mother tongue has rather powerful ideological effects. Once the notion of mother tongue circulates, there is the potential for people to identify with it so strongly that they might sacrifice much for its defense. Less dramatically, they might come to identify with it, but also with an institution and a group, such as the case of schools discussed below.

Before moving to the ways in which people talk about mother tongue and schools in the same breath in Varanasi, it is useful to explore why such associations might be missing in the large body of work on sociolinguistics in India. Indeed, scholars of language variation in India have been especially adept in describing the bewildering number of meanings and uses of mother tongue. They have been adept at tracing the ways in which certain meanings of mother tongue can be linked to the context in which they are used. The primary context on which their investigations are focused is not the school, but the census. Scholars were willing to explore the ways in which the Census of India was an institution in whose hands the meanings of mother tongue might change, and in which the enumeration of language varieties might be demonstrated to be inaccurate. In other words, sociolinguists rightly saw the census as an especially complex space for the production of language ideology. The same scholars were unwilling to explore another institutional domain, the school, with the same intellectual distance. In discussions of schooling, they have tended to treat mother tongue as something excluded and in need of valorization. In their discussion, the mother tongue emerges as something to be upheld and praised as Indian in opposition to the language of the school, something to be dismissed.

In a classic examination, Pattanayak (1981) presents a great number of possibilities for what mother tongue can mean. He decries the commonplace understanding of mother tongue as "one's own language" as too vague for scholarly use because two or more languages might fit definitional criteria (47). The gloss "language of nature," applied to the deaf and their "language of signs," he explains, presupposes no community at all (47). He invokes Rabindranath Tagore's assertion that "Sanskrit is the mother of Indic languages in the same sense as the earth is the mother of the worm" to critique the idea that the mother tongue is "the original language from which others spring" (47). Pattanayak explains that "learning a language without formal training" can be understood to make a language a mother tongue, but falls short of endorsing the meaning (50). He questions the idea that "language which allows one to have the cognizance of the world is the mother tongue" by pointing out that "cognizance" is vague (51). He proceeds to explain that mother tongue has rested on the emotional attachment one feels to a language that is often grounded in "mother land," one's nation or would-be nation (51). Often mother tongue implies the capacity for "cognitive development" and "creativity." Pattanayak makes explicit a commonly held belief that "precision of thought and clarity of ideas are considerably hampered without the ability to speak effectively and to read and write correctly and lucidly in one's mother tongue" (52). Finally, Pattanayak notes that mother tongue can mean something like "home language," and argues that the meaning can be challenged by the existence of more than one language spoken in the home (53).[1]

Pattanayak illustrates the institutional vicissitudes of the meanings of mother tongue by examining the changing linguistic descriptors and questions meant to solicit responses:

> In the census of 1881, 1931, 1941, and 1951 a question on mother tongue was asked. In the 1881 census mother tongue was defined as the "language spoken by the individual from the cradle." In the 1891 census the term was changed into "Parent tongue" which was defined to mean the language spoken by the parents of the individual. In the 1901 census it was further modified into "Language ordinarily spoken in the household." In the case of bilingual respondents, the language used with the enumerator was noted. In 1921 the question was simply "language ordinarily used." (1981: 47–48)

The very notion of mother tongue as well as the descriptors used for the notion shifted from census to census.

Pattanayak proceeds to demonstrate that the instructions given to census enumerators treated the idea of mother tongue in such a way that different answers might emerge for the same respondent: "According to the instruction given to the enumerators in the 1961 census, 'Mother tongue is language spoken in the childhood by persons' mother. If the mother died in infancy write the language mostly spoken in the person's home in childhood'" (1981: 48). Pattanayak illustrates the potential for different census results

> in the case of a Bihari mother tongue speaker (as declared in the census) marrying a Hindi speaker. Assuming that the mother was a speaker of

> a language/dialect which she could have declared Bihari in the census, then if she were living that would probably be recorded as the mother tongue of the child even if she was married to a man who would have recorded his mother tongue as Hindi. However, if at the time of recording the mother tongue the mother was dead then the language mostly spoken in the person's home being Hindi would be recorded as the "Child's mother tongue" (1981: 48).

Downright arbitrary is the procedure described by Pattanayak whereby "two languages were recorded by the census enumerator [in the 1961 census]" in the case of "respondents who spoke and understood more than one language in addition to their mother tongue" (1981: 49). Pattanayak notes that "the tabulation was based only on the language recorded first by him" (1981: 49).

The elegance and attention to detail that Pattanayak exhibits in his discussion of mother tongue in the Census of India disappears in general considerations of schooling and language. Key to understanding why is the pervasive argument in the work of Pattanayak and other sociolinguists that there exists in societies such as India the possibility of lasting and contextually appropriate multilingualism. Pandit (1977, 1979), for example, argues that language maintenance is the norm in India (unlike in the West), such that displaced groups simply gain languages rather than assimilate. In their review of sociolinguistic work on India, Agnihotri and Khanna claim that:

> In heterogeneous societies such as that of India, languages are learnt in non-authoritarian contexts leading to continuous sociocultural and cognitive enrichment. Variations in linguistic behavior act as facilitators rather than as barriers in communication. Languages are kept distinct as they perform different functions in different domains. On the other hand, there are several domains in which different languages converge towards a common lingua franca.... Although there is an underlying sociolinguistic unity that characterizes Indian multilingualism, it is this unity that nurtures rather than forbids flexibility and variability (1997: 33–34).

The depiction of India as a place of lasting multilingualism where languages are learned outside of authoritarian contexts is characteristic of the sociolinguistic scholarship reviewed herein in that the nation as a whole frames the discussion. Against the backdrop of flexibility and variability that Agnihotri and Khanna create, the implication is that the school is an institution that does not fit.[2]

The implication emerges as an explicit argument. In Agnihotri and Khanna's review, schooling is an institution alien to India. They turn to policy measures undertaken by the Government of India during the

1960s (discussed more extensively in the next chapter) in order to critique what they see as artificial, arbitrary impositions of schooling on students: "Two assumptions that have often guided the deliberations of these [government] committees are firstly, that every child in the country should learn the same number of languages and secondly, that learning Hindi and English are of paramount importance to everyone. Both of these assumptions militate against the fluid plurilingual texture of Indian society" (Agnihotri and Khanna 1997: 35). Here, Agnihotri and Khanna contrast the languages found in school with the sociolinguistic situation in India generally, outside of school.[3]

In another classic critique, Probal Dasgupta draws on well-established sociolinguistic concepts to characterize the language found in schools in India. He draws on the distinction between "high" (H) and "low" (L) varieties of language in Fishman's (1967) sense of extended diglossia. In Ferguson's (1959) original formulation of the concept of diglossia, "high" and "low" are varieties of the same language. Thus, Classical Arabic might be considered "high." Its emblem is the Koran. In its shadow, Egyptian Arabic can be considered "low." In Fishman's reformulation, "high" and "low" can be different languages. In the discussion below, Hindi might be considered "high" because it can be used in schools and can be found in textbooks, whereas languages like Bhojpuri, associated with the home and the village, might be considered "low." Thus, Ferguson argues that there exist linguistic distinctions like textual versus oral, formal versus vernacular, and institutionally acquired versus mother tongue within the same language, whereas Fishman argues that different languages could come to inhabit the oppositions. Dasgupta invokes the distinction to depict relationships between language and education, "high" and "low" emerging as something like styles of cognition. One is reminded of Bernstein's (1971) distinction between "elaborated" and "restricted" codes, respectively, wherein communication in the restricted code assumes prior experience in some social group or event and communication in the elaborated code does not.

> Education is thus a relation between two discourses. The H discourse level of systematic knowledge codifies and organizes the technical and practical complexes in terms of the simple primes into which serious and systematic thought analyzes the complexes. The L discourse level of the learner—and, in his or her ordinary life, the teacher—conceptualizes items as being difficult, or remote from experience, versus easy, or accessible to common perception. Education is a mapping between the simple primes of the H world and the easy precepts of the L world. (Dasgupta 1993: 104)

Dasgupta's usage differs from Bernstein's in that, in India, the classroom and, ultimately, the textbook become the locus of the "H world," whereas the "ordinary life" of teacher and student becomes the locus of the "L world."

Much later in Dasgupta's book, the "H world" and the "L world" come to rest on another distinction. Like in Agnihotri and Khanna's work, the nation frames the discussion. Drawing on the first line of the Constitution of India, Dasgupta argues that the referent of "India" is the "H world" and the referent of "Bharat" is the "L world." In the usage of the Constitution of India, "India" and "Bharat" refer to the same entity. The inclusion of "Bharat" would seem to make a gesture to a precolonial means of referring to "India" via Sanskrit, indicating that India's past is still relevant. In Dasgupta's rendition, "India" is juxtaposed to "Bharat" as the "Indian elite" are juxtaposed to the "people." Rather than bemoaning the advance of standardizing tendencies in government policy and the threat of school language to India's plurilingual ethos as Agnihotri and Khanna do, Dasgupta celebrates the resurgence of a plurilingual ethos in the return of "Bharat":

> As a consequence of this shift from the teaching mode, where the Indian elite took the social and cognitive initiative, to the learning mode, in which Bharat's many collectivities unevenly and regionally initiate processes of learning whose very brokenness reflects the (plural) pleasure of the people and marks the limits beyond which the modernization project cannot proceed, the nation-image of Bharat begins to emerge as a new reality, capable of constructing a credible past and future for itself, and of contesting the India image's presence as well as its projections into the past and the future. (1993: 182–183).

Thus, Dasgupta equates the high (H) variety with the "teaching mode," "India's elite," and a singular "modernization project" and the low (L) variety with the "learning mode" and "Bharat's many collectivities," which are "regionally" situated. The school is an institution that helps to constitute the difference between the high and low varieties, and only outside of the school do teacher and student have the ability to engage with "pleasure."

Once schooling emerges in the classic sociolinguistic works mentioned herein, the notion of mother tongue ceases to be relevant, much less to have the range of (standardized and non-standardized) linguistic possibilities that can be found, for example, in the Census of India.[4] When schools become the focus of discussion, language is not treated as a category of folk designation, but rather the knowledge that exists in the shadow of policy and modernity. Scholars contrast the "mother tongue" to that language found in schools, described as the "other tongue" (Pattanayak 1981) or the "auntie tongue" (Dasgupta 1993), the former rendering school language alien and the latter rendering it colonial. Pattanayak sums up the set of oppositions supporting the construction of the "mother tongue" as that language variety quashed by the school: "Schooling is a major break in the natural acquisition of language where ignorant pedants teach the non-existent logic, identify varieties as incorrect, create a low self-image by branding the home language as non-standard and try to establish their right to teach the correct [language] as the standard" (1981: 63). The language of schooling marks a break with the natural and the home.

The Mother Tongue and Language-Medium Schooling

It is not my intention to contest these scholars' assertions that processes of standardization present hurdles to policy makers, those who are charged with carrying out policy measures, or those who lack access to or control of standardized varieties. As will become apparent in the discussion below, many of the assertions made by the scholars cited herein ring true. Schools do indeed exclude certain language varieties, especially those that policy makers do not recognize as standardized. Talk about schools reflects this.

The most common way in which people referred to schools as types of institutions in Varanasi was to call them Hindi-medium or English-medium. Many language varieties are excluded when the question of medium arises. Bhojpuri is one of these languages. Bhojpuri is a language variety that exhibits regional variation different from Hindi, yet both Hindi and Bhojpuri can be found in locations far afield of India as a result of migration, often underpinned by indentured servitude of the nineteenth century or later policy shifts concerning immigration (Barz and Siegel 1988; Eisenlohr 2006; Gambhir 1981; Mesthrie 1991; Mohan 1978). The allure of employment opportunities has drawn speakers of Bhojpuri to various urban areas of northern India, especially Delhi, and away from the area still associated with Bhojpuri, which includes the western part of the state of Bihar, the eastern part of the state of Uttar Pradesh, and the northern part of the state of Jharkhand. In that region, from the colonial period to the present, officials and linguists have identified regional variation in Bhojpuri (Grierson 1967; Masica 1991). The relationship between regional linguistic variation and names that people use to identify language varieties is, of course, complicated, and sometimes contested. Some laypeople, officials, and scholars alike use "Bihari" to refer to the Bhojpuri found in parts of the state of Bihar and Jharkhand or in the speech of migrants from such areas residing in eastern Uttar Pradesh and beyond, while other scholars dispute the term's reflection of sociolinguistic variation (Masica 1991). My purpose is not to weigh in on such discussions, but rather to acknowledge that Bhojpuri is a language with complex variation that has been the focus of some controversy in the scholarly literature. Adding to Bhojpuri's complexity of nomenclature is that the city of Varanasi is associated with a variety of its own: "Banarasi Boli" or "Banaras Talk" (Simon 1993: 246–249).[5]

Hindi differs from Bhojpuri in two respects, among others. First, Hindi covers a much wider territory, stretching across entire states in northern and central India. People across this massive *Sprachbund* typically speak a language such as Bhojpuri, Avadhi, or Marwari in addition to having some level of competence in Hindi (Gumperz 1958, 1964).[6] Shapiro and Schiffman explain: "In large portions of South Asia it is difficult to construct a model of standardized languages directly subsuming discrete classes of regional dialects. Most of the spoken vernaculars of North India, for instance, comprise a virtual continuum of speech forms extending across the subcontinent from Bombay to Ahmadabad in the West to Calcutta in the East" (1981: 65). Hindi encompasses Bhojpuri geographically. And, unlike Bhojpuri, Hindi is recognized as having a standardized variety. This has implications for the relationship between the two languages because, as Michael Silverstein writes, "[any form considered] standard is endowed with claims to superiority as a 'superposed' register for use in those contexts of interaction that count in society" (1996: 286). Hindi has undergone standardization for use in domains such as the newspaper, government publications, and school texts (Dua 1994b; Gumperz 1961; Orsini 2002).[7]

Bringing together the notions of *Sprachbund* and standardization, John Gumperz locates the standard within a three-tier model for the large Hindi-speaking region in which Varanasi is located. He sees (1) a more or less unified phonological, morphological, and syntactic system constituting a standard; (2) more regionally delimited languages within the area of the standard; and (3) phonological distinctions within single villages (Gumperz 1958, 1961, 1964).[8] Sudipta Kaviraj provides a sweeping description of the colonial process by which the linguistic situation came to be: "In less than a hundred years an area which was covered by a mass of small dialects gets restructured linguistically into two or three regions using the highly self-conscious languages [Bengali, Oriya, and Hindi] of their respective high cultures" (1992a: 24).[9]

Many people call the standardized variety *śuddh* Hindi (pure Hindi). Some people praise and some people complain about its use of Sanskrit-derived elements (Al. Rai 2001).[10] The use of Persian- and Arabic-derived elements will often cue the language label "Urdu." What distinguishes Urdu and Hindi has become an increasingly complicated issue over the late-nineteenth and twentieth centuries (C. King 1994; Lelyveld 1993; Am. Rai 1984). Some stress similarity and mutual comprehension, especially in spoken forms, while others stress difference and even incompatibility. Certainly, script has come to demarcate one from the other (C. King 2001). The use of the Nastaliq script has come to be associated with Urdu and the use of the Devanagari script with Hindi.[11] Tariq Rahman accounts for the multiple dimensions involved in a demarcation of Urdu from Hindi when he writes:

> The separation of Urdu from Hindi ... is contingent upon the script (Devanagari for Hindi; Perso-Arabic for Urdu); lexicon (borrowings from Sanskrit from Hindi; Arabic and Persian for Urdu); and cultural references (Hindu history and beliefs for Hindi; Islamic history and ideology for Urdu). The language-planning processes led to the splitting of a language (Hindi-Urdu) into modern Persianized and Arabicized Urdu at one extreme and modern Sanskritized Hindi at the other. Between the two ends is a continuum which veers towards one end or the other according to the speaker, the occasion and the environment. (2011: 99)

Simon (1986, 2003) shows that the ways in which people use Bhojpuri and Hindi are complex. Bhojpuri and Hindi can be recognized as distinct in talk, but they embody a distinction whose pragmatic dimensions speakers can partially manipulate in a given context. For example, Simon notes that Bhojpuri can connote that something talked about, including a person, is Banarsi or Varanasi-like, especially when the particular variety, Banarsi Boli, or Banaras Talk, is used or mentioned. What is focused on becomes local against the backdrop of a more universal and encompassing Hindi. But, in certain situations, Hindi can connote something particular to Varanasi vis-à-vis Bhojpuri, associated with Bihar, the state several kilometers to the east.

While the pragmatic possibilities of Bhojpuri and Hindi are constrained in ways, the two language varieties are equals through the lens of the mother tongue. Indeed, all of the names for language varieties mentioned in this discussion emerged in talk about one's mother tongue: Banarsi Boli, Bhojpuri, Bihari, and Hindi. Sometimes a person would claim that because Bhojpuri comes from Hindi, they are both her mother tongue. I commonly heard the line, *bhojpurī aur hindī donõ mātrabhāṣā hãi* (both Bhojpuri and Hindi are the mother tongue) and even *bhojpurī aur hindī ek hī hai* (Bhojpuri and Hindi are one). In one interview with me in 1997, a schoolteacher reversed the typical relationship between Bhojpuri and Hindi. She used Varanasi's association with the development of a version of modern Hindi to argue that Hindi comes from Bhojpuri:

> Teacher: *hamārī mātrabhāṣā bhojpurī hai.*
> Our mother tongue is Bhojpuri.
>
> CL: *hindī nahī̃?*
> Not Hindi?
>
> Teacher: *nahī̃. banāras kī bhāṣā se hindī āyī hai. hindī bhojpurī se āyī hai.*
> No. Hindi has come from the language of Banaras [Varanasi]. Hindi has come from Bhojpuri.

Dalmia (1997) chronicles the late-nineteenth-century efforts of Bharatendu Harishchandra to shape a variety of Hindi through editorial work and publication. His efforts emanated from and became associated with the city of Varanasi. Dalmia shows that Harishchandra's preference was to draw on Sanskrit lexical items and morphology. In my own fieldwork, people recognized such language as *śuddh* Hindi. The schoolteacher has foregone the involvement of Sanskrit with the variety of Hindi associated with Varanasi and Harishchandra's efforts. Rather, she has made Bhojpuri the connection between the city and Hindi. People also commonly claimed an adjective used to describe language in the area—especially language thought to emanate from further east in Bihar—to be one's mother tongue. The language label was *mīṭhī bhāṣā* (sweet language). When I asked for people to describe what made the language sweet, they most often produced some rendition of a simple greeting or query with singsong intonation, always ending quite high. I was the only person said to have English as my mother tongue.

In the realm of schooling, only Hindi stands as the mother tongue.[12] The school with its textbooks and exams rendered in standardized language, Hindi, Urdu, or English, banishes the presence of Bhojpuri.[13] In turn, the knowledge that standardized forms are appropriate in educational domains far exceeded institutional boundaries. I often asked about the possibility of using Bhojpuri in schools. My queries were met with an absolute stance, always negative and sometimes peppered with amusement. In every school in which I worked, I noticed the principal and several teachers issue commands in Bhojpuri to non-teaching staff on occasion. I also noticed principals speak to relatives in Bhojpuri, whether in person, on the phone, or on a cell phone. When I commented on my observations, my interlocutor would say that the language is not appropriate for "schoolwork" (*skūl kā kām*). People found the idea of Bhojpuri in school texts and exams, much less in classroom interaction, ridiculous. They had at their disposal a whole set of descriptors to explain why Bhojpuri is not meant for school. People consistently contrasted Bhojpuri as *gā̃v kī bhāṣā* (language of the village) and *ghar kī bhāṣā* (language of the house) to Hindi as *rāṣṭrabhāṣā* (national language) or *deś kī bhāṣā* (language of the land/nation). As such, Hindi could stand proudly next to English, often described as *antarrāṣṭrabhāṣā* (international language).[14]

Schoolchildren and teachers alike described Hindi as *mātrabhāṣā*, or mother tongue. Toward the beginning of my year of field research, I came to know of student reflections on the idea of mother tongue when the principal of the private section of the Saraswati School suggested that I create a questionnaire on Hindi and English. So consistent were the answers to hundreds of questionnaires that teachers had distributed in classes six and nine in Saraswati and Seacrest that I feared that the teachers had perhaps told the students what to write. Consistently, the students used the words *mātrabhāṣā* (mother tongue) and *deś kī bhāṣā* (national language) together to describe Hindi. They wrote that English, in contrast, is an international language (*antarrāṣṭrabhāṣā*). In retrospect, I came to the realization that the students' reflections, even if coached, were consistent beyond the context of questionnaire answers. In conversations with me, students expanded on such notions by arguing that Hindi is the mother (tongue) of the nation (*deś kī mā*) and that the language deserves love (*pyār*) and respect (*arpit*). Thus, schoolchildren in Varanasi share the love and respect due a mother that Véronique Benei (2008) describes for Marathi in schools in the western Indian state of Maharashtra. But, unlike Marathi, the standardized language of Maharashtra, Hindi is equated with the nation as a whole via the notion of national language (*rāṣṭrabhāṣā*). Marathi, in contrast to Hindi, enjoys resonance in a single state. Thus, schoolchildren in Varanasi easily equate Hindi with Indians (*bhāratīya log*).

A teacher who, at the time of our interview, had been working in a government school in Varanasi for ten years equated Hindi with the mother tongue even as she claimed that people generally did not have control of the "correct" or standard form of the language, *śuddh* Hindi. The teacher had just been telling me that there is a "craze" (*krez*) for English and that people try to enter English-medium schools even when they should not be there. When I asked why not, she replied, "English is not in their background, not in the house" (*angrezī apne baikgraunḍ mẽ... apne ghar mẽ nahī̃ hai*). She explained that some English-medium schools put the students of poor backgrounds in a class together, segregated from other students. I then mentioned that I had heard that spelling and grammar in Hindi can be difficult for students too, and that it is not simply English that is tough for students. She replied:

> Teacher: *hā̃... aisā... lekin bhāratīya log nahī̃ socte hā̃i. ve socte hā̃i ki hindī hamārī mātrabhāṣā hai. kaṭhin nahī̃ hogī. lekin bī. e. mẽ īngliś se kaṭhin hogī.*
> Yes ... like ... but Indian people don't think like that. They think Hindi is our mother tongue. It won't be difficult. But in getting a B.A. it is more difficult than English.
>
> CL: *ṭhīk hai. śuddh hindī mẽ likhne cāhiye.*
> Okay. They have to write in *śuddh* Hindi.
>
> Teacher: *śuddh hindī. lekin ājkal koī nahī̃ bolte likhte hā̃i.*
> *śuddh* Hindi. But these days no one speaks or writes it.

The teacher's comments confirm what the sociolinguists whose work was cited above argue: schooling can alienate students from the language that they speak, especially as they advance in levels. Her comments also show that schooling renders Hindi—in the face of English—one's mother tongue. Schools thus shape people's ideas about the mother tongue—and the mother tongue shapes people's ideas about school—even in situations in which the vision is discriminatory and alienating. Indeed, the teacher claims that "no one speaks or writes" *śuddh* Hindi just after she has used the word "background" in our interview. Such words were common and could be considered to be Hindi when used as singularly as the teacher did. But such words could never qualify as *śuddh* Hindi. This might explain her use of *ghar* (house), unambiguously Hindi, after a pause following *baikgraunḍ* (background), a commonly used word, but most certainly a loan from English and not *śuddh* Hindi.

Just after arguing that a bachelor's degree in Hindi is harder for students than a bachelor's degree in English, the teacher offered an explanation that I heard frequently, whether from people involved in Hindi-medium or English-medium schools: Hindi is the mother tongue and therefore students do well in it. English, initially at least, is difficult. I begin our interchange by continuing what I understand to be the teacher's line of argument, that Hindi can actually be difficult.

CL: *jab hindī mẽ paṛthe hãi to kuch samasayẽ hotī hãi. matlab bhāratīya logõ ke liye.*
When they study in Hindi there are problems. Meaning for Indians.

Teacher: *nahī̃, hindī mẽ bhāratīya logõ ko koī dikkat nahī̃ hai.*
No, Indians have no trouble with Hindi.

CL: *nahī̃?*
No?

Teacher: *nahī̃. agar acche se ve paṛthe to koī dikkat nahī̃. īngliś unke liye muśkil hotā.*
No. If they study well then there's no trouble. They have trouble in English.

CL: *sac?*
Really?

Teacher: *sac*
Really

CL: *bolne mẽ yā likhne mẽ... sab cīzẽ...*
In speaking or in writing...everything...

Teacher: *donõ mẽ. likhne mẽ bhī bolne mẽ bhī, kyõki īngliś unke baikgraunḍ mẽ nahī̃ miltā hai ghar mẽ*
In both. In writing and speaking too, because they do not get English in their background, in the house

CL: *ṭhīk hai*
Okay

Teacher: *hindī to miltā hai to bacce bahut jaldī se sīkh jāte hãi. likhne bhī jaldī se sīkh jāte. mātrabhāṣā hai*
They are exposed to Hindi so the children learn it really quickly. They learn to write it quickly too. It's the mother tongue.

CL: *hā̃*
Yes

Teacher: *lekin īngliś mẽ nahī̃ sīkhenge*
But they will not learn in English

In this line of argument, the teacher reacts to my general assertion that "Indians" (*bhāratīya log*) would have "difficulties" (*samasayẽ*) with Hindi. In retrospect, it seems that I widened her restricted claim for the difficulty of Hindi at the university level too far—to Indians generally. This prompts the teacher to argue for the ease of study and acquisition of writing in Hindi by virtue of its status as mother tongue. English, in contrast, is difficult.

A "Complex" at the Intersection of Hindi- and English-Medium Schooling

One idea about Hindi- and English-medium schools is especially revealing of the trouble that can ensue when students from the two mediums are imagined to meet. The use of the term "complex" invokes the institutional labels of Hindi- and English-medium schooling, but focuses on the student, specifically the student's psychological disposition and emotions. A complex can "develop" either when a person moves from a Hindi-medium school to an English-medium school, or when the person who has been educated in an English-medium school comes into contact with someone who has been educated in a Hindi-medium school. The person in the former situation is said to feel "inferior" and the person in the latter situation is said to feel "superior."

The notion that a student can develop a complex rests on the distinction between Hindi- and English-medium schools, but does not emerge from associations with either type of school. The notion of a complex thus exhibits features of what Paul Willis calls "cultural production," "the profane, living, properly fertile, often uncontrollable combination of elements in real cultures, actual collective life projects, decisions and changes" (2003: 200).[15] The complex is a symptom of the contradiction between love for the mother tongue and the mother tongue's subordination in further and higher schooling. Furthermore, the complex is a tool by which people struggle to make sense of the world when language mediums, usually separate and oppositional, come into one another's presence.[16] The notion of a complex is a cultural form produced by educated people to make sense of a situation fraught by contradiction (Levinson and Holland 1996: 14). Willis explains that cultural production is neither "simple reproduction" nor "simple opposition" (2003: 201). That this is true is made especially apparent in the next section where two examples illustrate people claiming exception to the complex or turning its logic on its head.

A complex is likely to develop at specific points during a student's progression through school. Students can develop a complex at any age, and some teachers at English-medium schools did use the term to describe youngsters who had transferred from Hindi-medium schools anywhere from the first level all the way to the ninth level. Transfers after the ninth level were less common as students were fast approaching board exams given at the tenth level, and schools, especially those that are private and English-medium, wanted to ensure high scores. And though most teachers chalked up a reticence to talk on the part of children in the first, second, third, and fourth levels to bashfulness and to the lack of confidence of the very young, a few claimed the culprit to be a lack of practice in talking in English that attendance at Hindi-medium schools is said to entail. The complex is said to strike most commonly, however, at the point when students educated in Hindi-medium schools most often find themselves amid students educated in English-medium schools for the first time, the university classroom. Even those people who talked about a complex being relevant at the high school level, such as the woman in the second example to be presented below, noted that the shift from a Hindi-medium to an English-medium high school was undertaken in anticipation of minimizing the possibility of developing a complex in forthcoming university courses.

Vaidehi Ramanathan offers a description of the institutional forces that contribute to the dilemma facing Hindi-medium students desiring higher education:

> if the proficiency of students educated in the Vernacular [Gujarati in the case Ramanathan describes; Hindi in the case described herein] is deemed insufficient at the end of the 12th grade, which by and large is the case, they are denied access to these "prestigious disciplines" [science-based]. Furthermore, in instances when VM [vernacular-medium] students are admitted to EM [English-medium] colleges, they face the uphill task of not only taking classes with their EM counterparts but of having to make the same set of state-mandated examinations in English. In many cases, this proves to be insurmountable for many low-income VM students and many of them drop out of the education system during and after college. (2005a: 6)

Ramanathan's mention of "prestigious disciplines" draws attention to yet another way in which the notion of complex emerges from the intersection of language difference and institutional structure. At Banaras Hindu University and at many other central universities around the country, courses in science, technology, medicine, and management are offered in English whereas many courses in the social sciences and the arts are offered in either English or Hindi. During my initial fieldwork in 1996 and 1997, students in primary and secondary schools claimed higher education and an occupation in the sciences to be their own or some "bright" sibling's ambition. By later fieldwork in 2005, the answers "commerce" and "computers" had taken the place of "science" entirely. The language deemed necessary for higher education in such prestigious fields has remained the same, English, and the notion still holds that students coming from Hindi-medium schools who want to study "commerce" or "computers" will likely develop a complex.

In 2007, I traveled to Varanasi with an undergraduate student from Hamilton College, Patrick Hodgens, who was interested in the study of English in a postcolonial society. During one of our visits to the Seacrest School, we were invited to talk with a group of five students in the tenth level who had earned especially high marks and who were predicted to do well on the CBSE exams. Patrick began by asking the students about English and Hindi. Their comments resonate with links between Hindi and mother tongue, on the one hand, and English and the makings of a complex, on the other hand.

> Patrick: So, what do you think of when you think of the English language?
>
> Priya: It's a, that's a, it's a very bold language, means you can express your feelings very freely, I feel like. So I feel like everywhere English is required. I feel like it's an administrative language and you need it everywhere. I feel it's a good way of explaining your thoughts.
>
> Amit: I think it's a global language and we can communicate in English everywhere. We can continue in our business everywhere, and English is always essential for us to do any global activities. So, English is very important.
>
> Raj: Sir, English is a language which is everywhere in the world so we will not face problems surrounding anything. We can express our views regarding anything.
>
> Ram: It is a backbone of industrialization and all over the world people are communicating with English. Without English, a person cannot build up his personality. It is very necessary for the personality development.
>
> Abhishek: Since English is universal it can be used anywhere in the world and so it is very easy to establish friendship with any person, I feel, in any part of the world.

Several qualities and possibilities converge, including an all-encompassing frame of reference, an association with business, and the ability to communicate with potentially anyone.

Before Patrick asks about Hindi, he asks about the students' grade levels. What the students understand him to be asking about shifts the direction of the conversation.

Patrick: And what grade are you guys in?

Priya: Careers, Okay. Let's talk about the careers.

Patrick [to CL]: What grade?

CL: Which level?

Patrick: Which level, which level, sorry, which level?

CL: Are you in tenth?

Priya: We are in tenth.

Other students: Tenth.

Patrick: Um, do any of you know what you want to do after your, after Seacrest? Do you have any plans, careers?

Priya: Yeah, yeah, mine is in engineering. Computer engineering. I am interested in maths.

Amit: My interest is computer engineering.

Raj: Mine too.

Ram: Mine too.

Abhishek: But I want to do game images. I want to create games, computer games.

Priya: That's the creative thinking of him, in arts.

Patrick: And English is important for all those?

Priya: Yes, I feel that the most important thing is building your personality. Having space for doing something. From a long distance someone can see your speaking well, so it makes a good impression. It highlights your personality.

Patrick follows the path set by Priya's understanding of "grade" as "career." All of the students answer that they are interested in computer engineering, save the last who expresses his interest in computer game design. Priya divulges that his line of study is arts.

When Patrick returns to his questions about language, he asks about Hindi, and the concerns with careers, personality, and communication more generally disappear.

Patrick: And when you think of Hindi what do you think of?

Priya: Hindi. Ah, Hindi has respect from me as well.

Raj: It's our mother language.

Amit: It's our mother language, so ... it has so much importance.

Priya: Yeah, its importance cannot be mentioned in words. In words ... it is not possible.

It would seem that in contrast to the multiple ways in which English provides a platform for the overt expression of language ideology, Hindi is something whose emotional resonance is incapable of being expressed. The contrast between being able to talk about English and being relatively unable to talk about Hindi can be seen as one manifestation of the notion of complex.

The "Complex" in Two Reflections on Schooling

Two extended examples illustrate the ways that people use the notion of complex to narrate students' experiences in school. In both, the idea of mother tongue figures prominently. In the first example, a university professor in Varanasi shows that the notion of complex rests on ideas about the mother tongue of students. The professor argues that university students coming from Hindi-medium schools are severely but unfairly disadvantaged. The professor later divulges that she studied in Hindi-medium schools. In order to account for the incongruity between her past as a Hindi-medium student and her present as a university professor, she invokes a status common to all schools, regardless of language medium: the "topper" who scores highly in school board exams.

In the second example, a government secretary, like the professor, draws on notions of mother tongue and complex, but for a different purpose. The secretary mentions Bhojpuri, the language banished from schools, in order to provide an ironic twist to her narrative. Though the notion that a student can develop a complex assumes the fact that Hindi is that student's mother tongue, the secretary leaves one wondering whether it is Hindi or Bhojpuri. When schooling is the focus of discussion, this should not be.

Shona Shastri: "I Was a Topper Throughout"

In December 2005 I met Shona Shastri in her office at Banaras Hindu University. Professor Shastri had taught at BHU for approximately twenty years in the social sciences, and had served as department chair and dean. I had met Professor Shastri at a conference on education, and I felt comfortable enough to ask her for an audiotaped interview. In the interview segment presented here, Professor Shastri crafts a textbook description of the language-medium divide, structured by the mother tongue, and the complex that emerges from it. She also offers herself as an exception, someone who had studied in Hindi-medium schools but escaped the complex. Professor Shastri's comments are important to consider because they show that one can subvert the logic of the language-medium divide by claiming membership in a category emergent from the school that has nothing to do with language difference. The language-medium divide does not exhaust the ways in which the institution of the school provides people the means to manage its contradictions.

The professor begins the interview segment by focusing on the complex as relevant to those students in her university who have studied in English medium at the undergraduate level who meet and feel superior to those students at the graduate level who have taken their bachelor's degrees in Hindi-medium courses. Thus, the professor shows that the most salient structural insecurity in schooling underpinned by the language-medium divide, the Hindi-medium intercollege student desiring admission to an English-medium undergraduate course of study, can be extended further upward to characterize the Hindi-medium undergraduate desiring admission to select disciplines grouped by the language—English—in which they are offered.

> Shona Shastri (SS hereafter): English still dominates. But, ultimately, the drawback, what is there, that here those students who come from lower-middle class or from the rural background, actually they do not, they do not know English. And because they are poorly nourished, their brains are also not that very sharp sometimes, you know, so they find it really very difficult to learn a new language. Yeah. And for them it is very easy to learn their own mother tongue, learn the subjects in their own mother tongue. Sometimes they are very bright, but they have not been exposed to English-medium education because in the villages where there is less facility of schooling it is so difficult to get the English-medium education, you know. These children, they pass out in under … in B.A., in undergraduate level, with good marks. But when they come to this university, ah, they find it very difficult. They generally … unfortunately, English-medium boys, they suffer from some kind of superiority.

The professor lumps together a lack of nutrition, a rural background, a lower-middle-class economic status, and access to education via the mother tongue, all in juxtaposition to an English-medium student (cf. Ki. Hall 2009; Jeffrey 2010; Sarangapani 2003a, 2003b). Hindi-medium education is "marked" in semiotic terms because its differences from some other possibility are described in detail, whereas the other possibility is assumed and not described. Furthermore, the professor's usage of "mother tongue" nicely captures the ways in which education involves the term in exclusions in which English-medium education (the university, in this case) also engages, but is not thought to. Reflecting its exclusion in Hindi-medium schooling introduced above, Professor Shastri relies on and reproduces the exclusion of Bhojpuri when she states that subjects are easier to study in one's own mother tongue.[17] The professor's explanation takes for granted that Bhojpuri is excluded from consideration as the mother tongue, and also excludes or erases claims made elsewhere about the difficulties of Hindi relative to English.

In her next few comments, the professor explains that she protests to her own students that the complex is unjustified because one's language-medium background is an inaccurate measure of one's intelligence. She explains that she chastises students coming from an English-medium background for "not knowing your mother tongue" at the same time that she "encourages" students coming from a Hindi-medium background, "try to learn that language [English]."

SS: What happens generally you will find that the English-medium students, uh, somehow or the other, they dominate other students.

CL: I see.

SS: Because, uh, uh, snobbish, snobbish is a word, *na* (no)? Snobbish, *hā̃* (yes).

CL: Yes.

SS: Yeah. Snobbish. A snobbish value comes to them that they, they are perfect in English, they know English.

CL: I see.

SS: *hā̃, hā̃, hā̃, hā̃.*

CL: What kinds of things do they say?

SS: Do they say because they will only mix up with those children who know English. They will not mix up with those children who know Hindi. And they form a different group, an elitist group.

CL: I see.

SS: You know? So that is exhibited through their behavior and other things, you know? So, those, those who are good in Hindi, uh, they feel bad about it. They complain. They come to us and then they say *ki* (that)

> they feel so sorry that they do not know English, you know? But what we try to do in the class, we give equal importance to both of them. And we always tell our English-medium students it is not a great thing that you know English, because you have been educated in English medium, that's why you know, but not knowing your mother tongue is not a thing to be complimented. If a Hindi-medium student asks a good question, I will always encourage him or her. So it very much depends on the attitude of the teacher also. How do you take them, you know? So they are ... and I always tell Hindi-medium students never feel inferior that you do not know that language. Try to learn that language. If I can learn French at this age you can learn English at that age, you know? And you should learn English because there is so much of literature. There is, you can get, most of the good books are in English. They have not been translated in Hindi. So for your survival and progress you should learn English. So try to learn English. Even at this stage you can learn it.

The professor wrestles with the language-medium divide and, in doing so, becomes entangled in some of the contradictions common to discourse about language, schooling, and notions of mother tongue in northern India. For example, Professor Shastri begins by arguing that the complex felt by students who have been schooled in English-medium schools can be chalked up to snobbishness. She then states that those students of hers who are good at Hindi feel bad about their proficiency. We gradually learn that proficiency in Hindi implies a lack of knowledge of English. She then asserts that those students who have been schooled in the English medium might claim not to know their mother tongue, but that this is not a stance of which one should be proud. In keeping with the ideological nature of the nexus of schooling and language medium, one has the impression that were students disabused of the complex—the superiority and inferiority associated with English-medium and Hindi-medium backgrounds, respectively—then one's ability in one or the other language would disappear as a concern. The professor's silence on certain subjects, however, hints at why this is not likely to occur. She does not, for example, explain the benefit of the mother tongue to students who have attended English-medium schools.

In the next section of the interview, the professor introduces a surprise: she was educated in Hindi-medium schools. Given that she is a professor at a major university, Professor Shastri's assertion embodies a contradiction. It flies in the face of what she had claimed thus far about the complex and its emergence from the language-medium divide.

SS: You will be very surprised to know, because you take up my case, throughout I studied in Hindi medium. Throughout. Because, not because I belonged to a lower-middle class, because the place where I was living, all the nearby schools were in Hindi medium.

CL: I see.

SS: English-medium schools were very, very, very far, you know? So, I studied there, but English I always learned as a subject. And because I learned...

CL: And which area are you from?

SS: Banaras [Varanasi] only. Banaras. The ghats (steps to the city from the Ganges River). I was living near ghats.

CL: In the old city.

SS: The old city, yes, very near ghats. And, but English I learned as a subject. And as a subject I felt that my writing in English was much better than those, you know? When I joined here in M.A., then I joined English medium because I thought I should also be good in the spoken English, so I should also learn, you know? Because unless you communicate, and if you are sharp you can pick up the things very fast, you know? So at the age of M.A. when I was studying then I joined English medium. And then I picked it up and then I started teaching in English and other things, you know? So I know through what stage the students go, you know, and feel, and all that, you know?

CL: Did you ever face this complex yourself?

SS: I, my case actually, you know, I was a topper throughout. *hā̃*, so actually to whatever language you may be, but if you are a topper, generally you are taken in high esteem, you know?

Although the professor uses the school medium as the basis for describing an essential difference between her students, and describes herself in terms of the medium divide, such distinctions disappear when she describes herself with a term common to both Hindi- and English-medium schools, the "topper." In every school, whether Hindi- or English-medium, those students who have "topped" their board exams at the tenth and twelfth levels have their names and photos displayed temporarily, sometimes permanently, in prominent places including the school's entrance, hallways, or principal's office. In the professor's rendition of the relationship between languages and schooling through medium designations, becoming a topper seems to offer the esteem required to overcome the complex. The professor thus demonstrates that schooling presupposes the idea that Hindi is one's mother tongue and that this understanding rests on an institutional juxtaposition with English. She also demonstrates that success in the institution can nullify the very challenges posed by the institutional distinction of Hindi and English. The professor emerges as an exception to the state of affairs she has just narrated because the institution of the school provides a category, the topper, that hides the contradictions at the heart of the language-medium divide.

Arti Aggarwal: "Like All Her Life She Was Speaking Bhojpuri with Her Parents, and Naturally She Would Have Not Known Any Hindi"

During fieldwork in 1996 and 1997, I would work in school until noon, return home for a quick lunch, and be back at school for afternoon classes. Occasionally I would take my lunch at the government office where Arti Aggarwal, a friend of mine from previous visits to Varanasi, and other friends worked. I asked Arti if I could record an interview with her and she readily complied. While Professor Shastri's interview exhibits some of the characteristics and contradictions of the language-medium divide, Arti's interview provides an ironic twist in which Bhojpuri, the language banished by the school, figures centrally.

Arti had a three-year-old daughter at the time of our interview, and I had attended the daughter's birthday party with my landlady days before. In the first part of the interview excerpt, Arti focuses on her daughter's forthcoming education and the decisions that she has already made about it. She then turns to her own youth to consider the medium divide.

> Arti Aggarwal (AA hereafter): And one thing is there that the public, though I want to send my kid to a public school, an English-medium school, that has several reasons that I told you, that, like for higher studies she will be needing this and, I mean, she should not be developing this complex that "my mother didn't send me to an English-medium school and now I don't know how to cope up with my further studies."
>
> CL: Right.
>
> AA: But, it's a, like, superiority complex.
>
> CL: The public school. Superiority complex.
>
> AA: *hā̃*, they think, they think they are superior to the other Hindi-medium school-going children.
>
> CL: How so? I mean, like, can you give an example?
>
> AA: Yes. Um, uh, for class ... I went to, uh, Central Hindu Girls School for Class IX and, uh, as I, as you know, I was studying in Kendriya Vidyalaya.[18]

CL: Right.

AA: And, the girls coming from, uh, Saint Paul's School, when they, when they got to know that I, Okay, I, I am, the medium of instruction I'm opting is English, they were just like, "you want to come in English-medium class?" I mean, they, they thought, "Okay, she's coming from Kendriya Vidyalaya, so no way she can do it in English-medium."

CL: Right.

AA: So it was like, "are you coming? In this class?" I said, "why not?"(2)

CL: In English, you mean, you said this?

AA: Yeah, yeah [clears throat].

Arti reiterates Professor Shastri's assertion that English is the medium of choice for higher, postsecondary education, and introduces another term, "public." The word is used for fees-taking schools in which the medium is English. Not all fees-taking schools in Varanasi are English-medium, but Arti illustrates that high cost, implied in her use of "public school," serves as a vehicle for language-based institutional choice, ignoring the complex ways in which fee structure and language medium vary among schools in the city.[19] Arti also illustrates the reproductive power of the language-medium divide by talking about it as a choice, one about which she has personal knowledge, and, therefore, one for which she can envision consequences for her three-year-old daughter.

Arti has, prior to the excerpt presented here, expressed her desire that her daughter be able to pursue education in science. This, she has explained, will necessitate attendance at an English-medium school. But what happens in Arti's interview excerpt presented here dramatizes the way in which a complex might develop in a student and the risk the development embodies for a parent. Arti shifts to the first person—from her daughter's perspective, that is—in order to explain, "my mother didn't send me to an English-medium school and now I don't know how to cope up with my further studies." In parallel fashion, Arti uses first-person quotations to animate her own pain involved in switching from Hindi-medium to English-medium education. Arti herself has been met with the question "are you coming? In this class?" It is a question posed by students coming from the English-medium St. Paul's School to her because she has come from the Hindi-medium Kendriya Vidyalaya. The Central Hindu Girls School, where the question was posed, is exceptional in Varanasi because it is a government school in which English-medium education is considered to be quite good. The question is one that Arti does not want her child to be asked. Indeed, Arti finishes her narration of the experience of changing schools and joining the students coming from the English-medium school by clearing her throat and pausing for ten seconds or so before beginning again.

As Arti continues in the next part of the interview, however, she complicates the depictions of the language-medium divide offered by Professor Shastri and herself by rendering the English-medium students' superiority complex as hypocritical. In order to accomplish this, she introduces Bhojpuri, one of the languages excluded from the Hindi- and English-medium school division. Particularly interesting is that she draws on distinctions such as those between the rural and the urban mentioned by Professor Shastri, but does so in order to destabilize the disposition of a student who claims sole knowledge of English.

> AA: And there were some uh, some students from Valiant School, Dehradun, it's called Valiant Girls School Dehradun, and her background was like she belonged to Ghazipur, it's a totally rural area.
>
> CL: Near Banaras [Varanasi], right?
>
> AA: Yeah, near Banaras [Varanasi], and she would tell other students of my class that she doesn't know a word of Hindi. She doesn't know a word of Hindi as she was in an English-medium school. And this, Chaise, she was very proud of this. Okay, "I don't know any Hindi." And as I belong to Dehradun, my hometown is Dehradun, the other students will come and ask me, "Arti, is this school like this that they don't teach at all in, any Hindi at all? Or the students do not know any Hindi?" I said, "it's not that." And then, they say, "but the girl who has come from Valiant School in Dehradun, she doesn't know a word of Hindi." I said, "of course, how do you expect her to know Hindi because she must be knowing Bhojpuri because she's coming from Ghazipur." And, the other day, her parents came, her father was wearing *dhotī, kurtā*.[20]
>
> CL: Right.
>
> AA: Very traditional dress. And then, they were, my friends were, they came running to me, "see her father has come, her father has come." I said, "so? What do you realize now?" They said like, "I think you're right."
>
> CL: Yeah.
>
> AA: Like all her life she was speaking Bhojpuri with her parents, and naturally she wouldn't have known any Hindi.
>
> CL: So it's a joke [laughingly].

AA: Yeah [laughingly]. So this is the kind of mentality these English-medium, uh, students have.

CL: Wow.

AA: I guess they think, as they can converse in English, they are very superior.

Arti begins by introducing the case of a student who has come to Central Hindu Girls School in Varanasi from Valiant School, a private, fees-taking, English-medium school in Dehradun. Some of Arti's relatives live in Dehradun while the girl's relatives live in Ghazipur, a town close to Varanasi. Arti uses her transcendence of her classmates' knowledge of other distant locations in order to lampoon the girl's claim that she cannot speak Hindi. The girl has claimed not to know Hindi, presumably to claim maximal identification with English. Arti, however, turns the girl's claim of superiority on its head. Bhojpuri functions—rather ironically in a narrative about schools wherein the language is deemed unfit for use—as the element that lends the story a ridiculous twist. The girl does not (even) know Hindi (much less English) because she (really) comes from Ghazipur, a place that is not (even) Varanasi. Certainly, Bhojpuri occupies the lowest position among languages because it is the secret that unmasks a claim to superiority. But its use in the narrative is unanticipated by the dichotomy of Hindi-medium and English-medium schools. Arti uses an association with Bhojpuri to show up the claim to not to know Hindi as utterly ridiculous. In the meantime, she critiques what the language-medium division assumes, the rather confident feeling that those educated in English-medium schools are superior to those educated in Hindi-medium schools. And just like in Professor Shastri's interview, this critique rests on the idea that Hindi-medium schools teach in one's mother tongue. Indeed, when I asked if anyone might really not know Hindi at a place like Central Hindu Girls School, Arti answered that the very idea is ridiculous given that Hindi is every student's mother tongue.

Conclusion

People in Varanasi see schools as a place where the mother tongue can be found. Hindi and Hindi-medium schools both can be relevant in people's reflections on the mother tongue. This insight challenges the construction of schooling in the sociolinguistic work on India reviewed herein. Such work saw a kind of multilingualism in India that renders it unlike the West, where languages emerge in and from an alienating institution—the school. What is alienated from school is the mother tongue. Ideas about schooling and its connection to language—as they might emerge in specific contexts of activity and reflection—are largely absent in sociolinguistic work conducted in India.

This chapter concurs with the sociolinguistic work reviewed herein in that it demonstrates that language is crucial to conceptualizing schools, but shifts the locus of ideology from scholars to people involved in schooling. The notion of the mother tongue matters to both groups, but differently. For people in Varanasi with whom I worked, the mother tongue was not that which was alienated from school. Rather, the mother tongue was part of what they used to identify a type of school (as well as a language spoken in it). Rather than associating schools with standardized language and, in so doing, relegating both to the (non-Indian) West, people in Varanasi saw schools as places in which the mother tongue is particularly salient. There is no question that the identification of Hindi as the mother tongue in the context of schooling significantly narrows the field of what linguistic varieties might serve as the mother tongue. Nevertheless, people claim that Hindi is the mother tongue, and that its difference from English—as a language and as a language medium—makes it so. People who are likely to neglect the mother tongue are themselves identified by a school type defined by language: the English-medium student. The "other tongue" of the mother tongue for people in Varanasi is not that of the West, but rather that of advancement in the university and that of connections to elsewhere. It is not embodied by an elsewhere such as the West, but rather by the English-medium school.

The institution of the school serves as a vehicle for language ideology because schools are identified by language distinctions, but also because discourse about language mediums as distinct is silent regarding Hindi- and English-medium students who find themselves in the company of one another—in schools. The complex is imagined to reveal the different school histories of students configured by language-medium difference. As those histories grow longer with advancing grade levels, the severity and consequence of the complex grow. The notion of the complex comes to reflect the relationship between class, educational attainment, and language in India. The complex can exist at any level at which Hindi-medium and English-medium students meet, but the university is the place where English-medium classes pose a necessary challenge to students with a Hindi-medium background. In preparation for university studies, students choose a line of specialization. Science and commerce, the most prestigious lines and the ones thought to be the most lucrative after graduation, often presuppose classroom interaction in English, while arts is a line in which Hindi-medium students are thought to be more appropriate.

The complex is a form of cultural production because the institutional differences and inequalities that underpin it do not account for the life experiences of everyone. The two people whose interviews have been explored at length demonstrate that the opposition between Hindi and English medium excludes experiences and narrows the field of what languages are relevant to people as they reflect on schools. Albeit in different ways, Shona Shastri and Arti Aggarwal establish themselves as superior to people who might suffer the complex. Both have attained class positions that hinge on their control of English just as they claim solidarity with the mother tongue. Noblesse oblige and anxiety lie at the base of the position the women take between the language mediums. More generally, one can say that as people in Varanasi use the notion of mother tongue to envision school difference, they enter a tangle of contradictions.

Notes

This chapter incorporates material from "On Mother and Other Tongues: Sociolinguistics, Schools, and Language Ideology in Northern India," *Language Sciences* 32: 602–614.

1. Many critiques of the census and the changing denotational values of its linguistic descriptors exist. A particularly rich example is Khubchandani (1983).
2. Aggarwal challenges the notion of Indian plurilingualism and calls for studies that take account of "the history and socio-cultural, economic and political dynamics of the multi-dimensionally diverse plurilingual settings in India" (1997: 47).
3. Agnihotri and Khanna's assertion, I would point out, begs the question of whether resistance to these tendencies—especially in the South, as noted by Brass (1990), Das Gupta (1970), and Ramaswamy (1997)—were indeed fueled by the "fluid plurilingual texture of Indian society."
4. Though he does not approach the relationship between languages and schools in a closely considered case, Khubchandani outlines some of the dimensions of the relationship: "One needs to adopt a pragmatic approach to linguistic usage in education (such as when phasing the shift and/or combining the mediums of instruction) and take into account the mechanisms of language standardization in plural societies when tackling the literary problems through varying demands in the spoken and written genre of the same language" (2003: 251).
5. Bhojpuri, through its eponymous variety Banarsi Boli, has a special relationship with Varanasi (Banaras): "Bhojpuri is the language of the people who run the city

– the launderers and boat-polers, the potters and weavers and barbers and street cleaners. It is the language of musicians and toy makers. The ritual priests, the funeral assistants, the untouchables who touch the dead, these are Banarsi Bhojpuri speakers" (Simon 1995: 207).

6. On the seminal attempt to map linguistic variation across (colonial) India, see Grierson (1967). For critiques of Grierson's model and methods, see Shapiro and Schiffman (1981) and Lelyveld (1993), respectively. For an overview of many attempts to account for variation among Indo-Aryan languages and the classifications they propose, see Masica (1991), appendix 2. For an account of linguistic variation (with much more of an emphasis on sociolinguistic aspects of variation) specific to Varanasi, see Simon (1986).
7. For historical accounts of the standardization of Hindi and its increasing employment in and association with official contexts, see Apte (1976a), Dalmia (1997, 2003), Das Gupta (1976), Daswani (1989), Dua (1994b), Khubchandani (1983), Krishnamurti (1979), K. Kumar (1991b, 1993), LaDousa (2004), Orsini (2002), Pattanayak (1985), Southworth (1985), and Sridhar (1987).
8. See also Kaviraj (1992b).
9. For another treatment of the ways in which the colonial encounter shaped language categories and their hierarchies in India, see Cohn (1985). For a set of interesting articles that consider the exercise of colonial power in the collection of lore and proverbs, see Raheja (1996, 1999).
10. One might argue that Hindi's ties to Hindu identity mimics Arabic's ties to pan-Arabic nationalism in Egypt. Niloofar Haeri notes, "Thus pan-Arab ideology *overrode* other ideologies on the issue of language. The language of pan-Arabism is not the various 'divisive' and 'lowly' dialects but the unifying and standard Classical Arabic" (1997: 798). Haeri notes another Egyptian parallel with medium discourse in Varanasi: In Egypt, elites often use languages other than Arabic; international linguistic capital is not made available by Arabic. What makes the case of Varanasi quite different, however, is that Hindi has not been able to provide a pan-Indian symbol for the unification of Hindu identity; its reach is relegated to the Hindi or Cow Belt of North India, and it is resisted in other areas. Furthermore, medium discourse subverts wholesale the ideological underpinnings of the government's language policy.
11. Ahmad (2011) notes that some people now use Devanagari such that Urdu features are represented. He calls the variety "Urdu-in-Devanagari." He also notes that the representation of Urdu in schools generally is "pathetic" (280).
12. See Benei (2008) for the case of the state of Maharashtra where Marathi achieves the status of mother tongue in a way very different from the case of Hindi and the languages in its geographic domain.
13. This is not to claim, however, that education provided the only vehicle for the development of standardized forms. Krishna Kumar (1990: 1247) argues that during the crucial period of Hindi's standardization, 1880–1950, there was an explosion of magazines and literature. Francesca Orsini argues that textbooks contributed vitally to the standardization of Hindi in a gatekeeping role: "The journal expanded and validated varied new [Hindi] literary forms and experiments, the textbooks codified some as the only legitimate forms, and downplayed the others by excluding them" (2002: 92).
14. Note the difference between the ethnographic account of the notion of language medium offered here and the account of Khubchandani: "Owing to the rigorous academic base and to selective education, English, in spite of such intense use by

non-native speakers, has not been so greatly pidginized in the Indian context, but it definitely has acquired a certain regional flavor which distinguishes South Asian English from native standard varieties (British English, American English, etc.). The most prominent characteristic of South Asian English is the cheerful acceptance of regional deviations in pronunciation" (1984: 55). To people in Varanasi with whom I worked, much more important than schools' effect on the nativeness of English was its juxtaposition with Hindi as a medium of instruction. I present Khubchandani as an exemplar because his is one of the most ethnographically sophisticated approaches in sociolingustic work in India.

15. Thanks must go to an external reviewer for suggesting this line of argument.
16. See Demerath (1999, 2000) and Stambach (2000) for particularly insightful discussions of processes of cultural production involved in situations in which development, modernity, and the nation are at issue.
17. This ubiquitous construction hides a claim that I heard frequently about the primary school, grammar school, high school, and even intercollege students in schools where I observed. Teachers told me that Hindi is often the most difficult subject for students, more difficult than English, because many students have a very difficult time producing the correct *mātrā* forms, or combinations of consonants and vowels. Many teachers identified the distinction between *i* and *ī* as particularly difficult for students. The difference is especially important in the realization of the feminine grammatically (Agha 1998; Ki. Hall 2002). Some teachers explained with a smirk or a giggle that students "do not know" or "cannot write" their own "language" or "mother tongue." In this explanation, of course, "language" and "mother tongue" means Hindi to the exclusion of Bhojpuri, but the amused exasperation about the situation in which students make mistakes in their own language or mother tongue would seem to support the argument that Hindi and not English is the more difficult subject.
18. A school run by a board common to central schools that are all meant to serve the children of central government employees who may be posted away from their last assignment.
19. The use of the term "public" to denote fees-taking educational institutions not administered by the government originates in the colonial period. In Varanasi, I met some people who used "public," but many more who used "private" to denote such schools. Perhaps this reflects the growing presence of U.S.-centered media and of transmigration in Indian society.
20. A *dhotī* is a piece of cloth that is worn around the waist and legs. A *kurtā* is the stitched shirt worn on the upper body. The *dhotī* and *kurtā* can be considered traditional and/or formal depending on the context.

Chapter 2

Disparate Markets

The Uneven Resonance of Language-Medium Schooling in the Nation

The idea of national language prompts attention to language policy. Whereas scholars have neglected looking at schools through the lens of the mother tongue, they have devoted a great deal of research to the development of policy related to the question of India's national language and the particular languages that should be offered in schools. During the 1960s, the Government of India created an educational requirement known as the "three-language formula" in an effort to facilitate communication between different linguistic regions of the country (Naik and Nurullah 1974). School boards, as part of a "syllabus" legitimating schools, began to require that precollege students study three languages, the particular combination of which would vary by region. During my fieldwork, I have found only a few people to be familiar with the requirement or its purpose, although for at least a generation every student has been subjected to it. I learned quickly, however, that people in Varanasi use language distinctions as a convenient shorthand for talking about education, the nation, and one's future.

Hindi- and English-medium schools can be differentiated by whether they are associated with the "mother tongue" (*mātrabhāṣā*), but also by whether they are associated with the "national language" (*raṣṭrabhāṣā* or *deś kī bhāṣā*). The notion of mother tongue and the related notion of complex focus attention on distinctions between students within educational institutions, whereas the notion of national language draws attention to the ways that Hindi- and English-medium schools attain value in the larger world of differences between the national and the international. The distinction resonates in reflections on school practices. People understand Hindi-medium schools to embody the government's presence in schooling. They point to the collection of modest fees and affiliation with the UP Board. In contrast, they see English-medium schools as expensive and affiliated to other school boards. Language-medium schooling in the rubric of Hindi and English creates a wedge among people seeking class-marked educational credentials. This is reflected in the languages and the circumstances for which people imagine them to be useful, and in the institutional infrastructure of schooling.

National policy measures and commentary by people in Varanasi envision different relationships among language, schooling, and the nation. As one moves from policy to personal reflection, notions like "Hindi," as in the last chapter, but also "English" and "India," shift in significance and meaning. Most basically, the national policy measures created by the Government of India rest on a unifying principle while the ways in which people reflect on schools have dichotomizing tendencies. School language policy is based on the premise that students should expand their linguistic capabilities so that they can communicate with people in places far from their own. In Varanasi, people's notions of *raṣṭrabhāṣā* or *deś kī bhāṣā* (national language) and its relationship to schooling resemble their notions of *mātrabhāṣā* (mother tongue) in that they believe that Hindi and English form an opposition, setting students, families, and employees on different social and economic trajectories. Discourse about language medium oriented to the idea of national language always includes reference to one or both of two options: Hindi, imagined as India's "national language" (*raṣṭrabhāṣā* or *deś kī bhāṣā*), and English, imagined as an "international language" (*antarrāṣṭrabhāṣā*).

I do not wish to argue that people in Varanasi suffer because they do not know about national language policy or find it meaningful. Inequalities inflected by language and schooling exist that do not intersect the goals of language policy. Varanasi can be characterized, for example, by its lack of ability to provide a quality education, and the reason has everything to do with language. Some relatively elite people living in Varanasi have decided to have their children schooled elsewhere because they find schools in Varanasi generally unable to provide students with the ability to speak English free of Hindi elements.

Such people can be considered to be involved in class aspirations of a higher level than those of people in Varanasi who send their children to the city's schools. To these elites, more important than English's institutional difference from Hindi is the type of English a school offers. In turn, more important than institutional linguistic divisions within Varanasi is the city's inferiority relative to other places.

The notions of mother tongue and national language differ in a crucial respect because they construct different possibilities for reflection on language-medium schooling. Chapter 1 was able to explore the complex as a way in which people struggle to make sense of students' and their own social locations in the shadow of the language-medium division. Reflections on school difference by way of the notion of national language offer no such element of cultural production. In order to bring language policy and people's understandings of schooling to bear on one another, this chapter uses Bourdieu's notion of language market. Bourdieu (1991) famously argued that the modern state, by virtue of its schooling system, has centralized and unifying control over the production of valued language forms and practices.

The existence of three ideological constructions—the three-language formula, dual language mediums in Varanasi, and criticisms of Varanasi for its educational inadequacies—provides evidence that there are multiple language markets in India.[1] Monica Heller's understanding of schools as "social institutions" that she defines as "conventionalized social structures which organize resources, behavior, and meaning in certain ways that can be defined by social groups in order to advance their interests" is helpful in conceptualizing the different constructions of the nation underpinning the markets (1995: 373). In the three-language formula, the government envisions itself as a provider, via schools, of capital in the form of languages different from that of a student's own region. People in Varanasi who send their children to local schools imagine the government and the nation to be embodied by Hindi-medium schools, one option in a bifurcated system. And people who live in Varanasi and send their children to school elsewhere envision the nation as a market wherein the ability to speak English free of Hindi is a particularly important ability unattainable in places like Varanasi. Finally, to show that a market exists in India to which no one I knew in Varanasi—including those people sending their children to school elsewhere—seems to have had access, I turn to commentary published in national dailies and prestigious journals. The authors of this commentary imagine India to be a place handicapped in a global market by the type of English spoken there, and they place blame on the government.

The uneven and shifting resonance of the government in the language markets identified in this chapter reflect Akhil Gupta's assertion that "There is obviously no Archimedean point from which to visualize 'the state,' only numerous situated knowledges" (1995: 392). Sam Kaplan adds that the school is a key site for the production of such knowledges (2006: 13).[2] By situating knowledges of the state within different language markets, this chapter describes the language dilemma of the Government of India as its inability to produce capital for use in a market of its design. Many of the Indian nation's citizens participate in markets other than the one that the national government has tried to create. Constructions of "nation," "language," and "citizen" within these markets demonstrate that many of the nation's citizens ignore, but also subvert, the logic of the linguistic capital the government has tried to produce. Especially problematic for the Indian government and people in Varanasi is the disparity of the market complexes described below.

Three Languages, a National Formula for Education

To understand the Indian government's efforts toward linguistic integration, one must consider their ideological underpinnings. Webb Keane describes the attraction a national language holds for a national government: "The notion of a 'rational' and 'modern' national language rests on claims to a universality that transcends local particularities" (1997: 46). The Indian government is no stranger to a desire to "transcend local particularities," but it has never tried to do so by focusing on a single language.

Many scholars have offered accounts of the debates and struggles over a national language that occurred within the young nation's political sphere. Mahadev Apte (1976b) gives an interesting account of the strategies different ministers of parliament used to introduce, debate, or table concerns about language legislation and parliamentary procedure. Focusing more on the language varieties discussed, Jyotirindra Das Gupta (1970) describes Mahatma Gandhi's desire that Hindustani replace English in importance and become the national language, but notes that increasingly salient associations of Hindi with a Sanskrit-derived lexicon and Devanagari script and of Urdu with Muslim separatism, Nastaliq script, and a separate Pakistan made these languages' incorporation by Hindustani impossible to realize. Paul Brass notes that Hindi alone stood as a viable option for status as a single national language but that non-Hindi-speaking states' governments objected vehemently to its imposition. In the meantime, Urdu, increasingly associated with a lexicon derived from Persian and Arabic and with the Muslim faith and, thereby, disassociated from Hindi, was hidden in such concerns (Dalmia 1997; C. King 1994; Lelyveld 1993; Al. Rai 2001; Am. Rai 1984). A compromise ensued with an agreement that Hindi would become the sole official language of India in fifteen years (by 1965). Several events made the transition impossible, and another compromise in 1965, becoming the Official Languages Act in 1967, guaranteed that English would be retained as an "associate official language."

On the heels of these language debates, the Education Commission, also known as the Kothari Commission, devised a unifying plan in keeping with India's then-official multilingual mandate. From 1964 to 1966, the commission included within its National Policy on Education (NPE) a plan for the linguistic integration of the nation. Known as the "three-language formula," the plan mandates the teaching of a combination of three languages in the pre-university curriculum.[3] The formula's goal is to achieve national unity by creating multilingual citizens, specifically, ones equipped with languages of other regions in the nation.

The three-language formula was developed in the wake of several successful claims that regional language difference should determine state boundaries. The national government slowly and begrudgingly allowed the formation of new states whose cases for legitimacy rested largely on linguistic evidence.[4] Thus, the Nehruvian government divided Telegu-speaking from Tamil-speaking Madras in 1953, Marathi-speaking from Gujarati-speaking Bombay in 1956, and Punjabi-speaking from Hindi-speaking Punjab in 1966.[5]

This is not to imply that all such claims have been successful. For example, the movement to have the Maithili-language area in the northern part of the state of Bihar recognized as a separate state failed, just as Maithili was added to the Eighth Schedule of the Constitution of India in 2003. The Eighth Schedule includes languages recognized by the central government as official languages that will enrich Hindi, that will be developed in terms of scientific vocabulary and coinages for contemporary use, and that will be available for examinations for public service. Twenty-two languages are included in the Eighth Schedule, the most recent languages, Bodo, Maithili, Dogri, and Santali, being admitted in 2003. Not all languages recognized by states are listed in the Eighth Schedule. For example, the state government of Sikkim recognizes languages that are not included in the national legislation. The goal herein is to explain the ideology of linguistic unity at the level of the national government. Its relationship to local levels is, no doubt, varied. For example, particular dilemmas and contradictions discussed later are typical of Varanasi, and dilemmas in locales in a place like Sikkim likely differ radically.

Despite such vicissitudes, two standardized languages differ from those associated with state boundaries. Hindi predominates in several states, some highly populated, covering a vast geographic area in the northern part of the country.[6] The national government had little worry about fracture in the Hindi-speaking area; regional languages (such as Bhojpuri), some with associated literary genres and substantial numbers of speakers (such as Braj Bhasha and Avadhi), were understood to be "dialects" of Hindi, already mutually intelligible with the standard.[7] English, unlike Hindi, is not associated with any particular region but, rather, with urban, educated, upper-class people. Indeed, an influential government report on the state of languages in schools lists English as one of the most important languages for use in education despite its absence in the Eighth Schedule (Chaturvedi and Mohale 1976: 43). This situation posed a dilemma for language planning, evidenced by the explicit mention of both languages in the 1968 National Policy on Education: "At the secondary stage, the State Governments should adopt, and vigorously implement, the three language formula which includes the study of a modern Indian language, preferably one of the southern languages, apart from Hindi and English in the Hindi-speaking states, and of Hindi along with the regional language and English in the non-Hindi speaking states" (1968: xvii).[8] Education makes a few constitutionally recognized standardized languages into emblems of the nation.

The three-language formula represents "unity in diversity," a Nehruvian motto that, Brian Axel (2002: 236) argues, continues to inform the Indian government's representations of the nation. One need look no further than the formula's encoding of diversity, however, to understand why serious disagreements arose among the states about the fairness of its implementation. Although the formula establishes states as the administrative units for linguistic legitimacy in India, it cannot implement a one-to-one connection between states and languages. The "Hindi-speaking states" compose the axis on which the formula is built. Whereas a "southern language" (Kannada, Malayalam, Tamil, or Telegu) should be taught in school in a Hindi-speaking state, Hindi alone should be taught in all non-Hindi-speaking states (including northern states such as West Bengal, Gujarat, Maharashtra, Orissa, and Punjab). Indeed, a few state governments (especially that of Tamil Nadu in the South) fiercely objected to the teaching of Hindi in their schools (Ramaswamy 1997). The formula includes a built-in contradiction with its encoding of linguistic diversity by means of state identification. Nevertheless, the formula continues to mandate, at a national level, that every student acquire a trio of languages in school.[9] In grades one through ten, one should learn in the language of one's own state. In grades five through ten, one should start the second language. In grades eight through ten, one should start the third (Sridhar 1991: 92).

The Lack of Resonance of the Three-Language Formula in Varanasi

Knowledge of the government's language policy for schools is largely absent among Varanasi's residents, regardless of socioeconomic or professional position.[10] Not one person with whom I talked in the city during a year of field research knew of the three-language formula. I asked about it often, and the first reaction of many was to reply simply that a student has to study three languages in school. Indeed, the most common way that students reflected on multilingual pedagogy was to complain about having to learn more than one language. They did so in interviews with me as well as in conversations with peers. Much more common, however, were complaints about math, physics, biology, or some other science. Not until I visited Delhi, the nation's capital, did I meet someone who knew about the formula explicitly. A retired administrator of the Central Board of Secondary Education (CBSE) explained the details of the formula exactly, including its date of ratification. When I told her that no one I had met in Varanasi seemed to know about the formula, she used my report to launch a general diatribe about the poor quality of schooling outside of the capital. I suspect, however, that she derived her knowledge of the policy from her rather high official post, and not from her residence or education in the capital, because I met many in Delhi who shared Varanasi residents' lack of knowledge.

In Varanasi, the three-language formula has an effect on schools' language requirements: in every school that I visited, the curriculum included instruction in three languages. A consideration of which languages, however, quashes the idea that the national government's ideology of national integration has been successfully implemented. In all of the schools that I visited in Varanasi, Hindi and English were two of the three languages offered. The third language was most often Sanskrit, although, at a few schools, some other language from the northern part of India was taught—Bengali, Urdu, and so on. No school that I visited offered any of the four southern-based Dravidian languages specified by the formula. A school in one neighborhood, I was told, offered Telegu, a Dravidian language, but the language primarily served to maintain the residents' already established competence. Varanasi's situation is reflected more generally in Brass's (1990: 143) discussion of the problems that the Government of India has encountered in implementing the three-language formula, including finding teachers competent in the required languages who are willing to move to other regions. I would only add that I was aware of schools in Varanasi that had teachers competent in a Dravidian language and capable of teaching it as the third language in the formula. The southern languages, however, were never taught; Sanskrit or another northern state's language always took their place. Thus, although teaching three languages has become a taken-for-granted aspect of school curricula in Varanasi, the national government has been ineffectual in inculcating the ideology that communication with southern states via a southern language might benefit the nation.

Hindi- and English-Medium in Varanasi: *Laḍḍu* and Toffee

While Varanasi's residents are largely unaware of the three-language formula, they care about the language medium of a school. Furthermore, they use the distinction between Hindi- and English-medium schools to invoke ideological constructions of language, nation, and citizen. In an ironic interchange I witnessed, students and parents reflected on a ritual at school and drew from several spheres of meaning to criticize the national government. Christopher Pinney argues that criticism is typical of reflections on the Indian government in public discourse: "The sense of a state which is not adequate to the needs of its nation is a recurrent trope in recent Indian public culture" (2001: 29). The people present at the interchange described here criticized the government through its institutional embodiment as one-half of a dichotomy, itself structured by education. A Hindi-medium school came to embody the government and an English-medium school came to embody the alternative.

I had just attended the Saraswati School's Saraswati *pūjā*. Saraswati is the Hindu goddess of learning and knowledge, and, in recent years, the puja, or festival, in which she is worshipped has grown in popularity and has come to be associated with students generally (N. Kumar 1988: 219). I headed for a tea stall to join two friends, Ramesh and

Ashish, whom I had met during previous visits to Varanasi. As I approached the tea stall, I spotted my friends as well as the stall owner's wife and her three daughters. I had come to know the three girls well, seeing them daily at the Hindi-medium government-administered Saraswati school from which I had just come, and, less frequently, helping their mother at the stall after classes. The three girls were still in their uniforms, having, like myself, just arrived from school. I greeted Ramesh and Ashish, exchanged a smile with the stall owner's wife, and sat on the stall's bench.

Figure 2. Receiving *laḍḍu* at Saraswati Puja.

The woman distributed tea as her youngest daughter blurted out, "Did you get *laḍḍu*?" (*laḍḍu mil gaye ha͂i*?). Everyone laughed, myself included. Many times during my morning walk to the Saraswati School, students had called out, "*laḍḍusā*!" (which, in Hindi, means "like a *laḍḍu*" [a sweetmeat], and is also my last name, LaDousa). My name had become a pun throughout the neighborhood. I answered that I had, whereupon Ashish remarked wryly, "I pay this much money and my son only gets toffee" (*itnā paisā dete aur hamāre laṛke ko sirf tăfī miltī hai*). Ashish mentioned money because his son was attending the Seacrest School, for which fees are extremely high, in contrast to the girls' school. All smiled when Ramesh, single and with no children, returned, "Yes, but one does not get sick from eating toffee" (*hā̃ lekin tăfī khāne se bīmārī nahī̃ hotī*). The stall owner's wife added with a grin that "things of the government" (*sarkār kī cīzẽ*) are "things of sickness" (*bīmārī kī cīzẽ*). The comment was less cryptic to my friends than to me because they laughed heartily whereas I politely and belatedly joined them.

I thought long and hard about the interaction after arriving home and scribbling down details of it. On further reflection, I began to realize that distinctions within and across several spheres of meaning helped to make some of the comments both humorous and serious. Ashish introduced the issue of cost. Toffees cost roughly fifty paise, or one-half of one rupee (in 1996–1997, approximately Rs 36 equaled $1.00 (U.S.)), making them a cheap treat for children to enjoy after school. Ashish had brought his son to the stall in the afternoon on several occasions still dressed in his school uniform, and everyone at the stall was aware that Ashish was talking about the distribution of toffees by his son's school for the puja. A *laḍḍu* cost more than a piece of toffee. The price of a *laḍḍu,* depending on the type, ranged from one and one-half to several rupees. Ashish's comment establishes as ironic the distribution by the Hindi-medium government school of the more expensive *laḍḍu* for the puja.

Other distinctions, however, were at play to enable the final joke-making allusion to health. A switch in parameters of difference created an ironic reversal, and the image made all present laugh. *Laḍḍu* is part of the larger food group *miṭhāī* (sweetmeat), which includes perishable and locally produced items; indeed, the *laḍḍu* distributed at the Saraswati School were made by the students on the premises. "Fresh" (*tāzā*) and "hot" (*garam*) are some of the attributes that make such sweetmeats particularly delicious. Toffees, in contrast, are produced in a factory and have rather long shelf lives; their production is seemingly standard, precluding their involvement in the aesthetic judgment open to sweetmeats. Irrelevant in the case of toffees is critique or praise that points to the time expended since production, quality of ingredients, and techniques of production, storage, and display.

Ramesh replaced the idiom of cost with that of health by noting that *laḍḍu* opens its consumer to risk. *Laḍḍu* may be more expensive or more desired than toffee, but it is also more dangerous. Ramesh's comment could be construed as inappropriate given that the *laḍḍu* is received by students as *prasād*, a gift from the goddess Saraswati "marking" students with her auspicious substance (Marriott 1976). Wrapped pieces of toffee are far less effective conduits of the goddess's blessing than an unwrapped *laḍḍu*. Thus, Ramesh, like Ashish, had reversed the logic of the puja by noting that a *laḍḍu* exposes its consumer to harm that is obviated in a piece of toffee with its mass-produced origins. The stall owner nailed home the conflation of the local with the government by attributing to it the risk of illness that the consumption of sweetmeats entails. Although consuming the local *laḍḍu* temporarily might seem like the better deal because it is more expensive and delicious, in the long run the non-local toffee is a safer bet.

The vignette is interesting not just for the ways that objects emerge in a reflection on the divergent values of Hindi- and English-medium schools, but also for the ways that the people involved are positioned in terms of social class. The attendance of the tea stall owner's daughter at a government-affiliated Hindi-medium school reflects the desire on the part of a working-class family to have their daughters educated in pursuit of decent marriages and, perhaps, employment. The social class positions of my friends were more solidly middle-class as they were engaged in occupations that paid much more than ownership of a tea stall. The language-medium divide is thus salient to a wide range of social class positions just as it can be used to make distinctions between middle-class pursuits and dispositions.

Fees, School Boards, and the Politics of Language

The dichotomous image built in the interchange described above introduces the bifurcated manner in which languages and schools are mutually imagined in Varanasi. Important to Varanasi residents is whether a school is Hindi-medium or English-medium. When people in Varanasi talk about schools, they often cast as oppositional schools like that of the tea seller's three daughters, the Hindi-medium Saraswati School, and that of Ashish's son, the English-medium Seacrest

School. The two schools constitute extreme possibilities along an axis of language ideologies focused on language medium.

The language divide among schools is underpinned by differences of administrative control and financing: Hindi-medium schools are usually less expensive and under government administration via the UP Board, whereas English-medium schools usually charge higher fees and are affiliated with one of the private administrative boards. The most prestigious English-medium schools in Varanasi are affiliated, like the Seacrest School, with the CBSE. Paraphrasing D.L. Sheth (1990), Rejeswari Rajan describes the "dual system" as "the existence of (a small number of) expensive public schools where English is the medium of instruction from the lowest classes, along with (a preponderance of) regional-language schools, for the most part run by governments or municipalities, where English is taught—badly—as a subject for a few years" (1992: 19). Manabi Majumdar and Jos Mooij argue that the dichotomy is a lasting one: "It is particularly the middle classes and the elites who have exited the government school system in large numbers" (2011: 8). The issue of cost in the interchange about treats, for example, evokes the heavy subsidies that government-administered schools receive and that greatly reduce the amount of "fees" (tuition) required for monthly attendance.

Fees: Cheap versus Expensive

The payment of school fees is one of the most important of the institutional practices that serve as means to differentiate Hindi- and English-medium schools. My assumptions about how people would reflect on fees, however, were only sometimes correct. I asked about fees often, assuming that reflections on them would elicit interpretive frames used to organize the stakes of school attendance.[11] My use of the term fees for understanding reflections on schooling and cost was largely inappropriate for conversations about schools with many of the people with whom I spoke in Varanasi.

For example, after a few weeks of residing in her house, I used the word fees to ask my landlady about the cost of her daughter's government affiliated Hindi-medium school, the downstairs Saraswati School. She looked at me searchingly, and smiled awkwardly. Finally, after an uncomfortable half minute or so, she replied, "Meaning one and one-half to two rupees?" (*māne do ḍeṛh rupaye*?). When I responded affirmatively, she giggled nervously and added, "yes, that's all" (*hā̃ bas*). The focus on fees produced the same dynamic, confusion coupled with nervous humor, with all of my initial interlocutors involved in some way with government affiliated Hindi-medium schools. What I began to realize is that people wondered why I was asking about school fees because the fees were so low. They were not exactly sure how to answer my question.

When I inquired about fees with parents of privately owned Hindi-medium schools (such as the upstairs Saraswati School), they simply told me the amount as a matter of fact. Most private Hindi-medium schools charged between Rs 20 and 40 per month in 1996–1997 while a few schools charged as much as Rs 80. By the time of my fieldwork in 2010, those amounts had doubled. The reactions of parents of students at private English-medium schools, where tuitions were up to five times that of their most expensive private Hindi-medium counterparts, mirrored those of parents at private Hindi-medium schools. The substantial amount of fees at such schools seemed to make for a reasonable topic of conversation.

I learned to ask the parents or other "guardians," those people responsible for the student's welfare, of Hindi-medium students at government-affiliated schools about "expenses" (*kharc*). In contrast to the tense and short-lived discussions of fees, discussions of expenses were extremely productive, prompting a predictable list of items such as "books" (*kitābẽ*), "notebooks," (*kāpiyā̃*), "paper" (*kāgaz*), "pens" (*ḳalamẽ*), "pencils" (*pansilẽ*), "cloth" (*kapṛā*), and "sewing" (*silāī*). Indeed, the PROBE (Public Report on Basic Education in India) Team comprising independent researchers who administered a survey in villages across the Hindi-speaking states of Bihar, Himachal Pradesh, Madhya Pradesh, Rajasthan, and Uttar Pradesh from September to December 1996 report that the 318 households sending their children to government primary schools found a similar set of expenses most dear. The PROBE Team reports that respondents listed "fees" at Rs 16, "textbooks/stationery" at Rs 99, "uniform/clothes for school" at Rs 159, "private tuitions" at Rs 25, and "travel and other expenditures" at Rs 19 (1999: 32).

The most costly expenditure related to schooling mentioned by people in Varanasi was "tuition" (*ṭuiśan*). This term did not refer to the payment for school attendance, but rather to the tutor in one or more subjects that is widely thought to be necessary for the student's success in school. Reporting from their fieldwork in Bijnor, a district in Uttar Pradesh several hundred kilometers to the northwest of Varanasi, Roger and Patricia Jeffery and Craig Jeffrey note: "Tuition is relatively uncommon for pupils in classes 6–8, but most pupils who can afford to do so take regular tuition in science, English, and maths for the class 10 exams, paying out a total of around Rs 500–700 per month. In classes 11 and 12, pupils in the science streams may pay up to Rs 1,000 for tuition in biology, physics, and chemistry, possibly also continuing with maths and English" (2005: 50). In Varanasi, I saw that students from the third and fourth levels utilized tuitions, and their families reported paying the tutor between several hundred and one thousand rupees per month (in 1996–1997). The upper range is several times the fees then charged by Varanasi's most expensive schools. A number of factors might explain the ubiquity of tuitions in Varanasi via-à-vis Bijnor. Varanasi is a much larger city. Perhaps more significantly, tuition is an employment niche very popular with students attending Banaras Hindu University and Kashi Vidyapith. Families considered themselves lucky if they had managed to find a relative, a "cousin-sister" or "cousin-brother," who might take less money because of the kin connection. Some parents and students of both Hindi-medium and English-medium schools explained that more than one tuition (referring to the person or the subject) can be required, making school an almost impossible financial endeavor (cf. N. Kumar 2007, chapters 10 and 13).

Devdas Singh, for example, had five children in 2005. Two of them (a boy and a girl) were studying in Hindi-medium government schools. When I asserted, "I have heard that many people use tutors" (*m̃ai ne sunā ki bahut log ṭuiśan kā istemāl karte h̃ai*), he replied,

> *yaha to sar karte h̃ai log ṭuiśan kā istemāl karte h̃ai lekin bahut mahangā paṛ jātā. ham garīb log ke liye nahī̃ h̃ai. ab ham log mān lījiye do hazār rupaye mahīnā kā kamāte h̃ai aur do hazār rupaye pā̃c bacce h̃ai. do bacce skūl jāte h̃ai. aur batāiye do bacce ko alag alag ṭuiśan paṛhāne. to ṭuiśan kā fīs itnā zyādā kahā̃ se āegā. tīn sau rupaye ṭuiśan kā fīs lag jāegā. usī mẽ bacce ko khānā khānā hai apnā bhojan kapṛā bhī cāhiye pansils noṭbuk.... har cīz mahangā hai sar har cīz mahangā hai sir. isliye ṭuiśan garīb log to nahī̃ kar sakte h̃ai.*
>
> As for this, sir, they do, people use tutors, but they are very expensive. They are not for us poor people. Now please understand that I make two thousand rupees a month and two thousand rupees and I have five children. Two children go to school. So please tell me where the money for tuitions for each child will come from. Where will this much come from? The tuition fees are three hundred rupees [per month]. For that, the children have to eat ... their own food [for consumption at school], they need clothing too, pencils, notebook.... Everything is expensive sir, everything is expensive sir. Therefore, poor people cannot hire tuitions.

Devdas likely underestimates the charges incurred in hiring a tutor because he is unable to do so. The amount of Rs 300 emerges as a costly sum in his estimation. Interestingly, it was the mention of a tuition that often prompted Hindi-medium students' parents or guardians, were they employing one, to liken their own financial burdens to those of parents or guardians of English-medium students.

While a discussion of fees seemed awkward to the parents of Hindi-medium students attending government schools, the topic could nevertheless arise when it invoked a contrast with English-medium schools. This was true whether the students' Hindi-medium schools were affiliated with the government or were private. Consistently, when the parents of Hindi-medium students contrasted the fees charged by English-medium schools with those charged by their own children's schools, they exaggerated the upper amount, sometimes reporting three times the amount of actual charges. For example, even the principal of the government-affiliated downstairs Saraswati School explained that an English-medium school nearby "takes nine hundred rupees [per month]" (*nau sau rupaye lete haĩ*). She followed with a rhetorical question about how anyone but "rich people" (*amīr log*) could send their children to English-medium schools. The fees for the English-medium school's upper grade levels (eleventh and twelfth), the most expensive, were, in reality, Rs 320 per month. When I asked the principal of the downstairs Saraswati School to specify the amount of her own school's fees, she stated, "one and one-half to two rupees" (*do ḍeṛh rupaye*), and, with a short pause, elaborated in English "free."

The differentiation of schools by fees, sometimes exaggerated, underpins the division between Hindi- and English-medium schools. There are Hindi-medium schools that are private and charge fees such as the upstairs Saraswati School. There are a few English-medium schools that are affiliated with the government where fees are nominal. But, in the rubric of Irvine and Gal (2000), these are "erased" in talk about schools because Hindi-medium and government affiliation, on the one hand, and English-medium and private ownership, on the other hand, align in conversations about schooling to characterize school types. I would gradually find out that those schools that charge a meaningful amount of fees, questions about which draw so much confusion (until English-medium schools are mentioned), are called "government" (*sarkārī*) schools. Indeed, the government provides a substantial subsidy to the schools, reducing their fees. In 1996–1997, many people used a kind of shorthand that I did not understand at first. People referred to such schools, along with telephone service, natural gas allotments, and pension funds, using a noun in place of an adjective. Thus, people sometimes called such things *sarkār* (noun) rather than *sarkārī* (adjective). With the preponderance of cell phones and the privatization of many government services, such expressions have faded, but the association of low school fees with government administration, and of both with Hindi-medium schools, remains.

Consistently, people drew a contrast between government schools and the handful of very expensive schools in Varanasi, most of which people could rattle off by name. I often asked about the language medium of expensive schools. People, even those involved with private Hindi-medium schools where fees are not insignificant, treated me as if I were a bit dense, noting that such schools are English-medium. Sometimes people assumed an ironic stance in discussions about schools, singling out the schools in Varanasi that charge the highest fees. People would sarcastically mention that even the children of rickshawallas attend the most expensive schools in Varanasi. The sarcasm would be followed by the comment that attendance by such students is "useless" (*bekār*). The children of rickshawallas, according to such people, would not benefit from the sacrifices entailed by exorbitant fees because they would not be able to find the type of job for which their education was ostensibly preparing them. It was in the context of such discussions that the issue of language medium emerged. Some people added a rhetorical quip about the child of a rickshawalla's need of English.

An encounter provides a prelude to the ways, treated in the next section, that the divide between the government and the private school, underpinned by differences between Hindi- and English-medium, can entail spatial logics in addition to notions about cost. During fieldwork in 2005, I was chatting with an owner of a pharmacy in New Colony near my place of residence from 1996–1997. We were talking about how the street in front of his store had been paved, and how the neighborhood was now joined to a bustling neighborhood to the south by a bridge traversing a large drainage canal. The cricket field on which boys had played after school ten years before was now a traffic-clogged road feeding rickshaws, auto rickshaws, and cars into New Colony for travel beyond. Just as we were talking about the marked increase in traffic, several buses rumbled by. These were not painted Seacrest's familiar blue, but bright yellow. I noted that Delhi Public School, the name written on the side of each bus, must be somewhat new because it had not existed in Varanasi during prior visits. He told me that Delhi Public School was popular with "rich people" (*amīr log*), and that the inclusion of the name of the capital was meant to trump the names of local schools in terms of prestige. A principal of an NGO school explained that Delhi Public School is indeed a chain that had arrived in Varanasi two years previously, and that the school can be found "in every city from Delhi to Varanasi and even beyond." Such a feeling is not universal. The principal of the Seacrest School explained that her school has many more students that the Delhi Public School in Varanasi, and that her school had started a branch in Lucknow, the capital of Uttar Pradesh. But all of the vignettes hint that private schools can derive part of their prestige by their association with elsewhere.

Boards: State versus Private

School boards are like fees because they too serve as a means to differentiate Hindi- and English-medium schools. School boards are also like fees because there is no direct connection between school board affiliation and the language medium of a school. Boards are administrative bureaucracies to which schools must apply to gain affiliation. A board requires that an affiliated school offers the courses comprising a "syllabus" (*silabas*); suggests, or, in the case of government-affiliated schools, mandates the books that a school can use; and oversees the distribution and grading of yearly exams. Results determine which students can proceed to the next grade level. Attaining board affiliation is notoriously complicated, difficult, and costly, and any school administrator sees her or his own board affiliation as an achievement or, if several decades old, as something thankfully accomplished by someone else. Such a feeling characterizes the administrators of Hindi- or English-medium schools, whether government-administered or private. Thus, in a sense, all boards fall under the purview of the Government of India in that all boards must meet a set of standards.

Yet, boards reinforce the division between Hindi- and English-medium schools in a way parallel to the way in which fees reinforce this division. For example, most government-administered schools are associated with what people in Varanasi call the "Allahabad Board," the designation focusing on the board's location in the nearby city of Allahabad. At the national level, the same board is called the "Uttar Pradesh Board" or "UP Board," focusing on the board's jurisdiction in the state in which both Varanasi and Allahabad are located. Affiliation with the UP Board enables a school to receive the funds not nearly compensated by the family's nominal tuition payment, the basis on which such schools are sometimes described as free, as well as teachers' salaries that tend to be four to five times greater than those received by private school teachers.

A contrast in boards parallels the contrast in fees because the CBSE is a board to which Varanasi's most expensive private schools are af-

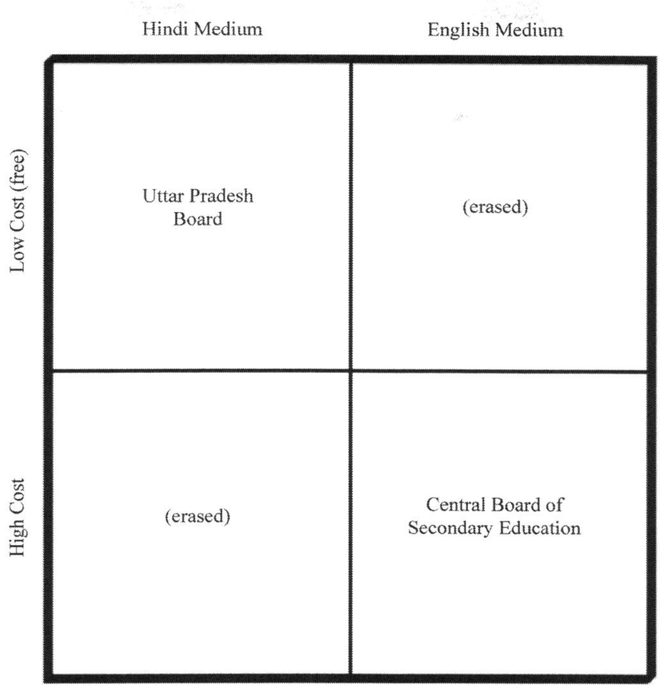

Figure 3. Relationship among language medium, fee expense, and board affiliation.

filiated. Indeed, affiliation with the CBSE, many school principals and teachers at all types of schools explained, allows a school to take high fees. Affiliation with the CBSE is a source of pride for administrators and teachers, and is noted on signboards and advertisements of many affiliated schools. Figure 4 depicts a signboard for Tulsi Vidya Niketan, a moderately expensive school located on the southern edge of the city. The sign also makes explicit that the school is affiliated with the CBSE at all levels, primary, secondary, and "up to class XII" that includes the intercollege levels eleven and twelve. These last two levels are crucial for students desiring university admission.

During initial fieldwork in 1996–1997, board exam results were posted on local buildings so that students could consult them for their results. Now, board results are posted online by both the UP Board and the CBSE. The UP Board's website claims to be the "biggest examining body in the world" and explains that it is "holding the examinations and preparing the results of nearly 32 lakh students [3.2 million students]." The website goes on to claim: "In Uttar Pradesh a

Figure 4. Tulsi Vidya Niketan signboard.

few secondary schools are being governed by the Indian Council of School Education (I.C.S.E.) and Central Board of Secondary Education (C.B.S.E.), but most of the secondary schools seek recognition of the U.P. Board. At present there are 9121 secondary schools recognized by the U.P. Board of High School and Intermediate Education" (Board of High School and Intermediate Education Uttar Pradesh, n.d.). While the date of exam results is current, the date of the information reported above is uncertain, though the homepage reports 2001–2002 as the current fiscal year.

While the UP Board claims (worldwide) supremacy in numbers, the CBSE's website claims a global presence. On reaching the homepage with a button for examination results, the word "India" appears. The names of countries, starting with Singapore, Russia, and Indonesia, fly across the screen until the message "21 countries" appears. This disappears and in quick succession the messages "More than 10,000 schools" and "Over 12 million students" appear. One finally reaches "Welcome to CBSE" with an option to replay the opening sequence.

The Seacrest School noted its affiliation with the CBSE on its signboards and advertisements during my initial fieldwork in 1996–1997. In 2005, I noticed that reference to the CBSE had disappeared from Seacrest's signboards and advertisements. The principal explained to me that Seacrest's reputation had grown so much that people assume its affiliation with the CBSE and, therefore, there is no need to include the affiliation on visual representations of the school. During my initial fieldwork, the principal spoke at length about the importance of affiliation with the CBSE, blending curricular requirements of the board with the high performance of Seacrest's students on the board exams: "We teach according to the CBSE board. The syllabus we follow, that is from the board, the CBSE board, and in the CBSE board, up to class ten, all the subjects are compulsory, and, besides those main subjects like Hindi, English, mathematics, social studies, and science, these are the compulsory subjects. I can say we have a very good reputation regarding all, hmm, they, our children have proven worth, they have shown very good results in the board examination." The principal went on to explain how difficult and expensive it was to build the school's curriculum to attain affiliation with the CBSE. The principal explained that the expense, coupled with the students' strong performance on exams, justifies the high fees charged by the schools.

By 2005, such board-related challenges had faded somewhat. The principal of Seacrest explained that the school's primary concerns have moved to other ventures to make the school distinct from others. The school, for example, had started a radio station. Students with special musical talents could thus be featured. Later, by 2007, the school had dropped its radio venture and had begun to buy time on a local television channel. Various programs, plays, and award ceremonies were aired on the television station. This in not to claim that CBSE affiliation is not important, however. One of the first things that the principal did during our reunion in her office in 2007 was to show me a signboard displaying the names of the school's toppers, students who excel on the CBSE examination. She noted how much longer the list had grown since my initial visits in 1996–1997. Indeed, on the school's website, students desiring admission to the eleventh and twelfth levels are informed that they must have a CBSE board exam result of at least 85 percent at the tenth level.

The division between board affiliations interpolates the division between Hindi- and English-medium schools along with the division between cheap and expensive schools. Just as "cheap" (*sastā*) (or "free") describes those schools affiliated with the UP Board and "expensive" (*mahangā*) describes schools affiliated with the CBSE, the schools are assumed to be Hindi-medium and English-medium, respectively. In one conversation, the principal of the Hindi-medium government-administered Saraswati School explained that the board affiliation and language medium of a school are "different issues" (*alag alag bāt h̃ai*).

She explained that "private schools" (*prāyvaṭ skūls*) take fees and that "government schools" (*sarkārī skūls*) do not. She was right, of course. Ravi Kumar, for example, asserts, "one finds that ... government schools are generally used by people who cannot afford the private schools" (2009: 151). Yet, when I asked her whether schools affiliated with the CBSE teach in English, she replied as if my assertion were a foregone conclusion: "yes, yes, what else?" (*hā̃ hā̃ aur kyā?*). I received a similar answer when I asked her whether schools affiliated with the UP Board are Hindi-medium. Associations between board affiliation and language medium thus exhibit a complex process of semiotic erasure whereby the low cost of government schools is taken to be indicative of Hindi-medium status and the high cost of schools affiliated with the CBSE is taken to be indicative of English-medium status. Private Hindi-medium schools and English-medium schools not affiliated with the CBSE are erased in discursive reflection on boards.

While the differences between schools configured by their board affiliations mirror the differences between schools configured by the amount of fees they charge, the issue of school boards shows that Hindi-medium and English-medium schools operate in different conceptions of spatial spheres. When we talked about the significance of board affiliation, the principal of the Saraswati School initially focused on the yearly exam procedure, whereby teachers from schools affiliated with the UP Board must travel to other UP Board schools in Varanasi to grade exams. This procedure, the principal explained, obviates bias in scoring exams. Later, however, she noted the many ways in which the Saraswati School has a "special relationship" (*khās riśtā*) with UP Board schools in its vicinity. For example, many times during the year of my visits, the principal showed me a trophy case in which the trophies that the school's students had won were displayed. She told me that the school has an intense rivalry in sports with schools nearby. She also told me something that I had seen enacted in school each day. The children who attend the Saraswati School (both levels, as I could see) are from the surrounding neighborhood, and one can see large groups of friends playing during recess and then walking home together, the groups getting smaller as particular students reach their destinations. Some students do travel to the more distant parts of the neighborhood by cycle rickshaw, but they are in the minority. Most students live so close that they can easily and safely walk. Such was not the case with schools affiliated to the CBSE. For example, the principal and owner of the Seacrest School explained that the prestige of the school draws students from all over Varanasi. Indeed, a huge traffic jam of cycle and auto rickshaws, cars, and the school's buses that now number over 100 occurred in front of the school morning and afternoon. Some of the branches of the Seacrest School have started accepting students who live at the school. They draw students from beyond Varanasi, something no school affiliated to the UP Board does.

Schools, Language, and the Nation in Varanasi

The process through which Hindi- and English-medium school identities are constructed relationally is anchored in mundane practices like fee collection and board affiliation, but also in a set of rather complex and uneven developments in the political and ideological dimensions of language in late-twentieth-century and early-twenty-first-century India. The opposition prompted by the mention of a school is informed by an increasingly salient linguistic opposition between Hindi and English in Indian society. Language-medium distinctions and political language developments resemble one another in the shadow of the three-language formula because in neither realm is national unity stressed. Rather, the realm of language-medium schooling and the realm of language politics both rely on oppositions as well as differences.

Richard Fox (1990) has identified the formation of a new identity, "Hindian," that comprises a mix of lower-middle classes and urban forward castes. Since the mid 1970s, the group so identified has felt increasingly threatened by rural class mobility, employment reservations for traditionally disadvantaged groups, and remittances that Muslims receive from relatives who live in the Gulf states. For the Hindian, the Hindi language—with a lexicon derived from Sanskrit (not Persian or Arabic, which for many people renders the language Urdu)—has become an icon for Hindu nationalism (*hindutva*), a project destined to undo the damages wrought by partition and secularism.

Fox explains that English provides Hindi and Hindu nationalism with an image of the alien transgressor. Indeed, Franklin Southworth argues, "The new Hindi [with a Sanskrit-derived lexicon] as developed by pandits and politicians, is one of the most important tools in the struggle to oust English from its position of importance in government, commerce, and elsewhere" (1985: 232). The rise of the Hindu-fundamentalist Bharatiya Janata Party in the 1990s, for example, saw many politicians speaking out against English as a language alien to India, bringing with it many inappropriate ideas and practices.[12] Sometimes politicians connected English to a fear of conversion to Christianity, and sometimes they connected English to the consumption of popular media and goods (Viswanathan 2007: 333). Sonntag notes that "the anti-English tone ... has won few friends for the BJP" given the party's base among the middle and upper classes and castes (2000: 148). Baral continues, "Even the Bharatiya Janata Party ... has recognized the primacy of the English language and has toned down its anti-English rhetoric, moving away from its advocacy of cultural nationalism borne out by the slogan 'Hindi, Hindu, and Swadeshi'" (2006: 476). Krishna Kumar (1991c) explains that English-literate elites have been unconcerned with Hindi's increasing Sanskritization and association with an essentially Hindu nation and that their lack of attention has exacerbated the increasing ideological divide between themselves and those Fox identifies as Hindians.

Much more sustained has been the political targeting of Urdu as a language of an alien transgressor in the form of Muslims in India. Anti-Urdu rhetoric could be interwoven with the 1990s attacks on mosques such as the Babri Masjid in Ayodhya, northwest of Varanasi, meant to reclaim birthplaces of Hindu gods. I have found a few people in Varanasi and Delhi who have talked about the division between Hindi and Urdu, especially the very visible issue of script difference. In a Saraswati Shishu Mandir, a school run by the Hindu-fundamentalist Rashstriya Swayamsevak Sangh (RSS), for example, I encountered someone who had strong feelings on the subject. The RSS is a Hindu-fundamentalist organization that runs a chain of schools across the nation popular for their inculcation of respect and discipline (Guichard 2010: 42–43). In the middle of a first conversation with the principal of the school, the man politely interrupted me and explained that my use of the word *ādmī* (man) indicated that I had studied Hindi first overseas because the word comes from Arabic. He explained that *ādmī* is Urdu and not Hindi. When I asked him what word I should use instead, he replied that *puruṣ* (man) is *śuddh* (correct) Hindi. I asked why people overseas might use a word derived from Arabic and he explained that many governments overseas support Arab nations by buying oil from them. I could not help but notice the large number of words and phrases that he used in our conversation with Arabic (or Persian) origins.

People also reflected, of course, on the distinction between Hindi and English, but most of the reflection I heard in Varanasi emerged through schooling and its relationship to labor. One of the most common reflections I heard during fieldwork was that English-medium schools provide a route out of Varanasi because they enable movement. Conversations about schooling in Varanasi often involved the verb *ghūmnā*, meaning to wander or to roam. A common refrain across

Hindi-speaking North India is that to get a job one must relocate. This is true for labor-intensive construction work as well as for desk jobs. People explain that education prepares one for the latter type of employment, yet the job is likely to be elsewhere. This is especially true when one is from a region like eastern Uttar Pradesh, which is largely left out of the information and digital technology sector. People in Varanasi told me as a matter of routine that education in an English-medium school would be necessary for middle-class employment elsewhere, whether secured beforehand or after relocation. Any office offering the type of work associated with a middle-class standing might demand competence in English. Furthermore, relocation might bring one into contact with others who do not share one's primary language, and mutual competence in English will serve as a communicative bridge. Needless to say, such ideas came with their own class-marked prejudices and blinders. Never, for example, did the manual labor for which so many move away from home figure into connections between movement and schooling. The erasure of manual labor from discussions of movement seems to constitute a silent connection between English-medium schooling and middle-class employment.

Some people explicitly contrasted the English-medium school's provision of mobility with Hindi-medium schools. Hindi-medium schoolchildren, such people explained, will not be able to move from the city and the region because English is necessary. Yet other people, mostly associated with Hindi-medium schools, turned the positive association with movement and English on its head. Many Hindi-medium-going schoolchildren's parents offered that attendance at Hindi-medium schools indicated "satisfaction" (*santuṣṭ*) with life. They noted that the need to leave one's home and family is missing. Satisfaction established Hindi-medium schools as an alternative to the desire for relocation's economic possibilities and indicated a laudable willingness on the part of Hindi-medium students to remain in the city or region. Many of these were the same people who scoffed at the efforts of the poor to gain economic benefit from English-medium schools. They explained that without the necessary connections, the poor would not be able to find jobs.

Another common reflection on schools, however, sang the praises of Hindi-medium schools for their support of the "national language" (*rāṣṭrabhāṣā*). In discourse that equates Hindi with the nation, Varanasi as a whole can occupy an important place by virtue of the publishing efforts there as well as its geographic location in the heartland of the "Hindi Belt." Some parents, and nearly all teachers at schools of either medium, explicitly identified Varanasi itself as a center of

Hindi, pointing to the city's role in the standardization of Hindi and the development of a literary legacy (Dalmia 1997; C. King 1994). All of the people who pointed to Varanasi as the origin of modern Hindi, however, acknowledged that such activities have now passed into the hands of the government. Many people, associated with either language-medium institution, explained that English is an "international language" (*antarrāṣṭrabhāṣā*). English-medium students described Hindi as their mother tongue, to be sure, but they never ventured toward Hindi-medium students' claims that English is "foreign" (*videsī*). Hindi comes to stand for the Indian nation and many Hindi-medium students went so far as to claim that English-medium students are "not Indian" (*bhāratīya nahī̃*).

I do not mean to argue that the relationship between schooling—via language medium—and nationalism is a simple one. For example, people in the middle classes attend Hindi-medium schools, but the ideological underpinnings of their attendance are specific and complexly informed by different and sometimes overlapping historical developments in Hindi's use in political and/or religious movements. The Bharatiya Janata Party, for example, used several political developments at both the national and state levels to extend its popularity among the middle classes, often in an idiom that used Hindi, whether Sanskritized or not, self-consciously (Rajagopal 2001). Setting the stage for BJP rhetoric at the national level, for example, was the announcement by Prime Minister V.P. Singh of the Janata Dal government in 1990 that the ten-year-old Mandal Commission's recommendation that 27 percent of government posts go to members of the Other Backward Castes (OBCs) would be implemented. The category includes a large number of moderately prosperous farmers such as Jats and Yadavs in Varanasi's state of Uttar Pradesh as well as in some surrounding states.

Around the same time, at the state level, Mulayam Singh Yadav, Chief Minister of Uttar Pradesh and member of an OBC, initiated a campaign called *angrezī haṭāo* ("eradicate English") that required all government correspondence in the state to be conducted in Hindi (Sonntag 1996; Zurbuchen 1992). The populist move was meant to appeal to those suffering from the state's high rate of unemployment and lacking access to English required by especially desirable jobs. The BJP worked on the fears of upper-caste, middle-class people who felt threatened by reservations for OBCs, and the party condemned the political moves of Mulayam Singh Yadav, not for their anti-English rhetoric but rather for their indication of what dangerous effects might result from the movement of members of OBCs—like Chief Minister

Yadav—into positions of political power (Hansen 1999). Thus, while the Hindu-fundamentalist BJP shared with Mulayam Singh Yadav an investment in Hindi for its political cachet, its call to resist the reservation for OBCs involved, implicitly, a defensive posture against its own constituency's loss of what was to be reserved. Such government posts often presuppose that one has had an English-medium education. And just as he was advocating his "eradicate English" campaign, Mulayam Singh Yadav was sending his son to an English-medium school.

From English Medium to a Kind of English

Although most people living in Varanasi send their children to the city's schools, a small number find it necessary to send their children away for schooling. The case of my neighbor demonstrates that not everyone in Varanasi focuses on medium differences within the city when reflecting on the significance of language in schooling. Indeed, my neighbor believed that Varanasi was a city unable to offer the kind of English that he saw as necessary for success.

The neighbor had been transferred from Delhi by the State Bank of India to train new employees in Varanasi branches for three years. People in New Colony referred to this man by his occupation, calling him "Bankwalla." He told me that he had taken up residence as a paying guest of a family in New Colony because of the cheap price, allowing him to send the bulk of his income to his wife and daughter in Delhi. Much anthropological work has been focused on the exodus of residents of Indian villages to small towns or cities in search of employment or higher wages. Most of the construction workers, rickshawallas, or petty merchants who worked in New Colony (but lived elsewhere in Varanasi) had moved to the city from villages nearby. Little work, however, has focused on people like the Bankwalla, who have been transferred to a position of authority as part of an employer's expansion or program of quality control. Commentary about language difference is likely to figure prominently in reflections on such transfers in relation to their geographic and hierarchical repositionings.

One day the Bankwalla visited my landlady's house while her daughter was studying in the next room with her tutor. Afterword, I accompanied him to a tea stall. He remarked that he had made the right decision in leaving his daughter in her school in Delhi, pointing out that my landlady's daughter had needed to speak in Hindi during her English tutorial. When I suggested that there are schools in

Varanasi in which classroom interaction occurs in English, he replied that no school in Varanasi could provide a student with the ability to speak in English without using some Hindi. He claimed that his daughter's education was taking place wholly in English, except for Hindi taught as a subject.

I describe the Bankwalla as an elite because residents of New Colony referred to him as a *baṛā ādmī*, literally, a "big man." This term is hardly indicative of a fixed social category, and its use varies by perceived difference in caste (*jāti*), occupation, or landholdings between user and designee. When I asked neighbors and friends to qualify their frequent use of the term for the Bankwalla, however, they mentioned a cluster of reasons that included his ability to speak English, his position of authority over most others at the bank, and his cosmopolitan Delhi origins, unique in New Colony in 1996. With these local rationales in mind, I call the Bankwalla an elite because he defines a place—in this case, Varanasi—as unable to provide its residents with a proper or valuable education in the form of English free of Hindi.

Disparate Markets

The three ideological constructions of language, nation, and citizen described above give evidence that each emerges from a discrete "market," in the parlance of Pierre Bourdieu (1977, 1991). Practices can be conceptualized as conferring symbolic capital in particular markets that are historically contingent. Symbolic capital has emerged within markets such as domains of religious practice or royal distinction, and regional spheres characterized by particular socioeconomic configurations. One peculiarity of the modern state, according to Bourdieu, has been education's ability to organize symbolic capital by training students in a particular type of language. Bourdieu explains that the educational system "has a monopoly over the production of the mass of producers and consumers [of linguistic capital], and hence over the reproduction of the market" (1977: 652). Bourdieu envisions the state's creation of a national system of education as a means to involve citizens in a unified market.

Some scholars have questioned the completeness of the process that Bourdieu describes. They contend that there are modern nations wherein multiple markets coexist. Taking Spain as such a case, Kathryn Woolard (1985) argues that whereas Castilian is the language of government, centralized in Madrid, Barcelona's history of industrial production and economic viability enables Catalan to be a vehicle of capital. Leigh Swigart (2000) reflects on a speech delivered in 1998 by President Diouf of Senegal, wherein he restated a French utterance in Wolof. He gaffed, claiming to be the television viewer's father (in his Wolof utterance), rather than the father of the nation (in his French utterance). Swigart notes that differences in reactions by Senegalese Francophones and intellectuals, who were angered by his incompetence, and non-Francophones, who were appreciative of his use of Wolof, give evidence of different capital values existing in overlapping but separate language markets.

The three market spheres presented in this chapter confirm Woolard's and Swigart's arguments for the existence of plural markets in modern nation-states. The three-language formula, for example, constructs the nation as a language market. One's linguistic capital is greater if it includes the ability to communicate across language lines—to be proficient in a language other than that of one's own state—and lesser if it consists only of the ability to use a single language. According to the logic of the formula, sole knowledge of one's state language is a sign of isolation, and to teach citizens only the standardized languages of their respective states is to handicap the nation. The formula encodes the future coordination of a national marketplace in which citizens stand to accumulate profit by their ability to traverse current linguistic boundaries, demarcating predominantly Hindi and the southern languages.

In Varanasi, however, the policy measure's vision of linguistic capital has little resonance. People understand two languages to dwell in two institutions, constructing each other in overt reflection and in taken-for-granted school habits. Among schools in the city, language medium constitutes "a sociolinguistic world of imagined dichotomies" wherein Hindi-medium comprises the half that is oriented to Varanasi and India and English-medium comprises the half that is oriented to Delhi and the foreign (Fenigsen 1999: 69).[13] The market for Hindi and Hindi-medium schools is the local and the indigenous whereas the market for English and English-medium schools is Delhi and "beyond."[14]

The case of the Bankwalla demonstrates that not everyone in Varanasi finds medium distinctions to be the most salient relationship between language and nation. The Bankwalla envisions India as a language market in which English free of the influence of Hindi serves as capital. The case of the Bankwalla shows the ways in which language ideologies call attention to the vertical, hierarchical arrangements of language markets. A number of scholars have developed the notion of scale to explore the unevenness of language ideologies and the forms of capital they assume: "social events and processes move and develop on a continuum of layered scales, with the strictly local (micro) and global (macro) as extremes, and with several intermediary scales" (Blommaert 2007: 1). Collins stresses the stratified quality of scales that are "layered into units of differing size" (2012: 197). For the Bankwalla, Varanasi emerges as a place unable to prepare students as well as Delhi, the national capital and city in which his daughter is being educated. Medium distinctions might matter to most people in Varanasi, but their ways of differentiating the significance of the local and elsewhere is irrelevant to the higher scale at which the Bankwalla's ideas about language operate. The difference between the scale gap between Hindi- versus English-medium schooling in Varanasi and the scale disparity between those mediums and the kind of English the Bankwalla wants for his daughter demonstrates that the "conditions of access" to different types of linguistic capital in Varanasi vary (Blommaert, Collins, and Slembrouck 2005: 213).

In many respects, the Bankwalla's emphasis on English was mirrored by many people in Varanasi who were sending their children to local schools. The potential of English to provide spatial mobility was important to Varanasi residents. Many, including Hindi-medium students and their families, told me that if one wishes "to wander" (*ghūmnā*), English is a necessity. By wander, some meant travel beyond India's borders, but most students mentioned Delhi as the ultimate destination for which English is required. Spatial mobility, in turn, provides opportunities for economic mobility.

Varanasi residents used schooling to make moral judgments about others in complex ways that served to reinforce local configurations of Hindi and English, their symbolic capital, and their markets. Some people used the topic of mobility offered by English-medium education to launch criticisms of the desire to get a job elsewhere, noting that such desire indicates a lack of concern for one's parents' welfare or a lack of satisfaction with a modest life. Some parents of Hindi-medium students decried as foolish the payment by poor families of massive bribes widely known to be required for entry to English-medium schools. Nearly everyone with whom I spoke, even those who had little or no prior schooling of any sort, knew these bribes to be outrageously high, counted in the thousands of rupees. These parents consistently pointed out that without proper connections, the poor, even if armed with an English-medium education, would not be able to find employment beyond Varanasi. "What is the use?" (*kyā fāydā hai*) many rhetorically asked.

But the English implicated in medium distinctions in Varanasi and the English important to the Bankwalla do not necessarily represent the same capital and certainly operate at different scales. Others in Varanasi share the Bankwalla's fear that the city's schools cannot teach an English valuable in a national market. Whereas the Bankwalla was unwilling to have his children join him in Varanasi, others in Varanasi were compelled to have their children sent away. A distant relative of the family that owns one of the most expensive (English-medium) schools in town, for example, explained that her own daughter was currently attending the first grade at the school. Her husband, however, was on the verge of getting a promotion and a transfer to Delhi. There, she said, her daughter would be able to attend a much better school. She expressed relief that she would not have to suffer separation from her daughter. When I did not understand, she explained that, were her family to stay in Varanasi, she would eventually need to send her daughter away to receive a better education than is available locally. I asked her what made some schools elsewhere better. She told me that attendance at university requires fluency in English, a cruel shock to all but the "most adaptable" children who do not come from the best English-medium schools. She then asked whether I had noticed that the children of the owners of her daughter's school (the speaker's cousins), five to seven years older than her daughter, did not attend the school. When I replied that I had not, she smiled ironically.

The relieved mother has in common with the Bankwalla an attitude that Varanasi cannot provide skills in English needed for future success. Furthermore, the shared attitude gives evidence that both belong to an elite—vis-à-vis people whose children are schooled in English-medium schools within Varanasi—because they envision education elsewhere as a tool of class maintenance and mobility.

Some people uninvolved in English-medium education expressed the notion that English-medium schools in Varanasi cannot provide the necessary linguistic capital to succeed in more central places. Partly as a result of her troubled teaching experiences, one woman had formed her own voluntary school for the extremely poor on the roof of her house. Most students came from a nearby slum, just a few blocks away from the school. The slum is occupied primarily by Untouchables, or Dalits, literally "the downtrodden." Krishna Kumar (1989: 59–77) explains that when they are mentioned in the curriculum's subject matter, Untouchables are generally derided as backward. Kancha Ilaih, who describes himself and the community in which he was raised as Dalit, reflects on his own alienation from the materials provided by schooling:

> What difference did it make to us whether we [Dalits] had an English textbook that talked about Milton's *Paradise Lost* or *Paradise Regained,* or Shakespeare's *Othello* or *Macbeth,* or Wordsworth's poetry about English nature, or a Telegu textbook that talks about Kalidasa's *Meghasandesham,* Bummera Potanna's *Bhagavatam,* or Nannaya and Tikkana's *Mahabharatam,* except the fact that one textbook is written using twenty-six characters and the other fifty-six? We do not share the contents of either; we do not find our lives reflected in their narratives. We cannot locate them in our family settings. Without constant recourse to a dictionary neither makes any sense to us. (1996: 177)

Notice that even though Ilaih decries formal education's exclusion of Dalits by the literary material it uses, he nevertheless invokes a divide between English and Telegu (the official language of Andhra Pradesh), the only standardized varieties present in school. Corresponding languages in Varanasi are English and Hindi.[15]

Voluntary schools are known in Indian educational parlance as belonging to the non-formal education (NFE) sector, and these are totally ignored in discursive activity related to language-medium distinctions. Yet, the teacher with the voluntary rooftop school criticized the owners of the most expensive English-medium school in town. She explained that the owners' children could not gain entrance to the "Doon School [in Dehradun, a city north of Delhi], Modern School [in Delhi], *vagaira* (etc.)" and had to attend the Woodstock School in Mussoorie instead. The Doon School, described in the introduction of the book, is known throughout India as an exemplary institution for instruction in English and for the provision of a cosmopolitan stance. The voluntary schoolteacher went on to explain that because the children had started their education in their own parents' school they could not pass the required entrance exams for the Doon School or the Modern School. She decried the desire to attend English-medium schools generally as "foolish" (*bakwās*).

Thus, reflections on language-medium schooling subvert the three-language formula in two ways. First, Varanasi residents conceptualize schools as embodying a duality that strictly divides what the formula strives to make complementary. Second, of the two mediums, only one—English—manages to offer capital within the market that the formula envisions as linguistically plural. Although Hindi represents the nation, English provides spatial and economic mobility within it.

Monolingual Ideology and Its Capital

Although an exploration of the lack of resonance between official policy and constructions of language, nation, and citizen in Varanasi reveals much about the complexities of language markets in India, it is not comprehensive. Published commentary shows that a market and a kind of capital exist to which people I knew in Varanasi, regardless of socioeconomic or ideological disposition, had no access. By criticizing the Indian government for allowing the growth of English corrupted by indigenous Indian languages, some published authors construct the Indian nation—and not locales within it—as a disadvantaged market.[16]

Such criticism invokes what Woolard calls the "monolingual point of view" (1999: 3). Pervasive in—but not confined to—regions once dominated by colonial powers is the strife wrought by the desire to coordinate nation and language (Errington 1998, 2001). In a well-known thesis, Benedict Anderson identifies the emergence of print capitalism as the process enabling the mutual imagination of the modern nation and a national language. Anderson describes the dilemma faced by regions dominated by colonialism: "The potential stretch of these [print language-based] communities was inherently limited, and, at the same time, bore none but the most fortuitous relationship to existing political boundaries" (1983: 46). Edward Gray notes more bluntly, "Contrary to the modern nationalist conceit—the boundaries of language and government almost never match" (1999: 9). Indeed, the ideological equation of "one language—one people" continues to pose "challenges" to nations and their governments, especially those once dominated by colonial powers (Woolard and Schieffelin 1994: 61). Independence from colonial powers, Woolard explains, has not lifted the burden of such discrepancies: "An ideology of 'development' is pervasive in postcolonial language planning, wherein deliberate intervention is deemed necessary to make a linguistic variety suitable for modern functions" (1998: 21). Development indicators, in turn, can be used to judge national governments as more or less successful at inculcating modernity.

Thus, the national government can become an actor whose disposition toward the relationship between language and nation is open to scrutiny. Whether a government can—or desires to—create and disseminate a unifying language can render it a success or a failure. One possibility is a nation that is envisioned—or a would-be nation whose spokespeople attempt to envision it—in terms of a unifying language. Jaqueline Urla notes that, in an effort to gain linguistic legitimacy, governments or would-be governments sometimes employ a census in which parameters of linguistic variation are narrowed. She states that in the case of Basque nationalism, "highlighting literacy and eliding dialects, the census categories refute the longstanding assumptions that Basque is not a fully modern language and that Basque speakers are not a single language community" (1993: 831). The linguistic regions making up the Hindi Belt have seen very different uses of census results, and only Maithili has achieved recognition in the Eighth Schedule as a recognized language.

Whether through a rhetoric of defense, revival, or creation, a language can emerge, with an often-undisclosed history of engineering, to standardize citizens' access to political information and participation. Kathryn Woolard provides an example from the United States. Although San Francisco, California, is associated with the support of pluralism generally, in 1983 the city's government passed Proposition O, prohibiting the use of languages other than English in the city's voting practices. Capitalizing on the assumption that "'Truth' is more likely to come in transparent English, free of the seductive power of foreign languages," Proposition O was able to construct monolingual elections as liberating ethnic voting blocks from their own manipulative leaders (Woolard 1989: 272). Such events show that assumptions about the need for a single language in activities of the government may be absent at a national level but can be mobilized locally at crucial moments to "erase" the salience of practices felt to threaten unity.[17]

Another possibility from a monolingual ideological perspective is a national government that fails to engineer and inculcate a national language. India is one of the most vilified examples. India's multilingualism serves as a foundation from which much criticism has been launched both outside and within India. Kailash Aggarwal, for example, decries the use in publications—even scholarly—of such terms as "linguistic laboratory" or, worse, "linguistic madhouse" to describe India (1997: 38). Some critics foreground the multilingualism of linguistic practice, especially when it is found in official contexts. For example, in an article entitled "Indish" (India + English), Khushwant Singh looks to the national government for reasons that Indians, even members of the parliament, are prone to speak "linguistic ratatouille" (1986: 37). The use of terms like *laboratory, madhouse,* and *ratatouille* fosters the idea that India is a place of linguistic confusion and disorder.

Some authors have written commentary published in English-language venues in India that specifies English spoken by Indians as a language whose very existence illustrates failures of the Indian government. Although none of these authors calls for the imposition of a single language in India, each uses an image of disorder to lambaste the national government and its educational system for failing to utilize and promote a legitimate language free from interference of other languages.

Such ideological positioning points to a particular group of elites that differs from others in India. Who is elite varies across India by region, the political histories of particular states in India, and the economic histories of villages, cities, or regions of residence. Such factors intermingle with linguistic practice in complex ways. For example, Braj Kachru notes that monolingual practice among Indian elites generally is almost nonexistent. Code switching and code mixing between English and indigenous languages such as Punjabi, Hindi, or Bengali is a normal feature of linguistic practice in many contexts for elites competent in English. Thus, regional elites have initiated the growth of regional varieties of English (Kachru 1992). I use Kachru's observation to argue for the distinctiveness of the authors cited in this section of the chapter. Indeed, the regional elites who have fostered regional varieties of English described by Kachru would seemingly be the most salient targets of the authors cited herein, given their concerns about the influence of other languages on English. Alok Rai notes, "The social presence of English in India is so varied that the notion of an English elite is self-evidently problematical" (2001: 8). Heeding Rai's warning, I argue that differences between English-literate elites in India can be identified broadly, albeit incompletely, by their access to positions in media and politics coupled with their ideological dispositions with respect to English.

Ideological variability exists among elites in India too. Braj Kachru notes that authors in India who have published in English exhibit a range of ideological stances with respect to the language. Some consider English just another part of their multilingual capabilities. Others consider English an Indian language. Some authors who write in regional Indian languages such as Hindi or Marathi feel betrayed by Indian authors who have gained literary success in English (Kachru 1996). My claim is that an ideological perspective that is concerned with (and nervous about) the English spoken in India emanates from the type of elite discussed in this section, and not from others.

For example, the authors cited in this section include, in order of citation, Khushwant Singh, who served as editor of the *Hindustan Times* as well as a member of the Rajya Sabha (Upper House) of the Indian parliament; Jug Suraiya, who has been an associate editor of the

Times of India as well as a columnist for many other newspapers, magazines, and journals; Romesh Thapar, who is cofounder of *Seminar,* a prestigious journal of national social issues; and H.Y. Sharada Prasad, who was press secretary to Prime Ministers Indira and Rajiv Gandhi. The daily English-language newspapers mentioned enjoy some of the highest circulations in India, and the political offices are situated at the highest levels of the national government. Finally, a few of the cited authors can be recognized from their best-selling books.

These elites differ from the Bankwalla and others who find Varanasi unable to provide English free of Hindi because their opinions have been published in major venues of pan-Indian distribution.[18] Ideologically, they differ from people like the Bankwalla by virtue of their use of an international frame for discussing (and disparaging) English in India. The Bankwalla does not point to the English spoken by Indians as a specifically Indian problem. Indeed, he believes himself to speak exemplary English and regrets having to leave his daughter in Delhi to be educated in a kind of English he finds unavailable in Varanasi. Thus, unlike the authors cited herein, the Bankwalla is concerned that one's shift in residence within India can deprive one's child of a kind of English and the capital it provides.

In an editorial that appeared in a nationally distributed daily, Suraiya concludes, "So-called 'Hindlish' [Hindi + English] lacks both reach and resonance, except within its own solipsistic context" (1990). Such statements about Indian linguistic disorder are quite similar to criticisms that have been made of the public use of Spanish by Puerto Ricans living in New York City. A boundary demarcates the acceptable from the unacceptable, the legitimate from the illegitimate, and the valuable from the flawed. Bonnie Urciuoli reports that "only within the [inner-city Puerto Rican] neighborhood (or 'around here,' as residents say) can English and Spanish safely coexist" (1991: 298).[19] Use of non-standard English outside of such contexts—especially English felt to be mixed with or influenced by Spanish—marks Puerto Ricans racially in relation to their unmarked counterparts, who are imagined to speak standard, unmixed English.

Whereas neighborhood boundaries provide the line between safety and danger for the Puerto Ricans with whom Urciuoli worked, national boundaries provide the line for the authors cited herein. And whereas the public use of English mixed with Spanish racializes Puerto Ricans and exhibits their lack of fit in the U.S. national market (Urciuoli 1996), the use of Indian English marks the Indian nation itself as inferior and illustrates its lack of fit in an international market. Thus, the government is often held responsible. Thapar, for example, associates a type of English with the nation and ascribes responsibility for it to the government: "It has to be recognized that for forty years we have refused to open our minds to the language tangle, and in so doing have fathered or mothered the bastard known as Indian-English" (1986: 3). Thapar invokes the period of the modern nation to portray an ineffectual government, unwilling and unable to produce legitimate language. Prasad portrays speakers of Indian English as ignorant dupes: "Indian English could perhaps be defined as a language written or spoken by Indians in the belief that it is English" (1986: 24). Variously coined "Hinglish" (referring to the English spoken by Hindi speakers) or "Babu English" and "Indish" (referring to English spoken by Indians generally), Indian English can be a symptom of confusion that points to the government's inability to foster (legitimate) English among its citizens.

Conclusion

People have the means of claiming a place in the nation through the notion that Hindi is the mother tongue. Teachers at Hindi-medium schools, for example, believe that their school is comfortable because their students speak the mother tongue. The institutional designation of a school by language implicates people in a national frame beyond the personal claim of mother tongue, however. When situated in a market wherein value emerges, people are implicated in a set of distinctions much more complex than that implied by the opposition between Hindi as mother tongue and national language, on the one hand, and English as other tongue and international language, on the other hand. National policy is national because it sees the nation as divided by standardized languages, many coinciding with state boundaries. Language value within the national policy of the three-language formula arises by learning a language of another state or region such that interstate communication might be possible. Language difference characterizes the nation, and one's ability to transcend some part of that difference brings parts of the nation into communication.

However, the ways in which people imagine the difference between Hindi and English, and the ways in which the languages are institutionally differentiated, inflect space in a manner very different from the three-language formula. Distant places resonate in the three-language formula via the control of a distant language. Distant places resonate in discourse on language-medium schooling through English. In turn, Hindi resonates with the local, or, at least, with a lack of movement.

Movement is imagined as important in the pursuit of a job—specifically, a job unavailable locally. Such jobs are primarily in the information technology sector, whether in the service-oriented fields dealing with customers, in the development-oriented fields dealing with programming, or in the maintenance-oriented fields dealing with troubleshooting and repair. The attainment of such jobs necessitates going far from Varanasi and attending the English-medium school to do it. Hindi-medium schools are not associated with movement and are described as being adequate for those who have little ambition to move. The institutional divide in Varanasi underpins language value through the association of Hindi-medium schools with cheap fees and English-medium schools with expensive fees, the association of Hindi-medium schools with the state's school board and English-medium schools with several private boards, and the association of Hindi-medium schools with stasis and English-medium schools with movement. Physical movement becomes a sign of ambitions of class mobility via English-medium schooling. The government's policy promoting interstate communication has not become a sign of class mobility because class mobility arises from the institutional divide between Hindi- and English-medium schools.

This is not the end of the story. The nation is a place fraught with contradictions for residents of Varanasi. There are people in town with employment that takes them to various places in the nation, not just Varanasi. The language-medium divide does not exhaust the value of languages for them. Some people do not find any school in Varanasi up to the task of offering their children the kind of English they see as available elsewhere, especially the national capital. Whereas the notion of the mother tongue resonates with people in Varanasi whose English might bear the traces of local education, they do not wrestle with their lack of a more cosmopolitan education because they have no access to the language market in which that education would be meaningfully deficient. That is to say, they sense threats to someone educated in a Hindi-medium school, and tell conflicted stories about the threat, but do not sense threats to someone educated in an English-medium school such that English might be seen as deficient.

People who have had their children schooled outside of Varanasi, in turn, can be relegated to a periphery by yet another kind of elite whose notions about language have found a public in the form of editorials published in nationally distributed newspapers and journals. Such elite authors use the nation itself as a frame for rendering a kind of English lacking the capital of English elsewhere. Whereas the sociolinguists whose work was reviewed in the previous chapter argue for India's differentiation from elsewhere because of its fluid multilingualism, the elites cited in this chapter argue for India's differentiation from elsewhere because of its English. Neither stance is typical of anyone I met in Varanasi.

Some people do care that their children be schooled elsewhere in pursuit of a specific kind of English, but the decisions are fueled by the deficits of Varanasi, not those of India. The dissimilar and uneven markets that I have identified confirm Thomas Hansen and Finn Stepputat's assertion that states are not uniform in the way they are mythologized nor in the way representations make them real (2001: 36). People in Varanasi associate the state with Hindi-medium schools, just as it is ultimately true that all school boards, state and private, are overseen by the state. This chapter has shown that there are several language markets in which the division between Hindi- and English-medium schools in Varanasi can be located such that they attain (or do not attain) value. For those who have sent their children to board-affiliated schools in the city, the distinction between Hindi- and English-medium schools intersects notions about the government and the private, the local and the global, the aspiring and the satisfied, and the distant and the near. Such distinctions have little resonance with those who have had their children schooled elsewhere. The salience of the language-medium divide, one might argue, locates one in a market—a market that does not resonate with others that are operative elsewhere vis-à-vis Varanasi.

Notes

This chapter incorporates material from "Disparate Markets: Language, Nation, and Education in North India," *American Ethnologist* 32: 460–478 and "Of Nation and State: Language, School, and the Reproduction of Disparity in a North Indian City," *Anthropological Quarterly* 80: 925–959.

1. Such a view helps to displace a rather naturalized focus on definitions of the nation in terms of its language or languages with a focus on definitions of the nation within different language markets.
2. Akhil Gupta and Aradhana Sharma invoke the school when they urge anthropologists to consider "everyday actions of particular branches of the state to understand what has in fact changed and at which levels and to account for the conditions in which discrepant representations of 'the state' circulate" (2006: 278).
3. For critiques of the three-language formula, see Gupta, Abbi, and Aggarwal (1995), Jayaram (1993), and A.K. Srivastava (1990).

4. Not every new state rested on linguistic evidence for its boundary. Some exceptions include Nagaland, which became a state in 1963; nearby Maghalaya, Manipur, and Tripura, which became states in 1972; and Arunachal Pradesh, which became a state in 1987. Sanjib Baruah (1999) notes that the creation of these states was partly caused by the unsuccessful imagination of Assam as a linguistic whole. Bengalis of the Cachar Region questioned whether Assamese should be the state of Assam's official language. Curiously, the inclusion of English as a compromise in the Assamese Official Language Bill of 1960 was similar in strategy to compromises reached at the national level just seven years later.
5. Other areas were subsequently joined with Telegu-speaking Andhra, including its capital city, Hyderabad, such that Andhra Pradesh became a state in 1956. Robert King (1997) attributes the rather gradual formations of linguistic states to Nehru's foresight that language might become a disintegrating feature of the Indian polity.
6. Shahid Amin cogently illustrates that India inherited this state of affairs from its former colonial ruler: "How artificial the provincial boundary was is evident from the ease with which Grierson could incorporate east UP terms into his *Bihar Peasant Life*" (1989: xlii). Among India's more populated states, Uttar Pradesh (UP) and Bihar lie in the Hindi region and with Chhattisgarh, Haryana, Himachal Pradesh, Jharkhand, Madhya Pradesh, Rajasthan, and Uttarakhand, share Hindi as the official state language. Standardized Hindi makes irrelevant the incongruity noted by Amin: the similarity of languages across the UP-Bihar state line in comparison to the difference between languages in western and eastern UP.
7. Lachman Khubchandani (1979, 1983: 112), joining sociolinguists with an interest in the census whose work is reviewed in chapter 1, notes fluctuating returns from census to census, which reinforced the notion that languages in the Hindi region were not going to be a source of fracture.
8. One motive for the formula's alignment of language and state can be derived from the text itself: education is largely in the hands of state governments. The national government, thus, was able to use state-demarcated and recognized languages to construct and manage linguistic diversity and to leave education in the hands of state governments without concern that education might serve as a site of struggle for linguistic legitimacy.
9. Harold Schiffman, following P.B. Pandit's comments on the suitability of multilingualism for India, argues that the three-language formula presents the best existing match with Indian sociolinguistic realities: "A policy that recognizes historical multilingualism, linguistic diversity, and reverence for ancient classical languages is more likely to succeed [in India] than an imported model of any sort" (1996: 168).
10. For the contrasting case of Corsica, where policy initiatives are quite salient and contested, see Jaffe (1993, 1996, and 1999).
11. I can only guess in retrospect that my focus on tuition as the relevant frame for imagining sacrifices involved in schooling was derived from my own upbringing in a predominantly Catholic area of a state in the southern part of the United States. There, relative to many other areas of the United States, private schools, most run by the Catholic Church, provided a popular but barely affordable option for people like my lower-middle-class mother who wanted their children to avoid an abysmal public school system (made more so by the growth and proliferation of private schools). I imagine that later, shared worries about financial aid for

college only made more probable my focus on tuition during initial fieldwork in Varanasi as the relevant concern for linking sacrifice and education.

12. For discussions of educational initiatives during the period of BJP rule, see Advani (2009) and Guichard (2010).
13. This is not meant to imply that ideological constructions are the same elsewhere in India. Thomas Hansen reports that Marathi's increasing association with Maharasthra and Maharasthrians rested, in part, on a competitive labor market specific to Bombay. Migrating there in the 1950s and 1960s, Marathi speakers met established groups such as "Muslim weavers from North India or literate South Indians whose skills in English gave them easier access to clerical jobs" (Hansen 2001: 45). Hansen writes of the Hindu-chauvinist group Shiv Sena's demonization of such people in a bid to crystallize and legitimate the Mahrashtrian Marathi speaker.
14. Rashmi Sadana writes, "Delhi has, not surprisingly, played a dominant role in defining the parameters of national culture, yet these definitions [of the regional, national, or global] are more often than not contested in regional milieus" (2012: 25). I would argue that Delhi's contribution to the national is partly constructed in such places as Varanasi.
15. Krishna Kumar (1989) confirms that these standard forms and representative literary materials serve to disadvantage and alienate Dalits in the Hindi Belt, regardless of language.
16. Monica Heller expresses her own surprise at hearing a song on the radio by the internationally known pop group Pet Shop Boys wherein lexical items of several Western European languages are included to highlight the value of multilingualism. The song, according to Heller, illustrates the possibility that multilingual productions are not necessarily "produced by marginalized groups aimed at fragmenting the unity of the dominant group," but can be used as "a marker of élite status in the new economic order" (1999: 270). Heller argues, however, that such developments must be contextualized. For example, she notes that the song emerges from socioeconomic shifts in Europe facilitating the formation of the European Union. The published elite commentary cited in this book reinforces Heller's call to contextualize ideological refractions of multilingualism. Although the elites cited are themselves multilingual, they nevertheless focus on English spoken in India as a language dangerously influenced by indigenous Indian languages. They envision India as a place isolated by the English spoken there.
17. Shirley Brice Heath explains: "The legacy of the language situation in the United States is ... the rejection of an official choice of a national language or national institutions to regulate language decisions related to spelling, pronunciation, technical vocabulary, or grammar. Yet Americans overwhelmingly believe that English is the national tongue and that correctness in spelling, pronunciation, word choice, and usage, as well as facility in reading and writing English, are desirable goals for every U.S. citizen" (1981: 6).
18. But see Chand (2011) for yet another elite position on Hindi and English not found in Varanasi.
19. This is true for racialized Puerto Ricans. When "Junk Spanish" is found in the discourse of whites, it has the potential to mark them positively (Hill 1998).

Chapter 3

Advertising in the Periphery

Modes of Communication and the Production of School Value

During a short school holiday in December 1996, I decided to take the fourteen-hour train trip to Delhi from Varanasi. I met with the retired official of the Central Board of Secondary Education (CBSE), introduced in the last chapter, who knew of the policy by which students study three languages in school. I was intrigued not just by her knowledge, but also by her statement in response to my explanation that people in Varanasi do not know about the three-language formula: "Education outside of Delhi is a disaster." Her statement constructed Delhi as a center, a place of order where the activities and aims of the government and educational bureaucracies are known to inhabitants; people who reside outside, in the periphery, are ignorant. On the trip home, I met a couple of middle-class appearance traveling from Delhi to Varanasi to visit relatives. The father had on a pressed pair of pants and a shirt with pens in a pocket protector, the mother had on a pressed sari, and they had good hard-shell luggage. As the train slowed on its entry into Varanasi, the man lifted the aluminum shade shielding us from the early morning sun. His wife, glancing out of the window as she readied her things to disembark, exclaimed, "We have reached hell" (*narak pahũc gaye h̃ai*). The clever woman enacted an arrival scenario whose ironic twist relied for its effect on Varanasi's place in the periphery. She toyed with potential meanings of hell (*narak*), one contradicting Varanasi's reputation as a Hindu holy site, and the other constructing the scene in front of her as unpleasant, and, as she told me moments later, "dirty" (*gandā*).

The train provided a conduit from the periphery to the center and back again. Although specific descriptions and constructions vary, the difference created by distinctions between a center and its periphery is often salient in conversations across northern India. Interchanges like those described herein intersect and reenact notions expressed in other places and times. A fairly common rendition, for example, is that Delhi, the center, is orderly and provides bureaucratic and commercial employment opportunity for migrants, but also heightened risk. In contrast, places outside Delhi are disordered, isolated, and economically stagnant, but also relatively safe on account of their well-entrenched notions about class and the potential for mobility. Talk about schools and languages often provides many realizations of relationships between central and peripheral spaces. The various comments offered in previous chapters have situated Delhi as central in terms of school board affiliation or the kind of English spoken there, but have also situated Varanasi as a central place via the mother tongue, or with respect to the rural periphery.

Constructions of center and periphery in northern India are not always played out in such discrete and neat juxtapositions of place. Hindi and English can be used to construct center/periphery distinctions in talk about schools located *within* Varanasi. Thus far in the book, when people have talked about schools in Varanasi, what resonates with the center and what resonates with the periphery has been variable. This chapter shows that when people read advertisements for schools that are displayed around town, they are much more constrained in what they can rely on to indicate the value of a school. Just like in spoken discourse, written words may confound the distinction between Hindi and English. Words such as "fees," "board," and "medium" could be identified as Hindi or English. But visual language requires the use of a script, and the primary choices for the schools considered here are Devanagari and roman. It is in the combination of language and script that advertising for schools departs from spoken language in what it indicates about schools.

Government-administered Hindi-medium schools do not advertise, but their signboards are always in Hindi rendered in Devanagari script, whereas private schools advertise vigorously in an array of combinations of Hindi and English rendered in Devanagari and roman script. Furthermore, the variability in spoken discourse does not exist in advertising for schools wherein there is a fixed association of Hindi with the peripheral and English with the central. This is because the most prestigious English-medium schools in Varanasi advertise in English in roman script, and less prestigious schools advertise in a variety of lexical and script combinations.

The newspaper embodies a much wider area of circulation than advertisements found on Varanasi's streets. This is because local schools advertise on the streets whereas schools outside of Varanasi advertise in the newspaper. Indeed, the only schools that advertise in the newspaper are prestigious English-medium schools located in other, metropolitan cities. This chapter argues that in the mirror of advertising in the newspaper, the wide variety of lexical and script combinations found on Varanasi's streets indicate that it is a peripheral place. In the rubric of scale, the newspaper is superordinate because the schools that advertise in it are located in metropolitan centers far from Varanasi, and advertisements found around town are subordinate because schools that advertise there are found locally. Messages at the superordinate level are conveyed in English in roman script, whereas, at the subordinate level, messages are conveyed in Hindi and English, in Devanagari and roman script. The possibility in spoken discourse that what is local might emerge as central via pride in the mother tongue or the national language disappears in the reflection of advertising around town and in the newspaper.

Gupta and Ferguson ask, "How are understandings of locality, community, and region formed and lived?" (1997: 6). Schools, via the language-medium distinction, play a major role in such understandings in Hindi-speaking northern India. Advertising presents lexical and script combinations that are tied to types of schools. Advertising, relative to spoken discourse, constrains people in constructing Hindi- and English-medium schools as central and peripheral. Thus, spoken discourse and written advertising offer different possibilities for the construction of the central and the peripheral, and the difference depends crucially on the semiotic tools provided by each type of communication.[1] My parallel consideration of spoken discourse and written advertising demonstrates that constructions of center and periphery are not always variable in language activity in Varanasi that involves schools.

Language-Medium Schools as Central and Peripheral, and Global and Local

Before considering how language distinctions are used to create centers and peripheries, it is necessary to understand that they reverberate with another distinction, that between the global and the local. The designation of something as "Hindi" can index it as local and indigenous, and "English" can index it as Delhi-like and foreign; "medium" transposes these qualities onto schools and those who attend them or are in their employ. An indexical relationship between an institution and the contrasting qualities it embodies is a semiotic one rooted in the context of schooling in northern India. One does not have to engage in overt descriptions of such linkages, for example, because they emerge already formed and tied together.[2]

Just what is global and local, on the one hand, and what is central and peripheral, on the other hand, can vary when schooling and language emerge in spoken discourse. One configuration of the two types of schools that has already been noted is indexical of a center and periphery. English-medium schools provide a route out of Varanasi because they offer access to jobs elsewhere, particularly in Delhi. In contrast, Hindi-medium schools do not provide access to a center defined, in Varanasi, by increased employment opportunities elsewhere. Yet, increased employment opportunities do not exhaust the ways in which constructions of language and education resonate with differences between a center and its periphery. In Varanasi, many Hindi-medium school-goers explicitly indexed patriotism and national loyalty with their mention of Hindi as well as their attendance at Hindi-medium schools. Hindi-medium school-goers and their families explained that Hindi is one's "mother tongue" (*mātrabhāṣā*) and India's "national language" (*rāṣṭrabhāṣā*). In discourse that equates Hindi with the mother tongue and the nation, Varanasi as a whole occupies a place of centrality by virtue of its place in the Hindi Belt.

Through notions like the mother tongue, fee structures, and board affiliations, language-medium distinctions constitute what Urciuoli calls a language "border": "Borders are places where commonality ends abruptly; border-making language elements stand for and performatively bring into being such places" (1995: 539). Mention of a school's medium launches the school into an oppositional contest configured by a language border dividing local Hindi from global English. Silverstein notes that any construction of locality is relational: "'Local' language communities do not exist in a state of nature; the very concept of locality as opposed to globality presupposes a contrastive consciousness of self—other placement that is part of a cultural project of groupness" (1998: 405). Discourse about language medium in Varanasi indexes the local in contrast to the global, but institutional examples of the global—English-medium schools—can be found locally (Silverstein 1976).

One of the most fascinating aspects of spoken discourse about medium is that speakers' transformations of the relationship between the local (Hindi) and the global (English) into distinctions between a center and its periphery are not always predictable. For example, a person might praise Hindi-medium schools as constituting the mother tongue and indicative of the nation (center), and disparage English-medium schools as not just foreign but indicative of apathy or avoidance of the mother tongue (periphery). Yet, another person might disparage Hindi-medium schools as tied to an isolated Hindi region (periphery), and English-medium schools as offering a language of pan-Indian or international value (center). The value of attending one or the other medium is constructed relationally, but it is variable in terms of just what is determined to be central and what is determined to be peripheral.

Central and Peripheral in Spoken Discourse and Advertising

Advertising for schools presents a sphere of linguistic activity in which dominance and subversion are not nearly so malleable as in spoken discourse about schooling. The fact that conversations about schools, on the one hand, and advertising for schools, on the other hand, provide different means of constructing relationships between languages and institutions indicates that they constitute different genres. Hanks, drawing on Bakhtin's (1986) writings on genre, notes that "conventional discourse genres are part of the linguistic habitus that native actors bring to speech, but that such genres are also produced in speech under various local circumstances" (1987: 687). The very possibilities of the construction of value in reflection on Hindi- and English-medium schooling thus vary according to whether the construction occurs within spoken discourse or in advertising. Language markets are accessed by certain genres of linguistic activity whose semiotic properties seem, potentially at least, to make all the difference in what may be dominant and what may be contested.[3]

In order to understand advertising's comparatively limited indexical possibilities, it is necessary to understand that certain semiotic features extant in advertising for schools are not available to speakers engaged in spoken discourse. Nowhere in advertising (as is quite common in spoken discourse) is the relationship between language variety and its appropriate use raised to the level of ostensive reference—for example, "English is the language of some in Delhi." Written language makes available a kind of semiotic relationship unavailable in everyday conversation; both Hindi and English lexical items can be represented orthographically in Devanagari or roman script.[4] This mixing is of a kind impossible to represent with the spoken word; speech can only describe the relationship between lexical affiliation and its scripted representation.

Advertising considered in the following discussion is circulated in two different ways: around town and in newspapers that reach Varanasi from Delhi or Lucknow, the state capital. School advertisements found around Varanasi contain all possible combinations of Hindi and English lexical items in Devanagari or roman script. School advertisements that reach Varanasi via newspapers, in contrast, lack such variability in combinations of lexical item and script; only one combination of lexical affiliation (English) and script (roman) is present in school advertisements in newspapers. The sum total of lexical and script combinations in school advertisements in the newspaper thus corresponds to only one of the possible combinations in Varanasi's streets—the combination that indexes the most expensive schools. Newspaper advertising thus renders the plurality of indexical possibilities in advertising found off the printed page—around town in Varanasi—itself an index (Silverstein 1996).

The lack of indexical play in school advertisements in the newspaper renders other combinations of lexical item and script, prevalent around town, indexes of Varanasi's peripheral status. Advertisements for schools in newspapers arriving from elsewhere are indexes of the center as a result of their paucity of lexical/script combinations. Varanasi's bid for centrality, in which the Hindi-medium school indexes the Indian nation, is subsumed in local advertising as but one participant in Varanasi's apparent diversity, and is altogether missing in advertisements in newspapers coming from more central places. Varanasi as a whole, from the perspective of indexical possibilities present in the newspaper, is a peripheral place where deviation exists.

Advertising Schools: Lexical Item and Script

All combinations of lexical affiliation (Hindi or English) and writing system (Devanagari or roman) can be found virtually anywhere in urban centers in India, where advertisements clog the visual field. Varanasi and other cities provide a "linguistic landscape" that includes "any written sign found outside private homes, from road signs to names of streets, shops, and schools" (Ben-Rafael, Shohamy, and Barni 2010: xiv). Anyone familiar with public spaces in India will recognize what Shohamy and Gorter call a "linguistic revolution" underpinned by practices of identity display and commodity consumption in the wake of economic liberalization, "allowing mixtures of languages, new linguistic rules, new spellings, new syntax, inventions of words combined with additional representations, those of sounds and images, and all displayed publicly" (2009: 3).

Advertisements created by schools, however, form a special group vis-à-vis other advertisements. Among school advertisements, the relationship between lexical item and script is a meaningful sign. This differs from advertisements generally, where lexical items and scripts are not necessarily coordinated. School advertising differs from other types of advertising because it presents predictable combinations of lexical item and script, depending on what school or board is being advertised. The combinations in advertisements for schools and tutorial services in Varanasi presented herein are indexical because English lexical items rendered in roman script and Hindi lexical items rendered in Devanagari script are present in advertisements that represent the most expensive English-medium schools and the Hindi-medium schools associated with government affiliation, respectively.

Deviations (other combinations of lexical item and script) are quite prevalent in Varanasi, but they are always subject to the charge of being "muddled." Parents, teachers, and principals associated with either Hindi- or English-medium schools were relatively unconcerned about combinations of lexical item and script in commercial domains exclusive of education. Advertising by educational institutions, however, was a different matter. Larger ideologies about the necessity of standard language for participation and success in school intersected with evaluations of lexical/script combinations in school advertising. Teachers and parents consistently identified spelling and grammar as two of the hardest things for students to master. Each of these practices presupposes a standardized form of language written in a standardized orthography. Notions of standard drew the line between inconsequential lexical/script combinations in advertising for commercial products, and lexical/script combinations in advertising for educational institutions in which pedagogical effects are thought to inhere. Thus, while the identification of the particular school is handled by the school's name, the combination of lexical affiliation and script identifies the school as belonging to a larger category divided by language medium. The ability of the combination of lexical affiliation and script to identify types of schools rests on the fact that it is an educational institution that is being advertised. Combinations of lexical affiliation and script do not function similarly in advertising for other sorts of products and institutions.

In Varanasi, as elsewhere in urban northern India, it seems that one is never out of sight of an advertisement for a school. There are cloth, paper, plastic, or metal signs hung over the street or affixed to walls; there are huge billboards set behind and high above the walls lining streets; and there are metal or wooden signs advertising schools nailed high on telephone, electric, or other kinds of poles. Perhaps most commonly, signs are painted directly onto walls lining the streets. I remember reading daily, while getting a *pān* (a betel nut and leaf packet with spices that is chewed) at the nearest crossing to my house, a sign, long faded, advertising a local school. It had been painted directly onto the neighboring *pān* stall before the one I patronized was built, obscuring the advertisement from all but customers who had visual access to the one-foot space between.

Advertising creates a stark contrast between government-administered and private schools. Most schools have a sign near the entrance gate, and government-administered schools are no exception, but this is the extent of government-administered schools' advertising. Private schools of either Hindi- or English-medium, in contrast, advertise vigorously. Besides the sign at the entrance, private schools have signs placed all over the city's public spaces, so that they are among the most advertised items in town. Both Hindi-medium and English-medium schools advertise, but in very different ways. An obvious difference was in the script used, and less variably, in the language in which the advertisement appeared. One might predict, as I did initially, that English-medium schools advertise in English, using roman letters, and that Hindi-medium schools advertise in Hindi, using Devanagari script, but this was not always, or even mostly, the case. My initial predictions did hold in the case of the convent school on the outskirts of the city and the fees-taking English-medium branches of the Seacrest School, one of Varanasi's most expensive. Their signage always looked the most expensive to produce, and their advertisements were the only ones to ever reach the domain of television. Among these schools, issues of language and its representation in script were moot, for no Hindi or Devanagari appeared.

Other schools were somewhat less predictable in terms of a match between the language medium of their pedagogy and that of their advertising. Some schools left the medium of pedagogy completely unmentioned. Their names might utilize Hindi words—बालक विद्यालय (*bālak vidyālaya,* "child school"), for example—or English words, such as "Toddler Convent." Sometimes the English words appeared in Devanagari renditions—टाड्लर कान्वेंट (*tāḍlar kānvent*)—and sometimes, though seldom, the Hindi titles appeared in roman renditions, such as, "Baalak Vidyalaya" ("child school"). Among these schools, there was no easy way to guess, unless it was explicitly stated, what medium the school being advertised belonged to. The sign in front of government schools, in contrast, was always in Devanagari, and in the few "Central Schools," regarded as the most prestigious of the government schools, the English name, "X Central School," was followed by its representation in Devanagari.

Rarely did schools advertise that they were Hindi-medium. Advertisements for hundreds of schools in Varanasi that I recorded included only one or two examples of schools that put "Hindi-medium" on their sign or in their roadside advertisements.[5] Self-declared English-medium status was much more common and many fees-taking schools stated explicitly in their advertisements that they were English-medium. Most often this was advertised in roman letters, though sometimes the lexical items were rendered in the Devanagari equivalent: अँग्रेजी मीडियम (*angrezī mīdiyam,* "English-medium"), *angrezī* being the Hindi for "English," or ईंग्लिश मीडियम (*īngliś mīdiam*), a direct transliteration. Not until much reflection on these possibilities did it strike me how ridiculous it would be to see "Hindi-medium" (rendered with English lexical items in roman script).

Some schools also advertised their board affiliation. Very few schools advertise their affiliation to the Uttar Pradesh Board (UP Board), however. Figure 5 shows the signboard for the Little Stars School. The signboard uses English lexical items transliterated in Devanagari for its name and then some English (pre-nursery) and some Hindi (*kakśā*), all transliterated in Devanagari.

Much more commonly advertised was a school's affiliation with the Central Board of Secondary Education. The acronym usually sufficed, whether in conversation or in advertisement; in advertising, one would see "CBSE" (Central Board of Secondary Education), or the Devanagari letters referring to the English letters of the acronym—सी बी एस ई (*sī bī es ī*). In the previous chapter, Figure 4 shows a signboard for a school, Tulsi Vidya Niketan (Tulsi Knowledge Abode), claiming affiliation with the CBSE. Although its name includes local personages and Hindu themes, most of the sign is rendered in English and all of the sign is rendered in roman script. Consistently, CBSE affiliation is claimed by the most expensive schools in town. In turn, the CBSE is juxtaposed to the UP Board in conversation. The two boards stand in opposition, parallel to the relationship between English- and Hindi-medium schools.

Figure 5. Little Stars School advertisement.

transliteration:	translation:
liṭil sṭārs skūl	Little Stars School
prī. narsrī se kakśā 10 (yū. pī. borḍ)	from pre-nursery to tenth grade (UP Board)
śivpurī kālonī, nagvā̃	Shivpuri Colony, Nagwa
hāī skūl mātra laṛkiyõ ke liye	high school for girls only

Whereas UP Board affiliation is rarely advertised at all, claims of CBSE affiliation are often the subject of comment and dispute. Figure 6, for example, is a signboard for Little Angel Convent School. It uses English lexical items transliterated in Devanagari to describe itself as serving "kindergarten to Vth" levels on the "CBSE pattern." No one to whom I mentioned the signboard believed that the school had board affiliation with the CBSE. People explained that the school refers to the board to claim prestige, specifically of an English-medium ambience. On the fourth line of the signboard, one discovers that the Little Angel Convent School shares an address with the Little Stars School. People targeted schools like Little Angel Convent School when they made accusations that English-medium, fees-taking schools' claims of board affiliation were false.

Some schools do not claim board affiliation in their signboards. They are typically unaffiliated with a school board. Figure 7 is the signboard for a school formed in a Dalit neighborhood in the southern part of Varanasi. The neighborhood began as a squatter settlement, and when the city government built a wall enclosing the neighbor-

Figure 6. Little Angel Convent School advertisement.

transliteration:	translation:
liṭil enjal kānvenṭ skūl	Little Angel Convent School
kiṇḍar gārṭen TO Vth CBSE paiṭarn	kindergarten to Vth CBSE pattern
ḍe-borḍing suvidhā upalabdha...	day-boarding accommodation available
patā—liṭil sṭārs skūl	address—Little Stars School
śivpurī kālonī, nagvā̃—vārāṇasī	Shivpuri Colony, Nagwa—Varanasi

Figure 7. Municipal Corporation Primary School signboard.

transliteration:	translation:
nagar nigam	municipal corporation
prāīmalī skul	primary school
safāī basti durgā kunḍ	sweeper colony Durga Kund
vārāṇasī	Varanasi

hood, the residents took the bricks from the wall one night and used them to build better housing. The school is meant for children who cannot afford the fees at private schools or even the uniforms and such at government schools.

These combinatorial possibilities are presented to demonstrate how advertising illustrates a difference in schooling through language use in visually represented form. Though types of advertising are many, most advertising forms utilized by schools in Varanasi include only written words in representing their commodities. Two exceptions are the photographs of particularly successful students that appear in the advertisements for tutorial services, and the school crest, which sometimes appears within a school's advertisement. Some expensive English-medium schools (the Seacrest School, for example) have begun to air television advertisements on local cable, but this is the only type of school to have done so. Most commonly, school advertising uses only written language in its representational form.

Script \ Language	Hindi	English
Devanagari	बालक विद्यालय (*bālak vidyālaya*)	टाड्लर कान्वेंट (*tāḍlar kānvenṭ*)
Roman	Baalak Vidyalay	Toddler Convent

Figure 8. The possibilities of language representations in school advertising in Varanasi (combinations of language and script).

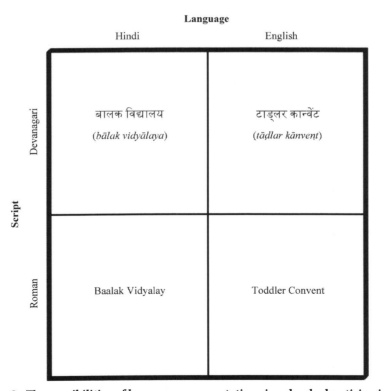

The correspondence between school medium and linguistic medium of advertising was not universal; however, two of the schools I focused on during fieldwork—Saraswati School and Seacrest School—represent end points in the spectrum of what happens linguistically in the public representation of schools through advertising. For these two schools, the relationship between school type and characteristics of advertising (language medium, language used in advertisement, script used in advertisement, and board affiliation) was predictable. For other schools like Little Stars School and Little Angel Convent School, these variables intermixed significantly, and some people used the "inconsistencies" to build a commentary on the school's legitimacy.

Considered together, lexical choice between Hindi and English and the script in which either is written illustrate particularly clearly the way that advertising constructs an index of language medium. In other words, the lexical/script combinations index the particular institution represented by the advertisement as belonging to a type.

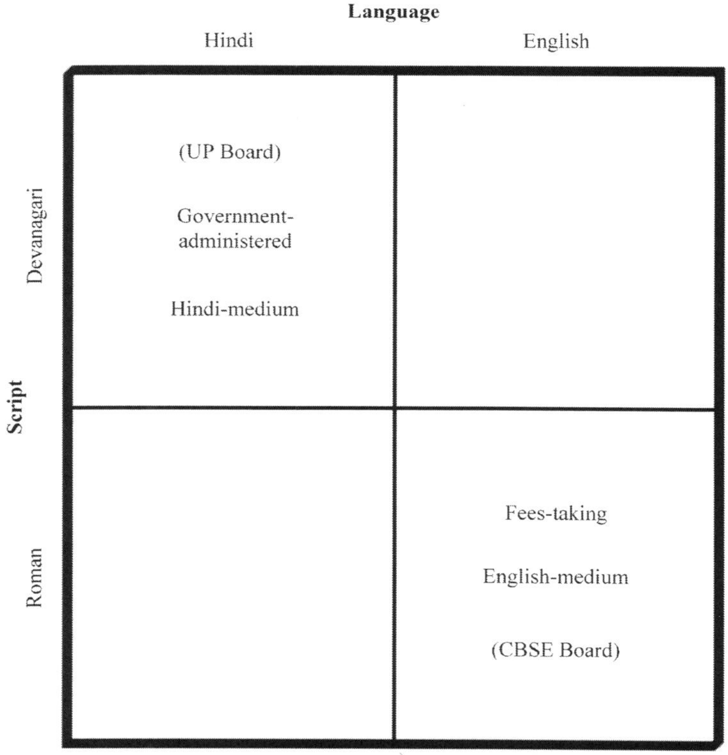

Figure 9. Relationship of script and language in school (and board) advertising, with predictable cases specified and cases erased in reflection left blank.

Two consequences result from a lexical/script combination's indexical function. First, the indexical nature of lexical/script combinations in advertisements for schools disregards linguistic complexity within the institutions indexed. The realm of advertising does not have to account for the more complex linguistic interactions that actually take place in all types of schools—for example, the linguistic maneuvering in Hindi and English that goes on in the Seacrest School's principal's office when parents bring their children for the entrance examination, or a rather complex discussion (presented in the next chapter) I had with a veteran government school teacher about the changing ways that Hindi and English have been used in government school teaching. School and tutorial service advertisements thus seem like particularly complete examples of what Gal and Irvine have labeled "semiotic erasure": "the process in which ideology, in simplifying the field of linguistic practices, renders some persons or activities or sociolinguistic phenomena invisible" (1995: 974). The end points of advertising's combinatorial possibilities of lexical and script choice erase the semiotic possibilities of the use of both languages in such conversations; consequently, advertising exists as a somewhat self-contained system of school differentiation. This is possible because advertisements for schools rely for meaning construction on differences that are not necessarily salient in advertising for other products. This is the second consequence of the indexical force of lexical/script combinations, and it illustrates why the indexical nature of medium distinctions in written advertising differs from that in spoken discourse. The two types of schools that stand as end points in the spectrum of possible combinations of languages and scripts do so precisely because, in their cases, those combinations are predictable within the larger linguistic scope of advertising, school-based or not.

The cases of other schools such as "Little Stars" (Figure 5) and "Little Angel" (Figure 6), where combinations can be called more variable and "muddled," are typical of the larger world of advertising in northern India. The lack of internal systematic correspondence between representation and language on the one hand and language and script on the other is unremarkable (see Figure 8). One might find examples in advertisements for products such as soap, matches, or even automobiles that are ubiquitous in northern India. Among such advertisements, it is possible that elements of a product's linguistic representation would draw comments about the correspondence between language and the product's symbolic consumption. There is nothing predictable, however, in representational choices between Hindi and English lexical items, and roman or Devanagari script.

Figure 10 shows the name of the store, prominently painted in Devanagari over the entrance—बर्मन स्टोर्स (*barman sṭors* (Burman Stores))—named after its owner. Just outside the store proper are many accoutrements of daily life—water buckets and plastic cricket bats, and just inside the entrance, hanging from the ceiling, are baby dolls and toy animals. Inside, one can find all manner of general goods, from paper to underwear. The photograph was taken in the monsoon season and an air cooler sits on the end of the counter for the clerk's comfort. The air cooler is a comparative luxury, complementing the ceiling fan found in most stores like this, but not in smaller stalls where more limited selections of household goods can be found. Painted with the store's name above the entrance is a symbol from a soft drink company and the address and phone number of the store. There is all manner of advertising, from a popular battery manufacturer (entirely in English) to a sign in the upper right-hand corner of the doorframe for सरल कोचिंग (*saral kocing*, "easy coaching"), an advertisement for a local Hindi-medium tutorial service. "Coaching" is borrowed from English, but it is a common term for tutoring across northern India.

Figure 10 shows a general store, while Figure 11 shows the larger group of stores in which it is situated. Burman Stores is the next store

Figure 10. Mr. Burman's shop.

Figure 11. A typical line of shops.

on the left, out of the picture. From left to right, there is a dry cleaner, another general store, a pharmacy, and a laundry service. Advertising abounds; logos and lexical items utilize Hindi and English, and use Devanagari or roman script as means of representing both. Figure 11 illustrates all possible combinations. श्री नाथ जनरल स्टोर्स (*śrī nāth janaral sṭors* (Shri Nath General Stores)) is painted in Devanagari just above the entrance to the store, just as in the case of Mr. Burman's shop, and written again, but in roman script, "SHRI NATH GENERAL STORES." This roman-script rendition is included on a plastic signboard for a soft drink whose consumption many associate with activities foreign or attributable to "big people" (*baṛe log*). (However, another sign for the same soft drink company, not more than a mile away, utilized Devanagari script to convey its English lexical items, *janaral sṭors* (general stores)). Just underneath is a cigarette advertisement, brand name in English (roman script) and accompanying slogan in Hindi (Devanagari script).[6] Painted on the head of the bench in front of the row of stores is यहाँ पर विडियो गेम किराये पर दिया जाता है (*yahā̃ par viḍiyo gem kirāye par diyā jātā hai*, "video games are rented here"), all rendered in Devanagari. As in the case of soft drinks, many people claimed that videos and video games are something foreign; nevertheless, they sit comfortably in an entirely Hindi sentence.

Advertising is susceptible to multiple interpretations and can trigger multiple commentaries or criticisms. What is possible depends on the historical circumstances of the viewer's life, current contextual factors, and the imagination of those engaged, but advertising done in the domain of schooling is less open to flux than are other kinds. The point here is not that school advertising comprises a domain in which script and language are in proper synchronization; linguistic play, as illustrated above, occurs in all domains of advertising in northern India and figures in commentary that links various contextual factors of the message, product, or location of advertisement with ideological dimensions of language. What is present in the domain of school advertisement, but not elsewhere, is a set of predetermined correlations (judged as proper) between linguistic representations of persons, objects, or institutions and their manifestations in advertisements, which, in turn, may be referenced in explanations of their correct functioning. Hindi lexical items in Devanagari script, on the one hand, and English lexical items in roman script, on the other hand, index polar opposites configured by language medium. This is possible because, within school advertising, nationally derived distinctions—school boards—find their place in local institutions—schools that claim school board affiliation.

Advertising Tutorials: The Language-Medium Division in Another Educational Institution

Schools are not the only educational institutions in northern India that utilize advertising to attract students. Many parents explained to me that, in order to pass their yearly exams, their children needed more instruction than school alone could provide. Many called on the services of a "tuition" (*tūiśan,* tutor). Most of the families I knew hired a tutor through family or neighborhood-based friendship connections. Many had a "cousin-brother" who was taking classes at Banaras Hindu University or Kashi Vidyapith, the two local universities, who was either willing to tutor or knew of someone else who might be. Families who approached a tutorial service were the exceptions.

Nevertheless, advertising for tutorial services is intense. Tutorial services largely utilize the same varieties of media as schools: signage around town and advertisements in the newspaper.[7] Some tutorial service advertisements index the school medium to which the service caters through the conjunction of lexical item and script. The Saraswati Study Circle, for example, claims to offer assistance to students in classes ten through twelve in the science and commerce "lines" (*lāyns*). The third line, arts, goes unmentioned. All of the words in the advertisement are rendered in roman script, and, apart from proper names, the lexical items are rendered in English.

Some tutorial services index parallel and discrete medium affiliations in their bid to attract students from both mediums—something that schools never do in their advertising, of course. The advertisement shown in Figure 12 demonstrates that tutorial service advertising is a realm for the creation of medium distinctions in which the salience of conjunctions of Hindi and English lexical items, and Devanagari and roman scripts, respectively, is apparent in a single message. This advertisement was displayed high over the road.

Abbreviations such as "M. S. S." are not uncommon in northern India. Nita Kumar's experience with such abbreviations is worth quoting:

> "I am the daughter of the I. G." The man was a fresh recruit and didn't grasp the meaning of what I said, but he took me through the inspec-

Figure 12. M.S.S. Tutorials advertisement.

transliteration:	translation:
M. S. S. TUTORIALS sāyākāl	M. S. S. Tutorials evening
kakśāyẽ III se VIII u. pra. borḍ CBSE	from level three to eight UP Board CBSE
māruti śikśaṇ santhān raji.	Maruti Learning Institute raji.
B-31/36 sankaṭ mocan mandir ke pās	B-31/36 near the Sankatmochan Temple
bhogābīr vārāṇasī	Bhogabir Varanasi

> tor's empty office, nodding at questioning countenances on the way, "She's a big person." In fact, it wasn't the I. G. that was crucial; any two or three initials would do. As for reaching closed places, if we had a jeep all we needed to do was to put a large plate on the front reading "R. S. C., Varanasi City" (Research Scholars from Chicago) to match such signs as "A. D. M." (Additional District Magistrate), "C. S. C." (Civil Surgeon City), "C. E. E." (Chief Executive Engineer), "U. P. S. E. B. M. D." and the plates of other VIPSs who could reach places. (N. Kumar 1992: 120)

Although Kumar is speaking of abbreviations attached to offices of power whose physical manifestations seem to require an automobile, her reflections nicely illustrate the degree to which such abbreviations are used in northern India. Perhaps what letters were actually used in her example was inconsequential precisely because their ability to denote power was presupposed, triggered by their presence on the plate of a car.[8] In other contextual renditions, what the initials stand for has a broader range than rank, government service occupation, or office; abbreviations are not confined to official, power-laden domains. Political parties, companies, and commercial products, as well as standard tokens of everyday reference (STD, standard trunk dialing, is used for the public pay telephone) are commonly named by abbreviations.

Figure 12 is presented here because it displays the conjunction of language of representation and script that one not well versed in the range of possibilities within advertising in northern India might expect. English terms are presented in roman script, and Hindi terms in Devanagari. Even so, interesting processes are at play in the advertisement, especially concerning the relationship between what is referenced and its appearance as Hindi or English. An abbreviation suffices as the name of the company; not until the third line does one find out what the abbreviation stands for. Roman letters come to stand for Hindi words (the last of which, *santhān,* is misspelled, and should be *sansthān*). The letters are followed by the roman-rendered English, "Tutorials." Without the information provided beyond the first line of the sign, one would have no idea that the company name is comprised largely of Hindi words.

The time of availability, "evening" (*sāyākāl*), is indicated in Devanagari-rendered Hindi, as is "levels" (*kakśāyẽ*) on the next line. Roman numerals denote the grade levels served. The abbreviations for board affiliations are telling: "UP Board" is rendered in Devanagari, but also in an abbreviated Hindi. The sign could have displayed यू पी (*yū pī bord*), which would have given a Devanagari rendition of the roman characters (not an unusual practice). For that matter, it could have said, "UP Board." However, it preserves a perfect dichotomy between Hindi/Devanagari and English/roman script, precisely because it depicts "UP Board" in a less abbreviated form in which Devanagari represents an abbreviated Hindi and not an abbreviated English. "CBSE," an abbreviation for a board that specifically oversees the requirements of some English-medium fees-taking schools, is left unexplained. The actual name of the institute comes next, but not until the third line of the advertisement. *Raji* most likely stands for "registered." The address is split between the block designation and the number (B-31/36) and the neighborhood (Bhogabir), typical in northern India. Finally, the location of the institute is placed near an important landmark, the Sankatmochan Temple, not far from Lanka.[9]

The only exception in the sign in terms of the correspondence between Devanagari and Hindi, on the one hand, and roman and English, on the other hand, is in the title of the company. The divergence is particularly apparent in a sign that otherwise preserves the correlation between Hindi and English lexical items, and Devanagari and roman scripts, respectively. Two factors lend the divergence meaning—one in the domain of linguistic practice within advertising in general, and the other present in the sign itself in its spatial configuration. Advertisements frequently use roman initials as a company's name, and these initials may stand for either English or Hindi lexical items. Advertisements may also employ Devanagari to represent Hindi or English lexical items.[10] The spatial configuration of abbreviation and corresponding lexical item in Figure 12 reminds one of Kumar's impression that the abbreviation itself carries persuasive force; here, it is what one encounters first in the sign, only later to be explained.

The relationship between abbreviation and the language it indexes is a bit more complicated in Figure 12 than in Kumar's examples for two reasons. First, the abbreviations do not index languages in the manner typical of the rest of the sign. In other words, "M. S. S." refers to the letters that would begin a roman script rendition of the unambiguously Hindi name of the company. An act of translation has occurred in the sign, one essentially different from that entailed in the rendering उ प्र (*u pra*) for Uttar Pradesh, or CBSE for the Central Board of Secondary Education (line two). Thus, within the rest of the sign's own construction of a properly functioning language-indexing script, "M. S. S." is marked or unusual. Second, the renditions in lines one and three do not match. One who understands both Hindi and English and the conventions for their abbreviation is left wondering whether the company's name is *māruti śikśaṇ sansthān TUTORIALS* ("Maruti learning institute tutorials").[11] But precisely this discrepancy exposes the language processes at work. The title as rendered on the first line is not an English equivalent of the information present in the rest of the sign (unreadable to anyone non-literate in Hindi). In fact, as shown above, the sign drives home the need to keep separate Hindi and English, and the scripts that properly index them. This makes the title odd and therefore noticeable.

That the marked or referentially charged item in the advertisement appears first is no accident: abbreviations are popular means of identification in northern India for everything from government offices to personal names. However, whereas those examples can demonstrate the easy representation of "Hindi sounds" with English-based orthographic representation, and "English sounds" with Hindi-based representation, such that scripts' language-indexing functions blur, the sign examined here represents a domain where those functions have been constructed "on the spot." Furthermore, it illustrates that in northern India, scripts' language-indexing functions can be used to effects other than indexing a language. A roman-script-based translation of sounds that begin Hindi words appears first in a sign that later works to keep script and language in strict correspondence (Devanagari/Hindi versus roman/English). For the Hindi-reading public implied by the sign's use of Hindi in all but two abbreviations and one word, English is the language of catchy identification and semiotic innovation.

Advertising the Local, Advertising the National: Schools in the Newspaper

The educational institution advertisements that clog Varanasi's public spaces are not the only such advertisements in town; newspaper readers encounter them, too. Newspapers, like schools, are divided according to language medium, available in Hindi, Urdu, English, and some other languages in Varanasi, even if they are not produced there. Educational advertising is confined largely to nationally distributed dailies, which contain sections that focus on major Indian metropolitan areas and their environs, apart from strictly national news. During fieldwork in 1996–1997, a daily from Lucknow had begun to include a weekly section specific to Varanasi. With the rise of web-based publishing, there are now Varanasi-specific pages online for all of the national dailies available in the city. Yet, the state of school advertising reported herein largely remains the same.

Most of the educational institutions advertised in the newspaper read in Varanasi exist elsewhere, in cosmopolitan cities like Delhi, Mumbai, and Chennai. Concomitantly, the indexical plurality provided by lexical/script combinations prevalent around town is missing in the newspaper. Only one possibility exists in the national daily: English lexical items written in roman script. Examples presented below demonstrate that advertisements emanating from the center for institutions located there serve to index Varanasi and its educational institutions in two ways. On the one hand, national advertising for educational institutions corresponds to the advertising practices of only the most expensive English-medium schools in Varanasi, because only they produce advertisements in English rendered in roman script. Expensive English-medium schools in Varanasi, thus, are indexical of the center, and other schools in Varanasi are not. On the other hand, national advertising indexes Varanasi as a place on the periphery, because medium distinctions, a large part of the indexical function of lexical/script combinations around Varanasi, are wholly absent in newspaper advertising for educational institutions. In Varanasi, some parents of children enrolled in English-medium schools and other people who read English newspapers explained to me that school advertisements encountered during a walk around town look disordered in comparison with newspaper advertisements for schools.

Like local advertising for education, advertising in the national daily is produced by both schools and tutorial services. In the newspaper, however, tutorial services' advertising strategies differ from schools' more significantly. No local schools advertised in the nationally distributed dailies widely available in Varanasi. No local tutorial services did, either, but, even at the time of my initial fieldwork in 1996–1997, the correspondence-based lessons offered by some tutorial services extended to Varanasi. Some prestigious schools with national reputations advertise in national dailies, but these differ from tutorial services' national advertising practices in one crucial way.[12] Prestigious schools that advertise in national papers ostensibly draw students from all over India (in the case of boarding schools) or from the major urban centers in which they are located (in the case of day schools). Nationally advertised tutorial services, however, may reach out to students living all over India. The latter often have branches in several urban areas, sometimes nationwide. Now, several nationally known tutorial services have offices in Varanasi. Sometimes tutorial services advertise nationally for only one location (usually in a major urban center), and sometimes institutes offer correspondence courses toward a degree, but these seem to be exceptions.

The prototypical elite schools for Indians are boarding schools, many established during the period of British rule. These schools draw students from all over India. They represent the paradigmatic institutionalization of English as a link language uniting state or region-based languages in the modern postcolonial Indian setting (see chapter 2). Some major urban areas have English-medium schools that advertise in widely distributed dailies but draw their students primarily from their own urban centers. Such a school's advertisement appears here as Figure 13.

Most attention-getting in the advertisement are the faces of students who have been particularly successful in exam scores. The first student is commended for her perfect score in biology, and the next two students for their high scores overall. Top-scoring students were not absent from Varanasi schools, but their pictures were not used in advertising.[13] Rather, photographs of students making top scores on exams, "toppers" (*ṭāpars*) would be published in the yearbooks produced by both the Seacrest and Saraswati Schools, which were distributed to students and their families and not used for general advertising. The rest of the advertisement in Figure 13 is typical for schools that advertise in nationally distributed papers. High results from class twelve are separated from class ten because these crucial exam-taking points in a student's career largely determine if, and in which "line," the student will continue. The actual percentage scores received are listed. All schools that advertise mention that their students receive top scores on exams, but not all are as meticulous or comprehensive as the one in Figure 13. The lines or "streams" are listed toward the bottom: "Commerce," "Science," and "Humanities." Class ten results are as crucial as those of college-bound class twelve students, and this fact is displayed by the announcement "ADMISSION OPEN FOR CLASS XI." Entrance to class eleven is based largely on the results of exams taken on completion of class ten. "NO FAILURE" is proclaimed, and there is not a hint of Hindi in the advertisement.

What is immediately apparent in many advertisements for tutorial services is the bewildering array of educational boards across the country. Figure 14, an advertisement for a tutorial service that helps students gain entrance to colleges with a medical focus, is typical for tutorial services that advertise nationally. It emphasizes the success its students have attained. "First" is the largest word in the advertisement, and the explanation before the list of exemplary students

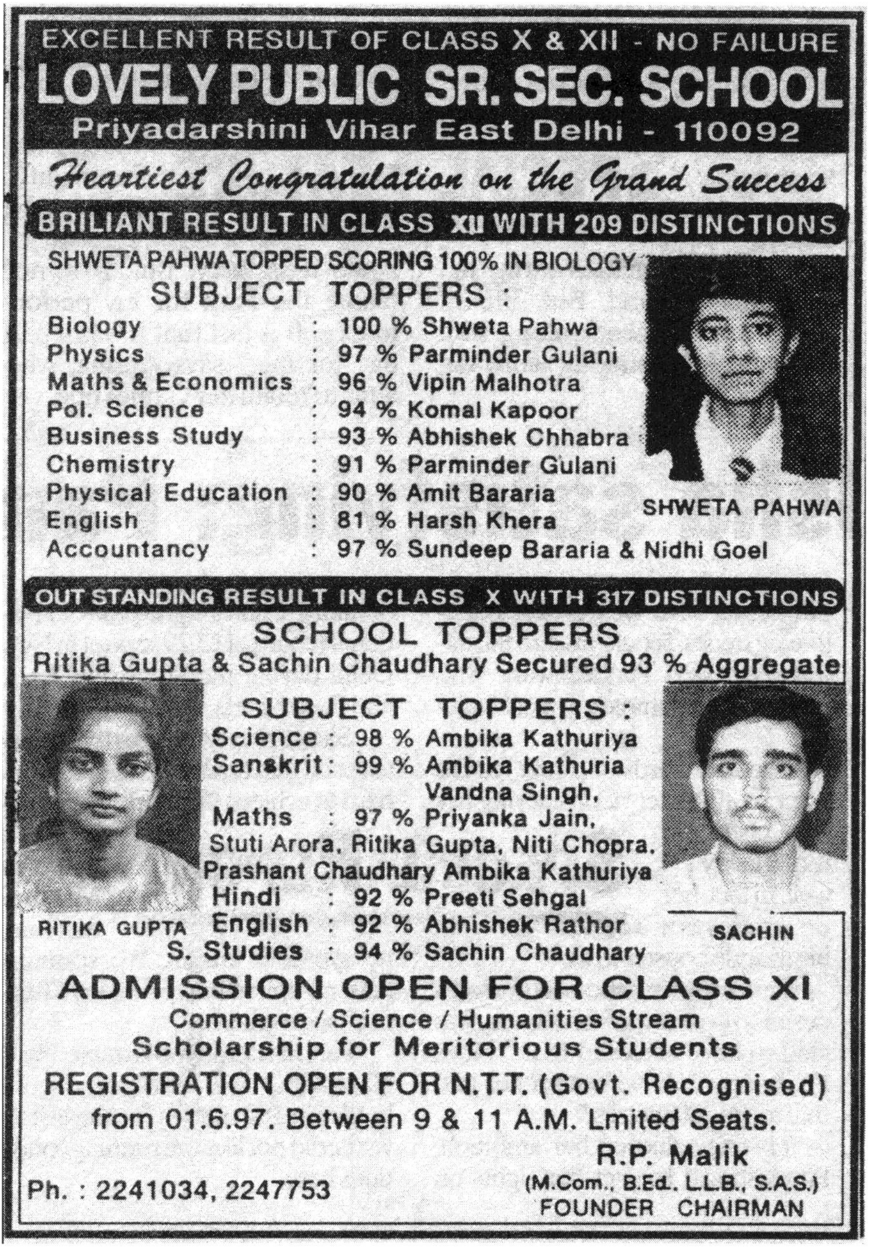

Figure 13. Advertisement for a school in Delhi in a locally distributed national daily; from *Indian Express,* Lucknow (8 June 1997).

focuses on success. The students are able to "hog the highest ranks" because of the "monumental labour" of the tutorials. Most relevant to this discussion of advertising is the next section, which lists the "firsts" in the medical entrance exam who have been associated with the tutorial service and the cities where the students took the exam. The most common city is Delhi, but there are others, giving the advertisement national appeal. The "rank" category is redundant, but this redundancy is effective as an advertising tool: all students have ranked "first." The last column translates location into the idiom of educational institutions, specifying the testing board for each student. As in Figure 13, more than one board is mentioned, but the boards in Figure 14 have lost the element of local competitiveness and, instead, are present to add to the tutorial service's proof of success. State boards and private boards mingle without any comparative frame.

Though many places and tests are named, the CBSE is mentioned first in the list. One cannot attribute that position to the student's home in the national capital, because many of the students taking other tests hail from Delhi. CBSE is also mentioned first in the box, just under the list of model students, and again later. It is the only board mentioned in the advertisement's copy. In light of the CBSE's national popularity, it is no surprise that, in Varanasi, it is the board to which schools' affiliations are often claimed to be false.

Although, at the national level of educational identity, the CBSE is particularly valued, it is only one board among many. The advertisement in Figure 14 mentions that one of the reasons that Brilliant Tutorials is so successful is related to the lack of uniformity among the boards' exams, referring to "the painstaking process of updating the Lesson Papers and Question Bank, based on the changing syllabi and testing patterns of the various Medical Entrance Exams." Here, the advertisement presents the nation's complement of educational boards as a disorderly bunch that requires diverse knowledge on the part of the centralized tutorial service. Most obviously, and most unlike the advertisement depicted in Figure 12, Figure 14 contains no Hindi. As in Figure 13, English is the sole medium of advertising. Figure 13 comes from Delhi, and Figure 14 comes from Chennai in southern India.[14] The school's and tutorial service's advertisements transcend the local, but in different ways. If one attends the school advertised in Figure 13, one might excel in Hindi, but only as one subject among many requiring examination in the board's framework. The message that English is the language of success is unambiguous. This is true also of the tutorial service. Whereas the school is a local institution of national (linguistic) scope, the tutorial service is simply

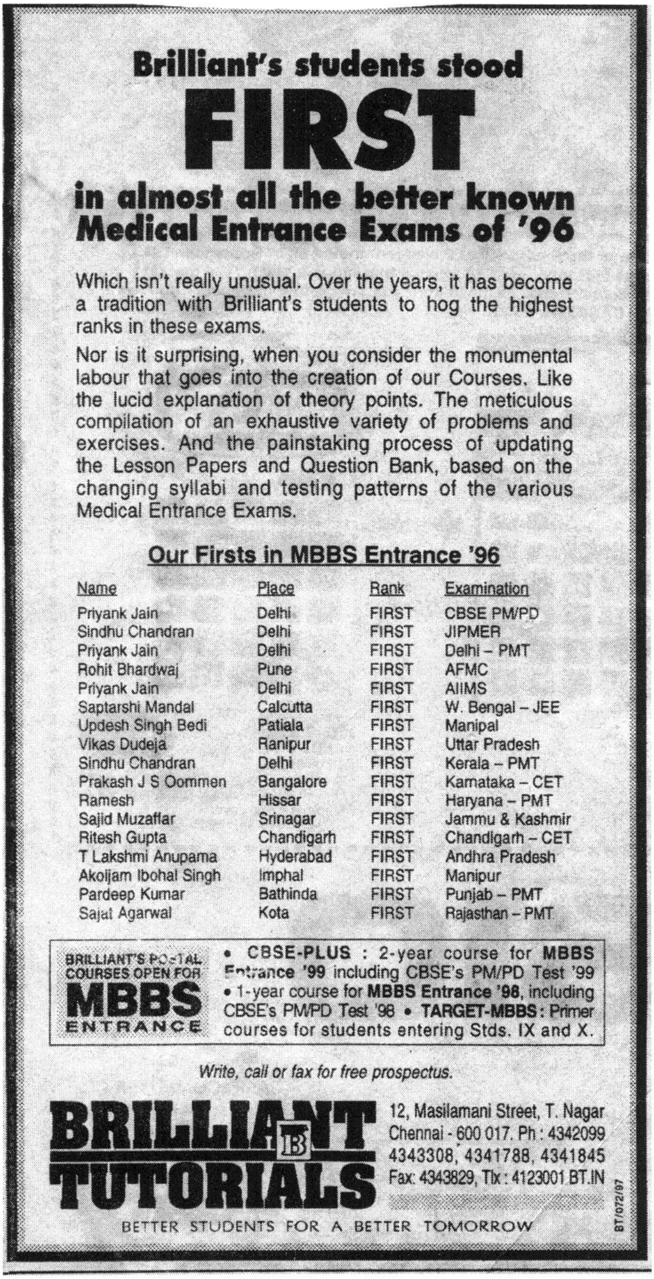

Figure 14. Advertisement for a tutorial service in a locally distributed national daily; from *Indian Express,* Lucknow (8 June 1997).

a national institution that has become so by catering to diverse exam requirement structures. Both have enacted their sales pitches through English; within these, a discourse of rivalry like that established in Figure 12 is not possible.

Conclusion

Whether discursive activity about schools occurs in Varanasi within spoken discourse or within printed advertising entails different possibilities for the construction of the relationship among language variety and language value. In spoken discourse, multiple constructions of Hindi- and English-medium schools as indexes of centrality and peripherality are possible. In terms of economic opportunity, English-medium schools provide conduits to a center to which Varanasi residents look, and Hindi-medium schools lie in the periphery because of their lack of possibilities. In terms of nationalism, Hindi-medium schools locate Varanasi in the center, and English-medium schools suggest a peripheral stance suspected of lacking patriotism. In spoken discourse generally, Hindi- and English-medium schools are bifurcated in an ambivalent way, and they are productive of differences that betray a unified hierarchical principle. There is the possibility that people can see Hindi and Hindi-medium schooling as an indication that their position is central in the nation as they pursue educational credentials.

In printed advertising, the centrality of English and the English-medium schools for which it is employed is more certain. In order to explain what makes English so decisively indexical of the center in advertising, one must include more than language distinctions per se. Script distinctions matter too, and they mingle with language distinctions to produce an indexical regimentation of the center and its periphery. A process occurs in advertising for schools in the newspaper in which adherence or non-adherence to only one possibility of lexical/script alignment (English/roman) establishes the indexical ground of the metalinguistic judgment of what is central and what lies on the periphery. Peripherality's indexical salience in advertisements for educational institutions in Varanasi is constructed by newspapers that are published elsewhere; advertising done by schools and tutorial services in Varanasi confirms that the city lies at the fringe of an all-English possibility. Consistently, a look in the newspaper, where advertisements for institutions at the "center" can be found, confirms that English lexical items in roman script are the only ones present, whereas a quick walk around town exposes one to other combinations. The message of school and tutorial service advertising for Varanasi's newspaper-reading residents is clear: places elsewhere are for an English unadulterated by Hindi, whereas Varanasi as a whole is subordinate to such locations precisely because, in Varanasi, languages and their institutions are visibly plural and in contest. Should one want to pursue employment options elsewhere, in larger, distant cities with larger communication infrastructures, English rendered in roman script would seem to be necessary. Hindi is nowhere to be found in advertising from afar in the newspaper.

Notes

This chapter incorporates material from "Advertising in the Periphery: Languages and Schools in a North Indian City," *Language in Society* 31: 213–242.

1. In sum, advertising for schools presents a domain of linguistic activity in which "structures of reception and evaluation" differ significantly from those in spoken discourse (Spitulnik 1993: 297).
2. An index is the relationship between a sign and its object of representation that is based on contiguity—spatial, temporal, or existential. Excellent discussions include Mertz (1985), Parmentier (1994), and Silverstein (1976). All draw from the work of Charles Sanders Peirce.
3. Irvine critiques Bourdieu's conceptualization of dominance across markets for his lack of attention to this kind of difference between spheres of communicative activity: "It [Bourdieu's conceptualization] tends to reduce language to presuppositional indexicality and to derive language's role in political economy entirely therefrom" (1989: 256).
4. Devanagari has as an ancestor the Brahmi script once modified for use with Sanskrit. For a description of Devanagari's evolution, see Masica (1991: 133–151). Masica explains that "Nagari (literally the 'city' or 'metropolitan' script < *nagar* 'city', also called Devanagari) is the official script of Hindi, Marathi, and Nepali, and of the new (or revised) literatures in Rajasthani, Dogri, Maithili (and other Bihari dialects), and Pahari dialects (e.g., Kumauni) when written" (1991: 144).
5. Notice the gap between the predominance of English-medium advertised schools and the virtual absence of Hindi-medium advertised schools, and the political rhetoric of officials (Mulayam Singh Yadav, former Chief Minister of Uttar Pradesh, was the primary official discussed in my 1996–1997 fieldwork) against English as the foreign language of the colonizer. Many middle- and upper-class people explained to me that such moves were useless because advertising showed that people obviously wanted English-medium education, or harmful because they only incited the uneducated to anger. Notice the process by which the government system of schools is left out of the picture by middle- and upper-class reactions to criticism, as well as by the practice of advertising. In turn, during my fieldwork, this gap was described as a "craze" for English-medium education.

6. This example illustrates particularly well the ways that visual advertising uses script difference to represent language difference. In interactions between clerks and customers, I heard entire conversations in Hindi in which the brand names of cigarettes or other items were the only lexical items that might be identified as English. These cannot be called examples of code-switching, but in their visual representations, such as the cigarette advertisement in front of the store, items' representations are clearly demarcated as English.
7. However, I never saw or heard of a television advertisement for a tutorial service that was broadcast in Varanasi.
8. Narayan (1993) writes of a village woman's performance of a wedding song (*suhāg*) in which she uses "V.I." and "V.P." to name the (fictional) educational degrees of the groom. Narayan poses the possibility that her own scholarly presence may have inspired the woman to speak of degrees; the singer, not familiar with their particular nomenclature, probably created "V.I." and "V.P." out of the familiar "V.I.P."
9. Maruti, a title of the deity Hanuman, may be used purposefully for the name of a company located near the Sankatmochan Temple, a home of that god.
10. The use of Devanagari seems to present more options for the representation of letters in an acronym. One never sees "yu pee" or "yoo pee" (roman-script-rendered transliteration of the letters), or either of the first of these with "p"; one only sees "UP" in public use. Acronyms for the state's name rendered in Devanagari sometimes represent the state's name (Uttar Pradesh) with the consonant-vowel combinations beginning the parts of the name, but sometimes represent the state's name by representing the sounds of the roman letters that can be used to for an acronym of the state's name (UP). Perhaps what accounts for the Devanagari-rendered English is that UP is the acronym for a political boundary, and is a part of official, English-medium nomenclature and the acronyms that N. Kumar (1992) describes. They are so common in everyday parlance that their Devanagari-rendered acronyms are widely understood.
11. The logic of the sign's linguistic construction, however, is that one must know only one or the other to identify, at minimum, what the company offers.
12. Schools with such national advertisements are generally boarding schools as well as English-medium.
13. However, a friend who had a television in his house with cable service told me that he had seen an advertisement for the Seacrest School on the portion of the programming designated for local sources. He told me that some children would feel very proud because their pictures had been displayed as a result of their good marks.
14. Chennai was once Madras. Across India, many city names have been changed from the names given to them in the colonial period; Mumbai was once Bombay.

Chapter 4

An Alter Voice

Questioning the Inevitability of the Language-Medium Divide

A school's language medium has become a major category of identity in Hindi-speaking northern India. People use the distinction between Hindi- and English-medium schools to frame a wide array of social entities and relationships: oneself, others, the place of Varanasi in the nation, and the place of India with respect to other nations. While the value ascribed to Hindi and English can vary greatly in spoken reflection on schools, nearly everyone I met during fieldwork has found in the language-medium divide a salient and convenient opposition. This chapter explores the case of one person who managed to complicate the very notion of language-medium schooling. A biology teacher working at a Hindi-medium government school reflected on schooling in a way that questions the inevitability of the language-medium divide.

In order to provide an explanation of how the teacher called into question the foundation of the divide between Hindi- and English-medium schooling, this chapter departs from the tendency of the discussion so far to note the distribution of identity categories across moments of interaction, and rather focuses on the emergence of identity categories in a specific and extended moment of interaction.[1] In order to explore the means by which the biology teacher casts doubt on the inevitability of the language-medium divide, this chapter employs Mikhail Bakhtin's notion of "voice." Bakhtin was unsatisfied with an approach to identity in discourse that merely records the use of identity labels and accounts for their use by sorting when and where they were used. Mediating the notion of an identity label and its use in discourse is Bakhtin's formulation of "voice." Scholars inspired by Bakhtin's writing on voice note that speakers "borrow" (Hanks 1996) or "rent" (Wortham 2003a) language from others such that any occasion of discourse involves relationships between voices (Bakhtin 1981: 279).

The sense of debt on which words like "borrow" and "rent" rest illustrates well that Bakhtin's writings about voice do not imply a world in which language can be used freely by anyone in any circumstance. James Collins and Richard Blot convey the spirit of Bakhtin's work on voice when they write, "The debate between those who emphasize discourse and fluid identity construction versus those who emphasize society and constraints on identity need not be polarized" (2003: 106). A central feature of voice as developed by Bakhtin is the principle that not all language lends itself with the same ease to what others might do with it. A "monologic" voice compels its users to take up a particular point of view (Bakhtin 1984). Bakhtin notes that discursive dynamics are at work in monologic voicing, though they might be hard to detect: "No one hinders this word, no one argues with it" (1981: 276). About such discursive dynamics, Webb Keane writes, "To speak in a singular or monologic voice appears to be a highly marked outcome of political effort rather than a natural or neutral condition" (2001: 270). The feeling that someone speaks on firm ground when they speak of the virtues of the mother tongue or the national language, for example, seems natural because a great deal of effort has been devoted to the language variety in question. It has been central to anti-colonial and nationalist struggles, it has been engineered for use in domains of political and educational authority, and it can bestow on its speaker merit and even patriotism.

"Dialogic" voicing, in contrast, is that in which contestation between points of view exists. In dialogic voicing, monologic voicing does not account for the tools by which speakers craft a point of view. In the example presented in this chapter, for example, notions like mother tongue and national language do not suffice to identify schools as types of institutions, nor do they enable the speaker to take up a typical stance toward schools. Bakhtin found dialogic voicing so fascinating because a point of view remains partial and unsettled. I conceptualize the burden of a dialogic approach as the ability to identify what Bakhtin calls the "centripetal" forces in language that make monologic voices possible, such that "centrifugal" forces, embodied by dialogic contestation between voices, might be identified and appreciated.

Bakhtin writes that centripetal forces are those "working toward concrete verbal and ideological unification and centralization, which develop in vital connection with the processes of sociopolitical and cultural centralization" (1981: 271). The uses of "medium" presented thus far in the book provide evidence that centripetal forces have been at work during the rise in popularity of English-medium education, and have gained strength since the acceleration of liberalization in the early 1990s. The language-medium divide is such a robust formation because it brings together so many aspects of social and national belonging, and prompts one to take one's place with respect to them (Kroskrity 2001). The discussion thus far has demonstrated that different people have used the language-medium divide between Hindi and English as a more or less ready-made opposition to serve various ends (Bucholtz and Hall 2004). Some have used it to differentiate urban and rural people. Others have used it to differentiate themselves from others living in their midst. And yet others have used it to uncover hypocrisy on the part of English-medium students, sometimes to argue in favor of the mother tongue, and sometimes to argue for one's own ability in English in the face of one's own school history. All of these examples are alike in the sense that they put in the spotlight the part played by the language-medium divide in the ways that "people are forced to situate themselves relative to what they are saying as being a particular kind of socially recognizable person" (Koven 1998: 413). Though people are—by design—differently positioned in the language-medium divide, the divide serves as a common frame with which to build images about centrality and marginality in the nation and world, as well as the ways in which one's own language practices and schooling histories implicate one in emergent commentary (Mendoza-Denton 2002).

Yet, Bakhtin's notion of centrifugal forces prompts me to ask whether all people use "medium" in the same way, presupposing the ideological salience of Hindi and English. Indeed, I met one person during fieldwork in 1996–1997 who, as a result of her experiences with schooling, was able to bring to bear voices in such a way that she threw into relief more monologic constructions of medium. In order to explore such dynamics, this chapter presents excerpts from an audiotaped interview I conducted with Madhu Khatri, a teacher. During the interview she deploys multiple voices, emergent from her past experiences with schooling, toward the production of complex "laminated identities" (Goffman 1981).[2] The chapter explores the discursive devices by which she is able to bring these voices to bear in such a way that they radically reframe what is important about language medium. She begins by deploying the voice of a parent, creating a vision of language-medium school difference much like that accounted for by centripetal forces. That is to say, she begins by deploying a vision of schooling that mirrors those presented in the book thus far. A division between Hindi and English structures school difference as well as the difference between those people involved. However, the language-medium divide so important in her first moment of speech fades as she juxtaposes her present difficulties in the classroom to the ease of her days as a student. And finally, she deploys voices made possible by another set of institutional experiences, the routine interactions in which she has been engaged as a teacher in the classroom. Arrangements and consequences of language-medium difference emerge that are utterly unlike those shaped by centripetal forces, such as those encountered in the book thus far.

By exploring the dynamics of voice fostered by the division between Hindi- and English-medium schooling, this chapter conceptualizes the relationship between institutions and identities as powerfully connected, yet hardly uncontested. Debra Spitulnik points out that, "It is only recently ... that scholars have focused their gaze below the level of the overall ideological function and effect of institutions to look more closely at how *specific practices* within institutions give value to different languages and to different ways of using language" (1998: 165). This chapter foregrounds the ways in which some people are able to question the inevitability of the institution's organization. Put in the rubric of a dialogic approach, centripetal forces in Indian society have brought together Hindi- and English-medium schools in a mutually productive opposition at the same time that the schools have involved some people in practices that allow them to exert centrifugal force on the mutually exclusive dichotomy of language and institution.

Discursive Evidence of Centrifugal Forces: The Malleability of Language Medium

The interview from which most of the transcription presented in this chapter comes occurred with a teacher named Madhu Khatri during the afternoon of 22 June 1997. She had come to pay a visit for several weeks in order to comfort her younger sister, my landlady, who was seriously ill. She had made the eight-hour bus trip north from her home in Rewa, a small town in the neighboring state of Madhya Pradesh. Her two nieces, daughters of my landlady, told me that she was a biology teacher, that she heard that I was studying schools, and that she was curious about my research. Though most of her attention was devoted to caring for my landlady and accompanying her to the doctor, her niece told me one afternoon that she would like to talk to me about schooling.

Mrs. Khatri began by explaining that she had been teaching for eighteen years in a Hindi-medium intercollege, a school for the final two years (levels eleven and twelve) of a student's pre-university schooling. Her opening comments about her background resonated with the division between Hindi- and English-medium schools in complex ways. For example, she spent several minutes talking about her own educational history, explaining that after attending a Hindi-medium government school, she completed a BSc (bachelor of science) degree in biology before going on to attain an MSc (master of science) in the same subject. While the inspiration for so much schooling came from her "interest" (*inṭrasṭ*) or passion for biology, she talked immediately afterward about the necessity of having educational credentials when applying for a job in "service," or government employment. She thus came full circle to describe the attainment of requirements for the job she occupied, teacher at a government school.

If the commentary on language-medium schooling presented thus far in the book can be taken as evidence that centripetal forces have been at play in Hindi-speaking northern Indian society, Madhu Khatri's interview provides an example of someone who disrupts connections between language and language-medium schooling and, in so doing, problematizes the convenience offered by medium divisions for representations of her world. Two moments in our interview, separated by approximately two minutes in which Mrs. Khatri talks to one of her nieces who has come to the room to offer tea, bring issues of voice to bear on the ways that people discursively engage social constructs like the language-medium divide. Asif Agha points out, "The typifiability of *voices* (whether as "individual" or "social") presupposes the perceivability of *voicing contrasts,* or the differentiability of one voice from another" (2005: 39). Further complicating the issue of voice, Agha explains, is that the participants can engage voices in different semiotic modalities. For example, people might describe the claims of another person, or make evident that they are re-creating them. Contrasts among voices and modes by which they are brought to life are both issues that must be considered in order to understand the way in which Mrs. Khatri is able to reconfigure what is problematic about schooling in the transition between the first and second moments of discourse presented below. For example, Mrs. Khatri inhabits radically different social identities (parent versus teacher), includes different actors (parents and children versus teacher and students), brings life to those actors and their opinions differently (direct quotes versus Mrs. Khatri's descriptions), situates the described scene differently (in the present versus in the past), and focuses the two moments with different problems (language medium versus technical vocabulary).

Mrs. Khatri, by virtue of her long-term involvement in parenting *and* practices of schooling, has at her disposal the ability to construct different voices for different periods of her life, one set of voices for the present and a different set for the past. These correspond to the two moments in the interview presented herein. In the first moment, a "voicing contrast" stages a disposition to the issue of language medium similar to that of people encountered in the book thus far. In the second moment, a "voicing contrast" radically decouples the issues of language and language medium as invoked in her first moment. The voices, those of teachers and students, operative in the second moment of discourse are unlikely to emerge in the discursive productions of people hitherto encountered in the book because they do not share Mrs. Khatri's teaching practices. In short, the institution of schooling provides the potential for centrifugal forces to question, at least within the confines of the interview, other people's taken for granted use of the Hindi- and English-medium school division.

It is to the first moment that we now turn, wherein a vision of Hindi- and English-medium difference is not only familiar, but also brought to life through something like a performance.

Interview Excerpt 1: "Hey, these are useless"

1 CL: *jī. aur, mə̃i ne sunā ki, ye angrezī bolne wāle skūlz krez hə̃i*
yes. and, I have heard that, these English-speaking schools are a craze

2 *yā ye faiśan hə̃i*
or a fashion

3 Mrs. Khatri: *hə̃, vahī to batā rahe hə̃i ham, na*
yes, I am saying exactly that, no?

4 *ki vaha krez hai aur, vaha ek kāmpleks banā huā hai*
that it is a craze and, it has given birth to a complex

5 *jo bacce ĩngliś mīḍiam mẽ paṛthe ha͠i,*
those children who study in English,

6 *ve hindī mīḍiamwāle baccõ ko bilkul aisā samajhte ha͠i*
understand exactly thus about the Hindi-medium children

7 *ki "are, ye to bekār ha͠i"*
that "hey, these are useless"

8 *unke gāṛḍianz bhī, thoṛā sā neglekṭ karte ha͠i*
their guardians too, neglect a little bit

9 *ki "ye to hindī mīḍiam ke bacce ha͠i."*
that "these are Hindi-medium children."

10 *ham log khud ghar mẽ dekhte ha͠i,*
we see in our home,

11 *ki "are, ye to hindī mīḍiam mẽ paṛthe ha͠i"*
that "hey, these study in Hindī medium"

In order to understand the ways in which Mrs. Khatri creates a vision of the world in which everyone disparages Hindi-medium children, it is necessary to introduce a few seminal ideas and their reverberations in studies of interaction. Such work understands representation of the self and others to be multiplex and to be emergent within interactions. Judith Irvine, in a discussion of Erving Goffman's work, exposes the inadequacy of focusing on "the isolated sentence tossed (like a football) by an anonymous Speaker, whose qualifications for play are specified only as 'competence,' to an even more anonymous Hearer who supposedly catches it" (1996: 131). Goffman (1981) complicates the notion of Speaker by proposing multiple interactional roles that might be operative in an utterance. For example, he notes a distinction between the participant who makes an utterance (Animator) and the party, present or not, who is responsible for the position represented by the utterance (Principal). One might also identify the party who crafted the utterance (Author) as occupying yet a different role. These distinctions can have consequences for the ways that participants engage social personae or, in the rubric of this chapter, voices (Agha 2007: 165).[3] The notion of voice allows for an appreciation for the multiplicity of ways in which "speakers engage in both explicit and implicit forms of social categorization and evaluation, attribute intentionality, affect, knowledge, [and] agency to themselves and others, and lay claim to particular social and/or moral identities" (Jaffe 2009: 9).

For example, whereas Professor Shastri and Arti Aggarwal in chapter 1 describe the "craze" and "complex" to inhabit English-medium and Hindi-medium students, respectively, Mrs. Khatri is able to create the impression that different types of people feel that the complex exists in Hindi-medium students. She is able to produce the utterances of different types of people as if she were those other types of people. In order to do so, Mrs. Khatri momentarily departs the role of "author" that Michèle Koven explains "indicates autobiographical continuity between herself as an author and herself as a narrated protagonist" (2002: 178). In the excerpts presented in chapter 1, for example, "author" is the role that Professor Shastri and Arti Aggarwal inhabited to attest to the historical details of their own competence in English and their knowledge of the "complex" suffered by Hindi-medium students who enter an English-medium environment, as well as the role with which they maintained the referential difference between themselves and others they describe, including students, daughter, and father. Earlier in our interview, before the excerpt presented here, Mrs. Khatri inhabited the same role, "author," to narrate the historical details of her own attendance at school and her emerging career as a teacher.

In lines 3 through 11, however, Mrs. Khatri inhabits a role that Michèle Koven calls "character," in which Mrs. Khatri speaks as if she is someone else, "reenacting their purported thoughts, speech, and other deeds" (2002: 188). Quoted speech is a particularly effective device for inhabiting the role of character because "direct quotations reproduce the reported speech as a fixed and authentic entity, clearly separate from the reporting context" (Lee 1997: 279). Margaret Trawick invokes the notion of boundaries in order to link reported speech to the deployment of alter voices—what Koven calls the role of character: "To the extent that the author distances his own voice from the voices of his characters, 'hard and fast boundaries' will be forged demarcating reported speech from its embedding context. As the distance is reduced, such boundaries dissolve" (1988: 202). Mrs. Khatri speaks, in turn, as English-medium children (line 7), as parents of Hindi-medium children (line 9), and finally, as people in her own household (line 11).

There are several features of Mrs. Khatri's discourse that facilitate her shifts in role. Mrs. Khatri occupies the perspective of different characters in a way described by Benjamin Lee (1997). First, a verb frames represented speech. Second, a vocative, "hey" (*are*), indicates the calling of another's attention (from the perspective of yet another, a type of person to which Mrs. Khatri does not necessarily belong)—further distancing the quoted utterance from the teacher's speaking stance (Urban 1989). Finally, referential indexes within reported speech are oriented from within the character's, and not the current speaker's, point of view. On this last point, notice how the way of referring to the Hindi-medium children remains constant among the changing represented characters, all done with the proximate form of the third-person plural (*ye*) (versus *ve*, the non-proximate form). The Hindi-medium children are experientially near to all of the various represented characters. This enhances the distance between the teacher's voice in her embedding utterances ("those children who study in English understand exactly thus about Hindi medium children that") and the characters' voices in the quoted utterances ("'hey, these are useless'").[4]

The maintenance of boundaries between author and character in Mrs. Khatri's discourse highlights the changes in perspective from which quoted speech is uttered. The first occurrence of quoted speech comes from the English-medium children. According to the language-medium divide, these are to be the quoted characters most different from Mrs. Khatri, who teaches in a Hindi-medium school. The second occurrence comes from guardians of Hindi-medium children, a group to which Mrs. Khatri belongs. The final occurrence is anchored within Mrs. Khatri's speaking perspective, made explicit by the first-person plural "we." The origins of the quoted utterances move "inward" in at least two senses. Mrs. Khatri begins by introducing the speech of people outside of the house, and ends by introducing the speech that takes place within her own home. Mrs. Khatri also begins with English-medium children, people who do not live in her home, and people she neither teaches nor raises. She moves on to the guardians of the English-medium children, and ends at home. By the third quote, members of the teacher's own family speak the quote.[5] Taken by itself, the third quoted utterance is neutral in its evaluation ("hey, these study in Hindi-medium"). However, taken in relation to the first quoted utterance, ("hey, these are useless") and the framing of the second ("neglect"), the third hints that simply noting that children are studying in a Hindi-medium school is disparaging in and of itself. The denigrating quoted speech moves "inward," and the similar quoted utterances that Mrs. Khatri launches via multiple character roles gain a sense of inevitability.

The linguistic component that accomplishes the negative evaluation also moves "inward," when understood through Bakhtin's notion of voicing (see Table 2). In lines 5 through 7, the character accomplishes the negative evaluation. In lines 8 and 9, the framing verb does, indicating a hybrid relationship between the character's speech and Mrs. Khatri's uptake of the role of character. Finally, in lines 10 and 11, the

Table 2. Mrs. Khatri's deployment of characters. The disparaging element is rendered in italics.

	Character	*Framing Verb*	*Quoted Utterance*
Lines 5–7	English-medium children	Understand	*"Hey, these are useless"*
Lines 8–9	Hindi-medium guardians	*Neglect*	"These are Hindi-medium children"
Lines 10–11	*We*	See	"Hey, these study in Hindi-medium"

quoted utterance remains similar in form to the preceding ones, but now is spoken by Mrs. Khatri as author ("we")—in other words, by the teacher's currently speaking self. The similar utterances become a palpable symptom demonstrating the pervasiveness of the complex.

Mrs. Khatri's discourse gives evidence that speakers can perform other personages through a shift in role: "Characters may be made to come alive as locally imaginable types of people, speaking in ways that contrast with the interlocutor's style" (Koven 2004: 484). That Mrs. Khatri's performance of the discourse of various types of people does not represent her own position on the language-medium divide becomes obvious approximately an hour after the excerpts presented here. Inhabiting the role of author, Mrs. Khatri revealed that she does not personally agree that Hindi-medium students are "useless": "It's not true that Hindi-medium children are dull. They are good" (*sahī nahī̃ hai ki hindī mīḍiamwāle bacce ḍal hãi. ve acche hãi*). Rather than provide a platform for the representation of her own opinions, Mrs. Khatri's use of characters in the excerpt above creates a universal refrain, so pervasive that there exists the possibility that it might be uttered in her own home.

The significance of Mrs. Khatri's animation of characters to the issue of voice cannot be fully appreciated until the next excerpt wherein Mrs. Khatri invokes a different set of personae and engages them in a different configuration of the roles "author" and "character." In so doing, Mrs. Khatri is able to destabilize the inevitability embodied in her just-prior animations of characters.

Approximately two minutes pass while my landlady's daughter, Mrs. Khatri's niece, offers us tea. She leaves the room and Mrs. Khatri and I resume.

Interview Excerpt 2: "Then it was really great"

12 Mrs. Khatri: *ab ham log kā to hindī mīḍiam skūl hai*
now ours is a Hindi-medium school

13 *is liye ham log ko sab kuch hindī...*
therefore everything to us [is in] Hindi...

14 *balki, ham logõ ne jab paṛhā*
moreover, when we studied

15 *to. bhale hī ham logõ ne hindī mīḍiam mẽ paṛhe*
then. it was really great that we studied in Hindi-medium

16 *lekin bī es sī em es sī kī jo buks thī̃ ve sab īngliś mẽ miltī thī̃.*
but BSc and MSc books those were all in English

17 *ham logõ ne likhe bhī pūrā māne,*
and we wrote too and could do it all,

18 *ham logõ ke mīḍiam mẽ īngliś rahatā thā*
English was in our medium

Striking about this second turn in comparison to the first is that Mrs. Khatri frames action temporally. Indeed, the first word is the temporal marker "now" (*ab*). In the first turn, in contrast, all activity takes place in the present; the past only establishes entities' existence in the present, as in "it [English-medium education] has given birth to a complex" in line 4. Whereas quoted utterances provide Mrs. Khatri a device for establishing perspective in her first turn, a contrast between the present and the past frames alter perspectives in this turn. She begins in the present in lines 12 and 13 but does not complete her utterance with a verb. On line 14 she begins again, but this time in the past. Only later will the significance of the switch in tense become apparent, as it emerges as part of the poetic structure of Mrs. Khatri's discourse.

After reframing her comments abruptly on line 14 with "moreover," Mrs. Khatri presents a state of affairs not possible in her first moment. What seems unthinkable in the present—that one might feel good about studying in a Hindi-medium school—was unremarkable in the past. She asserts that when she was a Hindi-medium student, the books that she used contained English. Furthermore, she had competency in English. Both of these assertions disrupt the stark divide between the linguistic affiliations of institutions that structures Mrs. Khatri's first moment of discourse, in lines 1–11. One cannot be sure just how she would have finished her abandoned utterance, but certain is that lines 14–18 establish that languages and institutions interpenetrated in the past, whereas lines 12 and 13 mirror the boundaries of Mrs. Khatri's first moment about the present.

Mrs. Khatri continues with a shift to the present, a disposition she will maintain until the end of the excerpts presented here.

19 *ab ājkal yaha itnī zyādā śuddh hindī ā gayī hai*
now these days there is this Hindi that is too pure

20 *jo sabhī logõ ko samajh mẽ nahī̃ ātī.*
that no one understands.

21 *ab bacce usī ko pasand karte hãi.*
now children like it.

22 *unko īngliś ṭarm ham batāenge to unko samajh mẽ nahī̃ āegā*
if we tell them the English term they will not understand it

23 *kyõki āj jo buks āyī hãi mārkaṭ mẽ. ve bilkul pyūr hindī...*
because now the books that are in the market. they [are in] pure Hindi...

24 *to ve usī ko zyādā acchā samajhte hãi*
so they really prefer that

25 *unko ek ḍar hai "īngliś kaṭhin hogī, īngliś kaṭhin hogī"*
they fear "English will be difficult, English will be difficult"

26 *jabtak ve yaha samajhte hãi. "īngliś ke ṭarms zyādā āsān hãi,*
until they understand this. "English terms are easier,

27 *ek kisī bhī cīz ke liye ek hī wārḍ hogī,*
for any one thing there is only one word,

28 *hindī mẽ to das wārḍs usī cīz ke milenge".*
as for Hindi there are ten words for it."

29 *lekin ve bacce nahī̃ samajhte hãi.*
but those children do not understand.

30 *unko lagtā hai, "īngliś kā śabd agar batāyā maiḍam ne*
they think, "if the teacher used an English word

31 *māne bahut kaṭhin hogā"*
it must be very difficult"

With a shift from the past to the present, Mrs. Khatri manages to identify a culprit responsible for the difference between herself as a student and current students (see Figure 15). With the return to the present on line 19, Mrs. Khatri introduces a new element, "this Hindi that is too pure" (*yaha itnī zyādā śuddh hindī*). *Śuddh* Hindi refers to Hindi lexical items that are derived from Sanskrit. Mrs. Khatri is not invoking *śuddh* Hindi's ability to distinguish Hindi from Urdu and index a parallel religious distinction between Hinduism and Islam.

Rather, on line 23, Mrs. Khatri makes explicit that she is talking about a more specific, institutionally bound type, Hindi words found in textbooks. The term that she uses for the variety shifts too, from "*śuddh*" on line 19 to "*pyūr*" (pure) on line 23. The shift in terms, coupled with the use of "*buks*" (books) and "*maṛkaṭ*" (market), mirrors the referential shift from Sanskritized Hindi to a variety used in schools. *Pyūr* Hindi refers to a lexicon that contains over three hundred thousand terms developed by the Scientific and Technical Terms Commission of the Government of India (Krishnamurti 1979). Scholars have attributed complementary motives to the government's desire to forge a scientific lexicon for Hindi. On the one hand, C.J. Daswani (1989) explains that the government desires an indigenous language equipped with the ability to match English in the scientific realm. On the other

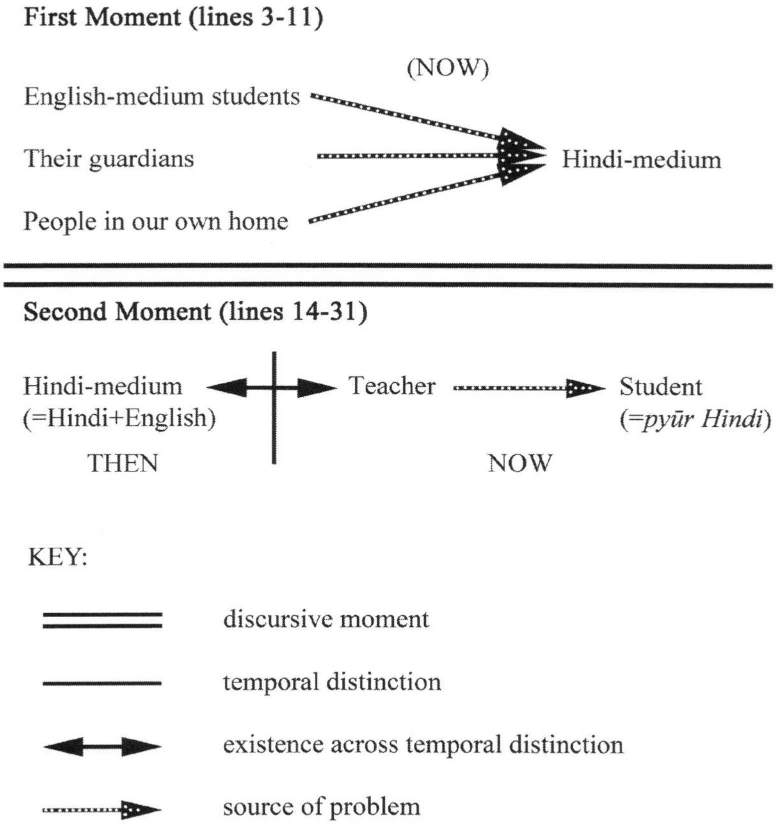

Figure 15. Mrs. Khatri's reconstruction of the "complex" and of what is problematic about language medium.

hand, S.N. Sridhar (1987) attributes the development of the lexicon to the government's wish to develop a technical language to distance itself from the possibility of English's influence.

In addition to mirroring her shift from talking about Sanskritized Hindi to Hindi developed for use in school texts (and other scientific endeavors), Mrs. Khatri's use of English lexical items seems to instantiate her claim that she attended a Hindi-medium school wherein English was used. This notion is reinforced by her shift from the use of "*ṭarm*" (term) on line 22, "*ṭarms*" (terms) on line 26, and "*wārḍ*" (word) on lines 27 and 28 to "*śabd*" on line 30. Her switch from "*ṭarm*," "*ṭarms*," and "*wārḍ*" to "*śabd*" mirrors a shift to speaking from the perspective of students studying in Hindi-medium schools today (versus students studying in Hindi-medium schools when she was a student).

Mrs. Khatri's overall focus shifts from distinctions between Hindi- and English-medium to the language affiliation of verbal practice within the Hindi-medium classroom. Language difference serves to differentiate teachers ("we"), who use English, from their students ("they"), who prefer the use of "*pyūr*" Hindi. Throughout lines 12–24, Mrs. Khatri consistently inhabits the role of "author" in Koven's framework. In other words, Mrs. Khatri's present speaking self is among the people referred to by her use of "we," while current students are referred to by the use of "they." The language preferences of "we" versus "they" locked in unsuccessful communication invokes non-referential aspects of voicing dynamics. Though Mrs. Khtari does not say so, lines 21–31 seem to resemble a classroom setting wherein interaction between teacher and students is highly orchestrated. Typically in the classroom, the teacher poses a question to a student of her or his choice or to a student who has raised her or his hand. The student stands, presents the answer, and sits when given permission by the teacher. Mrs. Khatri explains that a preference for *śuddh* Hindi and a fear of English could prove problematic in interchanges between teachers ("we") and students ("they").

Fascinating is that Mrs. Khatri leaves the role of author on lines 25–28, representing, in turn, a student's nervous self-talk, and the message that could assuage such fear. Mrs. Khatri says quickly, "English will be difficult, English will be difficult," the repetition mimicking someone silently talking to themselves. The repeated phrase embodies the "complex" felt by Hindi-medium students. But here the "complex" is found in the Hindi-medium school itself rather than in an alien and frightening English-language environment such as that described in chapter 1. After stepping into the role of character to represent the nervousness of a (Hindi-medium) student faced with an English word, Mrs. Khatri explicitly steps out of the role on line 26 by referring once again to the students as "they." The role she steps into, however, is ambiguous. One is left wondering who is responsible for the statements on lines 26–28: "English terms are easier, for any one thing there is only one word, as for Hindi there are ten words for it."

Although she never mentions the term in the interview, the teacher's discourse has implications for the notion of mother tongue too. One is hard pressed to imagine that the school that used to exist, wherein English words were used frequently, could be associated with the mother tongue. The very notion of mother tongue seems to presuppose the language-medium divide that the teacher works so hard to problematize. If anything, the mother tongue, represented by *śuddh* or *pyūr* Hindi, emerges in the teacher's comments as something alienating or manufactured, respectively. The notion that the mother tongue indexes pride or some sort of "we" opposed to English is not possible in the discourse of the teacher when she is representing the past.

Mrs. Khatri builds different depictions of the past and present through her multiplex engagements with schooling. Shaping her disparaging, multi-charactered portrait of Hindi-medium students is the cachet of English-medium schooling, the growth of which has been facilitated by the Indian government's policies of economic liberalization. Enabling the radical shift from a focus on language-medium schools as linguistic institutions to a focus on language used in the classroom is Mrs. Khatri's move from speaking as different characters to bringing to bear her own institutionally inflected experiences as student and teacher. Thus, Mrs. Khatri's experiences with schooling are involved in her discourse in a dual manner. On the one hand, the government's changing economic policies have reconstituted Mrs. Khatri's (and her children's) social position vis-à-vis English-medium education as well as the language she uses in the classroom. On the other hand, the school has involved Mrs. Khatri in a range of practices—from hearing disparaging gossip about Hindi-medium students to participating in the routines of classroom interaction.

One must beware of understanding Mrs. Khatri's discourse to be straightforward "resistance" to schooling or the government's policies, or to interpreting her construction of the past as nationalist sentimentality (Ahearn 2001). Many teachers in Hindi-medium schools expressed to me their frustration with the unfamiliar language that the government had designed for introduction in schools and pined for the time when they were students. They did not use language to align themselves with any parallel relation between language and national (or international) sentiment so much as to note that states of affairs were once otherwise. Careful attention to the discursive details of Mrs. Khatri's "solution" to the impasse between her students and herself, started on line 26, can avoid an alignment of her disposition with resistance. Note that the condition for alleviating what plagues Mrs. Khatri's interaction with students—that students understand that "English terms are easier"—is spoken as an authorless pronouncement. In the midst of statements that are carefully anchored by "we" and "they," and statements (on line 25 and 30 and 31) made explicitly from the point of view of students, Mrs. Khatri's statement on line 26 is anchored solely by "this." In contrast to surrounding discourse, the statement's authorship is obscure at the same time that its message is contradictory to educational policy. One possibility is that the authorless utterance is very much like a lesson—easy for the teacher to produce but difficult for the students to learn given the popularity of *pyūr* Hindi and the students' fear of English.

I also want to stress that my argument is not that teachers such as Mrs. Khatri are more knowledgeable than others about the history of the state's educational policy by virtue of their employment in its educational institutions. Indeed, when I asked Mrs. Khatri about the introduction of *pyūr* Hindi words in classrooms, she responded:

32 *patā nahī̃ kahā̃ se nikālte h͠ai,*
I don't know where they get them,

33 *sanskrit dikśanerī se ḍū̃ṛhthe yā hindī ke bhī rahate h͠ai,*
whether they search in the Sanskrit dictionary or if they are in the Hindi one too,

34 *usī se ḍū̃ṛhkar nikālte h͠ai,*
they look and get them,

35 *bhagvān jāne kaise nikālte h͠ai, bahut kaṭhin hote h͠ai jī*
God only knows how they get them, they are very difficult mister

Rather, the argument is that Madhu Khatri's location, both in a world of language-based school distinctions the social reverberations of which have altered radically and in a classroom in which she has been a student and a teacher, has shaped the means by which she envisions relationships between the present and the past. In short, her life achieves parallax with those of others via the dialogic relationships between present and past emergent in our conversation. This is made possible by both sociohistorical shifts in the salience of the Hindi- and English-medium divide and differences between the experiences with the people in the institution in chapter 1, for example, and Mrs. Khatri during these sociohistorical shifts. Mrs. Khatri's ability to reconfigure the relationship between the language-medium divide, and its usefulness in imagining one's own and others' pasts, presents, and futures, embody Bakhtin's notion that centripetal forces are never complete.

Conclusion

Centripetal forces have been at work in Varanasi such that a particular view of schooling circulates especially well. Language difference has come to differentiate schools. This is a matter of voice because when people reflect on society, a school and its language medium emerges as already tied to political-economic difference, disposition within the nation, and the attitudes of students, families, and employees. Earlier chapters showed some of the ways in which language-medium difference resonates complexly in the lives of people in Varanasi. Hindi and English themselves change in what they can represent depending on their associations with other distinctions such as rural and urban, national and international, and central and peripheral. Despite this ability, the distinction between Hindi and English remains intact. Monologic voicings, in the rubric of Bakhtin, rest on the centripetal forces bringing into alignment an institution, a language, and a person, and make possible the comparison of any one of these with an analogous feature of its opposed institution.

Fascinating about Madhu Khatri's interview is that, in one moment, she presents monologic voicings reminiscent of those employed by others. Indeed, Mrs. Khatri quotes other people to produce a particularly total scene in which voicings echo one another. Everyone seems to be ready to decry the Hindi-medium students, even guardians of such students. But these voicings do not exhaust the ways in which she reflects on schooling and language. By invoking her days as a student, she presents a voice that does not take for granted the alignment of language difference with language-medium difference. The voice represents an early time in her life but emerges relatively late in the interview. There is no easy way to explain where the voice comes from. Centrifugal forces seem not to emanate from a single source, but rather to emerge in the intersection between Mrs. Khatri's experiences with schooling (to which most others do not have access) and her deployment of voices in discursive activity. It seems that Mrs. Khatri borrows the discursive routine of the classroom to reframe the culprit for the difficulties faced by Hindi-medium students. To these difficulties, Mrs. Khatri juxtaposes her own student days in which the presence or absence of languages was an unreliable demarcation of which language medium a school belonged to.

The new assembly of voices that emerges—those of student and teacher in the classroom today versus those of Mrs. Khatri and people like her when she was a student—contrasts with Mrs. Khatri's earlier totalizing portrayal of Hindi-medium students because she develops different alignments between her speaking self and the characters she animates. A change in the dynamics of voicing coincides with a change in what is problematic about schooling (and language). Whereas earlier, the very designation "Hindi-medium student" brings derision, later, a certain type of language seduces schoolchildren. With this transition, Mrs. Khatri redirects the importance of the medium divide from its oppositional qualities (after demonstrating just how inevitable it might seem). She displaces a focus on medium with a focus on language and replaces a generalized world of impressions with the interactional routines of the classroom.

Notes

This chapter incorporates material from "The Discursive Malleability of an Identity: A Dialogic Approach to Language 'Medium' Schooling in North India," *Journal of Linguistic Anthropology* 16: 36–57.

1. Stanton Wortham (2003a), for example, points out that Dorothy Holland and Jean Lave (2001) ably describe the "thickening" of identity over time but do not specify how identities "thicken" in discursive interaction.
2. See Wilce (1998a: 249) for an approach using the notion with ethnographic work in Bangladesh, and Wilce (1998b: 34–43) for an application of the notion of voice to long-debated notions of the self in South Asia.
3. For example, in the interview transcript presented in this chapter, on line 3, Mrs. Khatri makes explicit that I have failed to understand her as an already-realized Principal for the utterances that I Animate on lines 1 and 2.
4. Hanks's (2005) assertion that deictics must be considered to be semiotically complex and multifunctional is salient here.
5. Our prior utterances are also engaged in a dialogic fashion, of course. Note the teacher's "I am saying exactly that, no?" (line 3). Whereas in lines 1 and 2 I report what I have heard without distance from my speaking self, in line 3 the teacher invites me to imagine that she has already complicated my authorial stance. My argument is simply that the dialogicality in lines 5–11 is of a distinct kind, emergent within the teacher's moment of discourse.

Chapter 5

In and Out of the Classroom

A Focus on English

While chapter 4 considered the case of someone who undercuts the foundation of the division between Hindi- and English-medium schools, this chapter considers whether the language-medium divide accounts for the value of languages as they are used inside the classroom and reflected on outside of schools, from the vantage of people in lower-class positions. English class at the Seacrest School—English-medium and private—and Hindi class at the Saraswati School—Hindi-medium and government-administered—exhibit the same kinds of interactions between teachers and students. Classroom interactions in the Seacrest School and the Saraswati School thus reflect the language-medium divide. English is used in the former and Hindi is used in the latter, and the interactional routines between teacher and students are strikingly similar. English class at the Saraswati School, however, finds the teacher using Hindi to frame interaction and to provide glosses for the passages from the textbook, which are in English.

All of these classrooms exhibit features of what J. Keith Chick calls "safetalk," a theoretical construct meant to account for classroom activity in the postcolonial world. Safetalk refers to students and teachers colluding in interactional routines so that they can engage in a language over which they have little control. Often decried as "rote learning" and "teacher-centered instruction," safetalk describes classroom activity in which few if any students initiate interaction, much less introduce new topics, but rather provide answers, often together, to questions designed by the teacher to prevent further talk.[1]

Scholars following Chick's lead (Hornberger and Chick 2001 in Peru; Arthur 2001 in Botswana) have argued that the structures that encourage safetalk underpin sociolinguistic and institutional conditions in most of the postcolonial world: "This particular style of interaction arises from teachers' attempts to cope with the problem of using a former colonial language, which is remote from the learners' experiences outside school, as the main medium of instruction and from teachers' efforts to overcome problems relating to class size, autocratic school management, and inadequate facilities for initial and in-service teacher education" (Heller and Martin-Jones 2001: 13).[2] Hornberger and Chick argue that safetalk provides a face-saving incentive, a "sense of purpose and accomplishment" (2001: 42), but also entails the "high price... of (a lack of) learning" (2001: 52).

Safetalk is a useful construct for relating classroom practices to ideology about language outside of the classroom. Safetalk and ideas that people have about classroom activity and language both find that the English class in the Hindi-medium school stand out as especially indicative of a desire on the part of the teacher and students to manage their lack of knowledge of English. But does safetalk account for the ways in which everyone reflects on English outside of the classroom? This chapter considers the cases of people in lower-class positions and the ways in which they find English to be important in order to question whether the theoretical construct of safetalk provides a comprehensive picture of the value of English. Their reflections show that English has a kind of value for people that is not anticipated by the language-medium division. Just as some relatively elite people bracket the language-medium divide in sending their children to schools for a particular kind of English, some lower-class people see a kind of value in English that the language-medium divide and its ideological underpinnings cannot account for. The value of English for people in lower-class positions emerges from the ways in which they find English useful, outside of school. Yet, some of the uses for which people find English valuable resemble the ways in which teachers employ English in the Hindi-medium classroom. This is a development that the notion of safetalk does not anticipate and that much ideology about language-medium schooling in northern India hides or openly decries.

Into the Classroom: Interaction in Language-Medium Schooling

Early on during fieldwork, I discovered that interaction in the Saraswati schools and at Seacrest exhibited what many scholars have argued regarding classroom interaction generally. Hugh Mehan (1979) notes that a common routine in the classroom is one wherein the teacher launches an "initiation," the student responds with a "response," and the teacher completes the routine with an "evaluation." So commonplace is this routine in classrooms that Courtney Cazden (2001) calls this sequence "traditional."[3] I found that this sequence accounted for interaction especially well in lower grade levels—those below the ninth level. The teacher picked a student, sometimes moving down a row of desks, and asked a question, usually derived from the book opened in front of the students. If the student could not answer, the teacher would move on to someone else. Sometimes the teacher would reprimand the student. If the student could answer, the teacher would "evaluate" the student's answer, and sometimes this evaluation would form the basis for the next question. Sometimes the teacher would evaluate the student's answer with a reprimand and move on to another student, and sometimes the teacher would acknowledge a correct answer without elaborating. The sequence identified by Mehan often achieved a corporeal dimension beyond the gaze or point of the teacher (accompanying an initiation) in classrooms in Varanasi. Often, when the teacher picked out a student, the student rose from her chair and stood to offer the answer or an apology for not being able to answer. In such classrooms, the student remained standing until the teacher had asked every student a question. The teacher would then command the students to sit and the routine would start again.

First Example: Fourth-Level Social Studies at Seacrest School

I witnessed the routine Mehan identifies often. An example comes from a fourth-level social studies class at the Seacrest School. In this example, the teacher asks students questions about a "general knowledge" lesson from the textbook.

Teacher: Srinagar is the city along which river?

Student: Jhelum.

Teacher: River Jhelum, Jhelum. What is the capital of Bhutan?

Student: Thimpu(3)

Teacher: Can you tell me Bangkok is the capital of which country? Bangkok.

Student: Thailand.

Teacher: Thailand, very good. Thailand. Yes. And Jerusalem is the capital of? Jerusalem?

Student: Israel.

Teacher: Israel. Canberra is the capital of, who will tell me Canberra is the capital of Australia? Canberra is the capital of?

Students: Australia.

Teacher: And which is the capital of Germany? Germany is the capital of?

Student: Bonn.

Teacher: Very good. Bonn, Bonn. Tell me, which is the smallest bird in the world?

Student: Amir bird, amir bird.

Teacher: Amir bird, amir bird is the smallest bird in the world. *Acchā*, tell me an animal that is the most destructive of man.

Students: [overlapping answers including "rat," "snake," and others I could not discern]

Teacher: An animal whose dead body can spread the disease.

Student: Rat.

Teacher: Can spread the disease of plague.

Students: Rat.

Teacher: And can you tell me, Gandhi-*jī* was assassinated by?

Student: Nathuram Godse.

Teacher: Nathuram Godse. Tell me, the first Indian who went into space?

Student: Rakesh Sharma.

Teacher: Very good, and first Muslim president of India. Who was the first Muslim president of India?

Student: Muhammad Ali Jinnah.

Teacher: No, no, who was the first Muslim president of India? Doctor Zakir Hussein.

Students: Doctor Zakir Hussein.

In this lesson, the teacher moves in topic from cities to animals to national figures. The teacher does not call on individual students to answer, nor does he make the students stand, but rather poses a question to the entire class and waits for a student to respond. The teacher evaluates the student's answer in several ways. If the student is wrong, the teacher calls attention to the fact with a negative response and poses the question again. This only happens once, toward the end of the excerpt, and the ridiculousness of naming the first Governor-General of Pakistan as India's first Muslim president seems to amuse the teacher. He laughs slightly as he says, "no, no." If a student's response is correct, the teacher either moves to another question without comment, repeats the answer and moves to another question, or offers some positive evaluation sometimes with and sometimes without repetition of the correct answer. In the one instance when the teacher reverses the capital and country, a student does not comment but rather provides the correct answer, Bonn, as though the question had been posed correctly. The teacher provides the answer to his own question about the capital of Australia, and the students seem to take this as a cue to repeat the answer together. In the case of the student's incorrect answer about India's first Muslim president, the teacher provides the answer. The students again take this as a cue to answer together. The one sequence in which the teacher elaborates on the theme of the question beyond a single turn at talk likewise provides the students with a cue to repeat the answer, rat, together.

Second Example: Third-Level English at Rajkiya Sarvodaya Kanya Vidyalaya (in Delhi)

In another interactional routine, especially common at the lower grade levels, the teacher would provide an utterance that the students would repeat verbatim. The routine resembles that of the social studies class in the first example in that students in the social studies class sometimes repeat the answer together and the teacher sometimes repeats the student's answer. The routine differs from that of the social studies class because no one in particular is supposed to offer an answer to a question posed by the teacher. The pattern is well known in schools in India, and Viniti Vaish provides an example from her fieldwork in a third-grade English class. Amarjeet, the teacher, prefaces her routine with brief instructions to the students:

> Amarjeet: *m͠ai read karungī. āp sunnā. m͠ai hindī m͠e bhī bolungī. ṭhīk hai? samajh m͠e ā gayā? bāt nahī̃ karoge. bas sunoge.* Keep fit miss.
> I will read. You listen. I will also speak in Hindi. Okay? Understand? You will not talk. You will only listen. Keep fit miss.
>
> Class: Keep fit Miss.
>
> Amarjeet: I have.

Class: I have.

Amarjeet: Good news.

Class: Good News.

Amarjeet: *mere pās ek acchī khabar hai. cīnā āī aur bolī* "mummy mummy *ek acchī khabar hai.*" "What is it?"
I have a piece of good news. Cheena came and said, "Mummy, mummy, there is a piece of good news." "What is it?"

Class: What is it?

Amarjeet: *kyā hai?*
What is it?

Class: *kyā hai?*
What is it? (adapted from Vaish 2008: 45)

In this particular lesson, the teacher pauses after phrases that she would like for the students to repeat, and the class does so readily. The phrases come from the day's reading. The teacher shifts from explaining what the students should do to offering the utterance from the textbook to be repeated by the students. At the same time, she switches from Hindi to English. Once the students repeat "I have" and "good news" in English, the teacher glosses the utterances in Hindi. She then translates "Cheena came and said, 'Mummy, mummy, there is a piece of good news'" into Hindi without having the children repeat it. Instead, they repeat her utterance "What is it?" Again, a shift from Hindi to English on the part of the teacher cues the students to repeat the teacher's utterance. The teacher then offers a translation of the question in Hindi and the students repeat it. The routine has, in the last interchange between teacher and students, led the students to produce an utterance not in the text, but rather its Hindi equivalent.

In her initial instructions, the teacher tells the children to listen and not speak. By this, she seems to mean for the students to repeat what she says rather than wait for a question, as they would were the initiation-response-evaluation routine being followed. Vaish calls the routine of repetition "chorusing" and explains that "From the perspective of ELT [English Language Teaching] in countries where English is spoken as a first language this will look like mindless chanting without comprehension" (2008: 46). She argues for the routine's continuity with precolonial pedagogical practices such as learning the Vedas. Whether such continuity exists or does not exist, the repetition of the teacher's utterances on the part of students begins to wane as a classroom practice by the fourth level.

Third Example: Ninth-Level English at Seacrest School

Another common practice that begins to emerge in higher levels is one in which the teacher explicates some key theme in the reading for the day. The teacher's turns at talk are much longer than in the first two examples because the teacher maintains the focus on topics as they emerge in the day's reading. After the teacher's rather lengthy explications, the teacher cues the students to speak by raising her pitch and volume. Rather than repeating what the teacher says, however, the students give evidence that they anticipate what the teacher will say, and join in to utter a word or phrase along with her. This results in a classroom setting wherein the teacher does most of the talking and the students participate in infrequent and short utterances.

An example comes from a ninth-level English class at the Seacrest School recorded in early 1997. In the example, the teacher prefaces a lesson on the reading assignment for the day, entitled "Abandoned Farmhouse." The title of the lesson is the name of a poem by Ted Kooser (b. 1939), and the poem is a common feature of English school texts around the world.

Teacher: Abandoned farmhouse. Do you know what abandoned means?

Students: Abandoned

Teacher: What abandoned means? Means?

Students: I know.

Teacher: Wait, wait. Abandoned, what does abandoned mean? Abandoned means. Left out. I mean. Your friend which you do not visit. Or. Uh. With. Rejected. Sort of rejected. You have abandoned him. You have abandoned your friend. You are ta.... You are not on talking terms. You have abandoned your friend. That is you are not you are no more on talking terms with him you have dejected him or. You are no more on talking terms with him. With him. Now if I say this is an abandoned house that is no one lives in that house. The house has been left out I mean no one is living here, there. That is abandoned. Can we think of something else which we can say? He. Is an abandoned child I mean he is having no more friends, no one, no one looks after him, he is an abandoned child. Abandoned house, abandoned, uh. Room abandoned, anything that is that is not visited frequently. You do not go inside it. If it is an office or house. Uh. Sort of room. That is it is not visited. Abandoned someone you are not in talking terms you are not looking after him. You are no more pally I think that is. You have left him. I mean. Uh you have abandoned your shoes you are not.
⌈Wearing it⌉

Students: ⌊Wearing it⌋

The teacher begins by stating the name of the story from the textbook and poses a question to the students. Unlike the fourth-level social studies teacher, however, the English teacher does not desire an answer. Rather, she commands the student who answers to be silent and begins an extended explication of the word in the story's title, "abandoned." Once she provides the words "left out" and the discourse marker "I mean," she repeats a construction. Each utterance begins with an address to the students wherein "you" also serves as the subject in the illustrating example. The teacher shifts reference with "Now if I say," and incorporates the other word in the story's title, "farmhouse." She concludes the sections framed by the shift from "you" to "I" with the utterance "That is abandoned," which is not anchored by "you" or "I." The teacher then shifts to framing the interaction with "we" and again asks a question to which the students seem to know—now, at least—that they should not answer. She revisits the meanings of abandoned that she has already introduced, including a break with social relations and a place's lack of visitation, and adds the sense of dispensing with something in her final example. She pauses at the mention of "you are not," her pitch rises, and her volume increases. Collectively, these aspects of her utterance cue the students to join in en masse with the teacher as she utters, "wearing it." The utterance is not part of the story, but rather emerges as part of the teacher's explication of the word "abandoned."

The lesson continues.

> Teacher: Anymore abandoned. Then what? Plenty of. ⌈Many⌉ abundances.
>
> Students: ⌊Many⌋
>
> Teacher: ⌈Plenty⌉ now we are. Did you remember?
>
> Students: ⌊Plenty⌋
>
> Teacher: Did we read that abandoned farmhouse that is? A farmhouse that. ⌈No one is staying⌉
>
> Students: ⌊No one is staying⌋
>
> Teacher: It is. Just a lonely farmhouse no one is going inside it no one is. Uh, staying inside it. So it is. Abandoned farm. No one is going inside that, house. No one stays there. Lives there. And yes, we, you are not having the book also just see. Okay. He was a big man. Says the size of his shoes. On a vine of broken wishes. By the house. A tall man too. Says. The length of the bed. In an upstairs room and a good. God fearing man. Says the Bible. With a broken lamp. On the floor below. A window. Bright with sun. But not a man for farming. Says the fields. Cluttered with boulders. This paragraph tells you about. How when you enter an

abandoned farmhouse. Though no person is living there, no person is there. But still his things are there. Now, there were. Big shoes were left there. So. This is a sort of place he has written of. There this. Where you enter a room. And you see the room is very untidily kept. And the tennis racket is there. Uh. Perhaps many cassettes are there. So if you don't, see the, owner you will say Okay he is a music lover because he is having. ⌈Cassettes⌉ there and all of the cassettes are [inaudible].

Students: ⌊Cassettes⌋

Teacher: So we can make a guess. ⌈That he loves⌉.

Students: ⌊That he is ⌋

Teacher: He loves Kishore Kumar's. Songs. So. We can guess this much. Now if you see that. Uh not really jeans and flowery shirts and. Are there so what we will see what you will find. He loves wearing flowery shirts and jeans. Okay now if you see that. The. Uh. Bed is unmade the pillow covers are very dirty. So what idea you will get about that ⌈person he's⌉ not a very tidy man.

Students: ⌊Yes ma'am ⌋

Teacher: Now. Just the reverse contrary. If you enter a house and see. The room is very neatly kept very tidily kept. And the, uh, and the bed is all made the clothes are. Properly. In a hanger in the closet or in the cupboard and. The books are piled very neatly. So what idea you will get about the owner of the house.

Students: Very tidy

Teacher: Very neat and tidy person. Okay. Now this is the difference. An untidily kept room gives you. Uh. An idea that the person is not very. ⌈Tidy⌉.

Students: ⌊Tidy⌋

Teacher: A very tidily kept room gives you the idea that the person is. ⌈Very⌉

Students: ⌊Tidy⌋

Teacher: ⌈Tidy⌉

Students: ⌊Tidy⌋

Teacher: And he knows where to keep the things. He doesn't scatter his things here and there. Yes. Yes the same way. And in an abandoned farmhouse a person enters. Now. It is a farmhouse. Farmhouse. Farmhouse

The teacher introduces the notion of abundance by shifting the students' attention with "then what?" The teacher introduces another notion in the poem with her "many abundances" and the students join her in uttering "many" and "plenty." It seems that the teacher has gotten ahead of herself, however, because she returns to the explication of "abandoned." She cues the students that she is about to read from the text by addressing me and noting that I do not have a copy of the textbook. I say nothing, but lean over to signal that I can read from my neighbor's copy. The teacher proceeds to read from the textbook. The end of her reading is made apparent by her utterance, "This paragraph tells you about," which shifts her stance from within the text back to her previous one alongside it.

In her utterances that follow, the teacher extends the items that one might find in "a room" that is "very untidily kept." The notion of untidiness is something introduced by the teacher, and is not to be found in the textbook. Given the utterances that follow, the teacher seems to introduce the notion in order to mention items not found in the poem. First she introduces "tennis racket," but, in comparison to the next item, "cassettes," the example is short-lived in its explication. I knew of no students who owned a tennis racket, whereas cassettes were a ubiquitous feature of life, especially in the world of students and their interest in film music. The teacher cues the students to say "cassettes" with her, but when the teacher cues the students to speak again, their utterance is a bit different from the teacher's. Whereas the students seem to be imagining a description for the owner of the cassettes with the verb "to be," the teacher uses the utterance to introduce a popular singer. That the students could not anticipate this move on the part of the teacher is unsurprising, but the routine allows for the difference between the teacher's utterance and the students' utterance to pass without comment. The teacher ends the exploration of the example of cassettes with "we can guess this much," and moves to another set of items, "jeans and flowery shirts." The examples are particularly interesting because neither jeans nor shirts with prints of flowers were popular among students at the time of the recording (1997). The examples seem to have been taken from the world of the cinema and fashion. The teacher seems to have picked these items to make a connection with the media the students might be consuming.

Next, the teacher begins to explore more explicitly the notion of "untidy." The teacher does raise her pitch slightly when she utters "about that," and the students take this as a cue to speak. The students do not have an obvious word or phrase that they expect the teacher to utter, however, so they simply express agreement with "yes ma'am." One might understand the teacher to mark the end of the discussion of untidiness with her cue of the students to speak. In any case, this is the second time that the teacher's and students' utterances do not match one another, and the second time that the lesson continues without interruption.

The teacher continues to explicate the notion of tidiness by offering "just the reverse contrary." She mentions the disposition of bedding, clothes, and books of a tidy person. For the first time in the lesson, the teacher cues the students to answer a question rather than offer an overlap with her utterance. She does so by using a phrase akin to the one with which she concluded her discussion of an untidy person. The teacher provided the cue to answer at "about that" the first time she asks, "So what idea you will get about that person he's." In contrast, she waits to raise her pitch and increase her volume at "about the owner of the house" the second time she begins her question, "So what idea you will get." There is no unmatching overlap the second time because the students seem to know what to answer and the teacher waits for the answer.[4]

The teacher proceeds to finish the discussion of the notion of a tidy person and his room, and her extension of the discussion of an untidy man and his room. That she is finishing this line of discussion is made evident by her switch from detailed examples to cues for the students to offer utterances. Indeed, the teacher cues the students twice, and the students repeat what they have just said for a third utterance because the teacher utters "very" instead of what they anticipated, "tidy." The teacher gives an indication that the larger discussion is about to end by reinvoking the name of the poem and lesson, Abandoned Farmhouse. She attempts to draw a parallel between her explication and the abandoned farmhouse of the poem with "Yes the same way" and blending the abandoned farmhouse of the poem and "a person enters" from her explication. She utters the discourse marker "now" signaling a change from her explicatory sequence and utters the word "farmhouse" three times. She then begins to introduce the focal topic of the next part of the poem, reads another section of the poem, and cues student utterances toward the end—a repetition of the cycle considered herein.

Fourth Example: Ninth-Level Hindi Class at Saraswati School

The next example comes from a ninth-level Hindi class at the Saraswati School. The class is at the same level as the English class from the example at the Seacrest School, and the focus, again, is poetry. Just as in the English class, the students in the Hindi class have the poem in front of them on their desks. And just as in the English class, the teacher focuses on topics that she draws from the reading. She cues the students to speak exactly as the English teacher does, by raising her pitch and her volume. Indeed, the only difference between the English class at the English-medium school and the Hindi-class at the Hindi-medium school is that the Hindi students answer a question posed by the teacher rather than anticipating the end of the teacher's utterance.

In this excerpt, the poem is by Sumitranandan Pant (1900–1977), a well-known twentieth-century poet whose work is often included in textbooks at the higher grade levels. The teacher begins the lesson with a rhetorical question and begins to explicate the image of a beautiful girl from the poem.

> Teacher: *samajh mẽ ā rahe hãi? rupak pant kā. ek sundar yuvtī kā rup diyā hai. aur kyā kahā ki vaha sundar yuvtī. yānī śaradarupī nāyikā. śaradarupī yuvtī ko kyā hai? ant sarohū caraṇ kar māne ye hāth yahā̃ se* [teacher motions with her hands] *aur caraṇ māne pair. to hāth aur pair donõ uske kaise hãi? ungliyõ hāthõ aur pair... donõ pair se hãi aur āruṇ. āruṇ māne?*
> Do you understand? Pant's metaphor. He gave the form of a beautiful girl. And what was said was that beautiful girl. Meaning to say that form-of-winter heroine. What about the form-of-winter girl? Finally lotus feet ... hands, meaning these hands from here [teacher motions with her hands] and feet meaning feet. So how are both her hands and feet? The fingers the hands the feet ... from both feet vermillion. Vermillion means?
>
> Students: *lāl*
> red
>
> Teacher: *kaise lāl? kamal ke swarup jaise alp sarohū kar caraṇ. kar māne hāth caraṇ māne pair panjā. to uskī donõ hatheliyā̃ aur panje donõ kaise lāl hãi? ab kaise?*
> Red how? In the form of a lotus just like little lotus hands and feet. Hands meaning hands, feet meaning feet, hands. So both of her palms and hands, how are they both red? Now how?
>
> Students: *kamal ke jaise*
> Like a lotus

In the excerpt, the teacher develops her own images to explicate the image offered by the poem. She explains that the poet has provided the image of a "beautiful girl" (*sundar yuvtī*) and then accomplishes the invocation of the phrase in the poem with "that is to say" or "meaning" (*yānī*). Not only does the teacher offer an explication, she does so by offering the students a phrase with which they might be familiar. By no means is *sundar yuvtī* colloquial Hindi, as it might qualify as *śuddh* Hindi (clear or correct Hindi), but it is much more recognizable than the phrase offered in the poem, *śaradarupī nāyikā* (awkwardly translatable as form-of-winter girl). She gives evidence of offering a more recognizable form by replacing *nāyikā* with *yuvtī* when she asks, again rhetorically, *śaradarupī yuvtī ko kyā hai* (what about the form-of-winter girl?). She offers a phrase of the poem and again offers more recognizable words and phrases in explication. First she offers *hāth* (hand) in place of *kar* (hand) as she uses her own body to point, and then makes explicit that she is glossing with more recognizable words when she utters *caraṇ māne pair* ("feet means feet"). Now that she has established the grounds for a routine whereby words and phrases in the poem are to be rendered in words or phrases more recognizable to the students, the teacher cues the students to provide an alternative to *caraṇ* by raising her pitch and increasing her volume when she utters *āruṇ māne* (red means?). The students take the cue and utter as a group the alternative *lāl* (red). The teacher goes on to introduce the larger line of the poem *kamal ke swarup jaise alp sarohū kar caraṇ* (In the form of a lotus just like little lotus hands and feet), introduces yet more alternatives including *panjā* (paws) and *hatheliyā̃* (palms), and cues the students to describe her alternatives in the phrase of the poem, *kamal ke jaise* (like a lotus).

The teacher continues the lesson using the alternatives for the poem's words and phrases that she has provided.

> Teacher: *lāl kamal ke samān uskī hatheliyā̃ aur uske panje. tum log jab dains kartī ho klais kartī ho yā koī prograim detī ho to hāth ko lāl rang se detī ho. unglī ko rangtī ho pair mẽ mahāvar lagātī ho. talvā ko bhī rang detī ho. gulābī rang. to ve pair aur hāth lāl lagte hai. dekhne mẽ sundar lagtā hai jab dains nṛtya kī posiśan jab hotī hai to usmẽ hāth aur pair vā dikhtā hai. bahut sundar lagtā hai. to us nāyikā ko sundar kahanā kā matlab vaha gorī hai aur gorī hone se uske hāth aur panje kī jo mānspeśiyā hai. vaha kaisī hai? lāl hai. kyõki jab kisī bahut gorī laṛkī kā dekhā hogā binā kuch lagāye hī uske hāth aur pair ke jo panje hãi ve lāl lāl hãi. samajh mẽ āyā? to itnā sundar rupak kavi ne bāndhā hai ki alp sarohū kar caraṇ. us śaradrupi nāyikā ke hāth kī hatheliyā̃ aur panje donõ hī kaise hãi? lāl kamal ke samān. netra khanjan aur netra kaise hai uske? khanjan pakśī ke samān ānkh hai uskī. iskā netra hī kyā hai? khanjan pakśī kā netra hai. itnā sundar hai. mukhcand. aur yaha mukhaṛā uskā kaise hai?*
> Like a red lotus her palms and her hands. When you all dance … do class … or put on a program you put red color on your hands. You color your fingers … you put red powder on your feet. You put color on the soles of your feet too. Pink color. So those feet and hands seem very red. They look so beautiful … in the *nṛtya* position the hands and feet are

> shown. It looks very beautiful. So saying that the heroine is beautiful means that she is fair and from being fair ... her hands and the muscles of her hands. How is it? It is red. Because when one sees some very fair girl even without any on her hands and feet those hands are very red. Do you understand? So the poet has made this beautiful form that little lotus hands and feet. How are that form-of-winter heroine's palms of the hands ... both hands? Red like a lotus. Eye ... *khanjan* ... and how is her eye? Her eye is like the *khanjan* bird. What exactly is its eye? It is the *khanjan* bird's eye. It is this beautiful. Moonface. And how is this lovely face of hers?
>
> Students: *candramā kī tarah.*
> Like the moon.

In this second excerpt, the teacher shifts activities from providing alternatives for the unfamiliar words and phrases of the poem, as she did in the first excerpt, to reframing the context of a theme from the poem. She makes the students relevant to the beautiful quality of the poem's heroine's red hands and feet. She does this by referring to dances that the girls learn in school and the school programs in which the girls perform. The teacher continues the pattern from the first excerpt whereby she asks questions of the students, but she often does not expect the students to respond. She reframes the context yet again with *to itnā sundar rupak kavi ne bāndhā hai* (so the poet has made this beautiful form), thereby leaving the explication of the beauty of the heroine and the comparison with the students' school activities and returning to the poet and his poem. The teacher revisits the figure of the form-of-winter heroine and the likeness of her hands and feet to a lotus before introducing a new image from the poem, the heroine's eye and its likeness to the *khanjan* bird. Again, the teacher asks a question, "*aur netra kaise hai uske?*" (and how is her eye?) but does not expect the students to answer. She does this again before cueing the students to answer by raising her pitch and increasing her volume with "*aur yaha mukhaṛā uskā kaise hai?*" (and how is this lovely face of hers?). The students answer "*candramā kī tarah,*" the correct simile for "*mukhcand*" (moonface) that the teacher has provided. Across the two excerpts in the ninth-level Hindi class, the students have spoken three times, first to render a word into its more familiar and less Sanskritic form, and twice to answer the teacher's question about an aspect of the subject of the poem.

Fascinating about the second excerpt is that the teacher uses words that might not be considered Hindi, much less *śuddh* Hindi. In redirecting the students from the poem to the context of their own lives, the teacher uses the words *dains* (dance), *klais* (class), and *prograim* (program). As in other parts of the book, I render these words in the transliteration conventions for Hindi because the words question any easy separation of Hindi and English. One hears them commonly in utterances and interactions in which they are the only elements not easily identifiable as Hindi. In the second excerpt, the teacher's use of the words parallels a shift to the present, and away from the temporal frame of the poem's creation. In other words, the teacher moves from the temporal frame created by "*ek sundar yuvtī kā rup diyā hai*" (he gave the form of a beautiful girl) to the temporal frame of "*tum log jab dains kartī ho*" (when you all dance). That is to say, the teacher moves from the perfect to the imperfect. Thus, one task in which the teacher engages is providing the students with less Sanskritized Hindi so that she can provide a rendition of the poem in language that the students might recognize; another task is to extend a motif of the poem to the students' lives. It is in the latter task that the teacher introduces words that some readers might identify as English.

Fifth Example: Ninth-Level English Class at Saraswati School

The final example of classroom interaction comes from a ninth-level English class at the Saraswati School, the same Hindi-medium school from which the fourth example was taken. In some ways, the lesson is like the third and fourth examples. The teacher draws from the textbook for the topic of explication and asks the students to provide very short answers. She cues the students to answer by raising her pitch and volume. In other ways, the lesson is quite different from the third and fourth examples because the teacher uses a good deal of Hindi in an English class. The teacher uses Hindi to frame the discussion of the reading. She also uses Hindi to provide glosses of her explication of the reading in English as well as of quotes from the reading in English. Through her use of two languages, the teacher in this example differs from those in examples three and four quite markedly.

The teacher begins the lesson by asking the students about a section of the textbook that concluded the previous class period, regarding the interests of Socrates.

Teacher: *zyādā* importance *diyā jāta thā. kaun, kaun* subject *thā*
It has been given much importance. Which, which subject was it?

Students: gymnastics

Teacher: *uskā nām* gymnastics. gymnastics means, the physical(3) the importance of exercises. he also learned some science. science *ke bāre mẽ bhī paṛhā.* and mathematics also. *kuch* mathematics *bhī paṛhe.* and

> he also knew about the stars, *aur kuch ākāś mẽ bhī itāre hote h̃ai. isko kyā kahate h̃ai. jo itāre h̃ai. usko, iske bāre mẽ kyā likh diyā.* but not nearly so much history and geography as children learn today. *ājkal ke jo bacce h̃ai ve abhigya h̃ai* social studies, *jaise* history *bhī hai* geography *bhī hai. ve pasand karte h̃ai. isko zyādā* importance *diya jātā.*
> Its name is gymnastics. Gymnastics means, the physical(3) the importance of exercises. He also learned some science. He studied science too. And mathematics also. He also studied some mathematics. And he also knew about the stars, and something else too are the stars in the sky. What is it called? The stars which. That, what has been written about this? But not nearly so much history and geography as children learn today. Children these days are knowledgeable in the social studies, there is history too, geography too. They like it. It has been given much importance.

The teacher begins the English lesson in Hindi, using a passive construction to focus the students' attention on what the lesson has emphasized. She then asks what subject is the focus of the lesson. The teacher expects a reply, something indexed by her rising pitch and increasing volume in "*kaun* subject *thā*?" (what was the subject?). The students readily understand the cue to answer and do so en masse, "gymnastics." Referring to her earlier "subject," the teacher confirms the students' answer "*uskā nām* gymnastics" (its name [is] gymnastics, the verb deleted and assumed). I render words like "gymnastics," "science," and "social studies" as English because the class is English and the teacher engages with the textbook's English. There is no possibility of her using English words that might be understood as Hindi, as in the ninth-level Hindi class (fourth example).

The teacher then engages in a routine reminiscent of the third and fourth examples presented above, introducing explication with the use of the verb "to mean" or "*mānnā*" (to mean). She offers the gloss "the physical importance of exercises." She then invokes Socrates, the central figure in the lesson, with "he also learned," and introduces another "subject," "science." This time, rather than glossing the term, she provides a Hindi translation for what she has just said, but does not translate the focal part of the utterance, "science." The routine of offering an utterance in English and providing its translation into Hindi will occur again, though the translations are not always so parallel. For example, her offer of "and mathematics also" is rendered "*kuch* mathematics *bhī paṛhe*" (some mathematics also studied, inflected for perfect and plural) wherein the verb is provided for the Hindi, and the subject deleted and assumed. Then, the teacher's "and he also knew about the stars" in English becomes "and something else too are the stars in the sky" in Hindi.

The teacher more explicitly refers to the textbook lesson when she utters, "*isko kyā kahate hãi. jo itāre hãi. usko, iske bāre mẽ kyā likh diyā*" (What is it called? The stars which. That, what has been written about this?). This sequence of utterances is especially complex because she begins by talking about something in the book and then making explicit that, whatever it is, it is related to the theme of stars. She asks a question about what has been written about "this" in the textbook. If one were to imagine that the referent of "this" is the teacher's last utterance in the sequence involving the stars—astronomy perhaps—one would be wrong. Instead, the referent of "this," the phrase in the textbook, is, "but not nearly so much history and geography as children learn today." The phrase satisfies the teacher's claim in that the phrase comes from the textbook, but the phrase is not related to what one would expect, a word or phrase that somehow relates to the stars.

The teacher never does return to the theme of stars, but rather proceeds to offer a translation of the phrase from the textbook: "*ājkal ke jo bacce hãi ve abhigya hãi* social studies, *jaise* history *bhī hai* geography *bhī hai*" (Children these days are knowledgeable in the social studies, there is history too, geography too)." The translation is not exact, of course. First, the teacher introduces the term "social studies" that is missing in the phrase from the textbook. Second, the teacher offers a grammatically complete sentence in Hindi for the line from the textbook that she relates as a sentence fragment. Finally, unlike the teachers in examples three and four wherein they extend elements within the textbook's context to the students' lives, the teacher in this example maintains the referential stance of the textbook with the construction *jo bacce ... ve ...* (relative pronoun children ... third-person plural pronoun). That is to say, the teacher does not address the students and involve them in the elements of the textbook lesson with the second-person pronoun. She continues the excerpt by stating something not present in the text, "They like it," thereby maintaining third-person reference for people like the students sitting in front of her. She thus remains faithful to the frame of reference contained in the lesson.

She concludes by offering a construction similar to the one that she used to introduce the segment of the textbook lesson. Whereas she begins the segment with "*zyādā* importance *diyā jātā thā*" (much importance gave goes was) wherein the object is left unexpressed, she ends the segment with "*isko zyādā* importance *diya jātā*" (this+dative much importance gave goes) wherein the object is expressed. What is fascinating is that the referent of the first utterance is provided by the students with their utterance "gymnastics," whereas the referent of the second utterance seems to be "history" and "geography." While the teacher never returns to what was studied by Socrates, the difference between referents of her initial utterance and her final utterance—when considered with the discussion of Socrates—does parallel the difference between the temporal period of Socrates and the temporal period of the present. Though she struggles with the explication of the subject related to the stars, and presents a sentence fragment in English, glossing it with a complete sentence in Hindi, she manages to use a parallel construction to scaffold the distinction between the time of Socrates and the present, a major point of the textbook lesson.

The English Class at the Hindi-Medium School as a Special Case of Safetalk

All of the interaction that I recorded in schools—regardless of the subject or language medium of institution—exhibited some features of safetalk. Teachers controlled classroom interaction and students contributed relatively little. As in the excerpts presented here, students sometimes answered questions posed by the teacher that were oriented to specific aspects of the lesson and not emergent in the teacher's exegesis; they sometimes joined in with the teacher's ongoing exegesis when cued to do so, and sometimes answered the teacher's questions in the midst of ongoing exegesis. Never did I see a student contribute an utterance that produced anything other than praise, acceptance, or rebuke on the part of the teacher, all in response to an evaluation of how the student had satisfied or failed to satisfy the teacher's command. While the question-and-answer format in the first example allows for the provision of answers that can be evaluated as incorrect, the routines of the other examples makes an incorrect response less likely. Even in the event of an unanticipated answer—as in three instances in the ninth-level English class at the Seacrest School (example three)—the teacher is able to continue without breaking the routine. Indeed, the answer is unanticipated rather than incorrect. In contrast to the question-and-answer format of the first example, the routines of the other examples would seem to embody safetalk because they offer little possibility that a student could be singled out as incorrect.

In other respects, the argument for the existence of safetalk in the excerpts presented above is problematic. When one considers the relationship between the textbook and the teacher's discourse, the ninth-level English class at the Seacrest School (example three) and the ninth-level Hindi class at the Saraswati School (example four) resemble one another. In both cases, the textbook provides the anchor for classroom interaction and teachers orient most of their activity to it (K. Kumar 1988; Ramanathan 1999). Yet, in the examples, the teacher elaborates on passages in the textbook by introducing elements not already present. In the third example, the teacher introduces the image of a tennis racket, cassettes, and a popular singer in order to reframe, albeit momentarily, the notion of abundances within the students' lives. In the fourth example, the teacher invokes the dance classes and programs in which the students engage in order to involve the students in the images of beauty and redness from the poem. The extension of images from the context of the textbook lesson to the context of the students' lives overruns the boundaries of safetalk. Indeed, part of the interactional routine that the teachers use to involve students is oriented to that part of the lesson. Thus, the teacher enriches the lesson beyond the textbook, however modestly.

Indeed, if there is a case to be made that safetalk occurs in a certain type of class, the relationship between teacher and textbook must be invoked. In comparison to the English class in the English-medium school (third example) and the Hindi class in the Hindi-medium school (fourth example), the English classes in the Sarvodaya School (second example) and in the Hindi-medium school (fifth example) find the teacher extending the information contained in the textbook so that it might be relevant to the students to a much lesser degree. In both cases, the teachers are much more inclined to offer translations of the textbook's English messages in Hindi.

In this respect, the teachers in the second and fifth examples are participating in a kind of interactional safetalk described by Martin (2005) from his fieldwork in schools in peripheral areas of Malaysia. There, some teachers use other languages, a local language as well as the national language, to accomplish interaction in English class. Martin argues that the use of other languages helps the teacher to accomplish the work of the lesson, as well as providing glosses for English words and phrases to which the students otherwise lack access. The translations offered by the teacher in the fifth example are not exact, of course, but they do tend to maintain the referential stance of the textbook's message and do not attempt to extend it to students, even when doing so would be easy. Indeed, the teachers in the second and fifth examples use Hindi to explain the desired interactional pattern, frame questions, and gloss English passages from the text. Renditions in Hindi are much more elegant in the emergence of the lesson than are the phrases repeated from the textbook. Thus, the teacher and students in English class in the Hindi-medium school engage in safe-talk of a different kind than those in English class in English-medium schools. In the former, Hindi is the language in which the teacher directs the lesson and English is the language for which an alternative in Hindi is to be provided. In the latter, the teacher uses English to direct the lesson and provide exegesis of the passage from the textbook.

There is no doubt that safetalk can be used to understand differences between the interaction routines of the classrooms presented here. The notion of safetalk can reveal classroom dynamics as important because interaction in the English class of the Hindi-medium school differs from that of the English class of the English-medium school or the Hindi class of the Hindi-medium school. Were we to limit our perspective to classroom interaction, one could imagine the teacher and students in the Hindi-medium school colluding to save face by discussing a monolingual English textbook in a manageable way.

Ideas about English in the Hindi-Medium School

A number of scholars (Pérez-Milans 2012; Weber 2008) have argued that when classroom interaction is understood from the point of view of language ideology outside of the classroom, the notion of safetalk might not account for all of the ways in which classroom interaction might come to have value, whether pedagogical or otherwise. Thus, the notion of safetalk is useful in thinking about the relationship between discourse that occurs in the classroom, in the interactions between teachers and students, and discourse about schools that occurs outside of the classroom, in people's reflections about schools and languages. Safetalk is relevant to reflections outside of classroom discourse too because comments about English question whether safetalk accounts for the value of languages as they are differentiated by and used in language-medium schools.

There are several ways in which reflections on schooling outside of the classroom resonate with or recall the routines of the English class in the Hindi-medium school presented above. Emergent in various discussions presented in the book thus far is how people talk about the importance of English-medium education in Varanasi and across the

Hindi Belt of North India. Conversations about schooling in Varanasi often involve the verb *ghūmnā*, meaning "to wander" or "to roam," a notion explored in chapter 3. People explain that education prepares one for employment, but that the job is likely to be elsewhere. This is especially true when one is from a region like eastern Uttar Pradesh, largely left out of the information and digital technology sector whose growth has fueled fantasies of class advancement and growth in the last twenty years or so. Many scholars have attested to the links between English and employment in India's new middle classes, and people in Varanasi told me as a matter of routine that education in an English-medium school would be necessary for middle-class employment elsewhere, whether secured before or after relocation.

Many people used the English class in the Hindi-medium school to shore up the notion that an English-medium school was the place necessary for the acquisition of a job-getting mastery of English. In a manner reminiscent of descriptions of the complex suffered by Hindi-medium students in an English-medium environment, some people argued that Hindi-medium schools drew students who would never be able to "cope up" with the English necessary for a middle-class job, and referred to the English attained at an Hindi-medium school as *bekār* (useless). Furthermore, such people lampooned the massive rise in English-medium schools in the city, its surrounding area, and all over the northern-Indian Hindi Belt in the last twenty years by describing the ambitions of students and their parents as exceeding the English taught at the school.

People drew on a common set of school routines to illustrate the limitations of many English-medium schools. People argued that some English-medium schools taught students to utter greetings such as "good morning ma'am, good morning sir" to their parents, and "yes ma'am" and "no ma'am" to their teachers, and claimed that such abilities made the parents and teachers happy because they convinced the parents of their family's increasing "modernity" and the teachers of the English-medium status of the school. Some people pantomimed such greetings in a particularly biting and vicious manner. Many people went on to explain that students' abilities often ended there, and argued that just like in Hindi-medium schools, Hindi would come to be the most useful and used language in such English-medium schools. Unsurprisingly, the people who launched such critiques were comfortably middle-class. Some had attended relatively prestigious English-medium schools, but some had attended Hindi-medium schools. The former seemed to be poking fun at people who might think that they attend the same kind of institution but cannot speak English, while the latter seemed to be poking fun at what they saw as the hopeless incompatibility of lower-class backgrounds and the promises of English-medium education.

There is another understanding of English's place in ideas about movement, however, and it is one that emerges from a lower-class position—one that someone educated in a board-certified English-medium school would likely decry. Safetalk helped me to begin to pay attention to such lower-class understandings of English because they were not oriented in a defensive posture to English—as the notion of safetalk would have it—but rather pointed out English's benefits. Indeed, from the perspective of such lower-class ideas about English, the routines of the Hindi-medium English class emerge as something other than a method of hiding a lack of learning. It is not a position that I heard valorized or acknowledged explicitly by anyone, to be sure, but it is one worth considering lest understandings of language and language difference that rest on institutionalized forms of class reproduction be the only ones acknowledged.

A Missing Stance in Reflections on Language-Medium Schools

It was not until I started to think about classroom interaction in Hindi and English classes in Hindi- and English-medium schools in terms of safetalk that I turned my attention to the relationship between classroom discourse and the language ideology emergent outside. The notion of safetalk and language ideology outside of the school find the practices of the English class in the Hindi-medium school to be marked vis-à-vis those of the English class at the English-medium school, safetalk in a sympathetic mode and language ideology in a disparaging one. Neither sphere of interpretation, however, allows for the perspective held by some people outside of the classroom: that English, as it is used in the Hindi-medium school, for example, is indeed valuable. A shift in perspective allows classroom interaction in English class in the Hindi-medium school to emerge as something other than a face-saving technique.

Priti Chopra writes of Laila, a woman living in Mandaltola village in Bihar, a state bordering Uttar Pradesh to the east. Laila works as a sharecropper with her five children, and her husband is a migrant laborer living hundreds of kilometers away in Punjab. Chopra describes the lack of resonance between literacy programs in the non-formal educational sector and "everyday life practices that were more meaningful and relevant for her [Laila]" (2011: 636). Laila "claimed that learning to read and write takes too long" (2011: 636). Nevertheless, literacy would be helpful to Laila in certain respects: "She felt that it would be useful to read the names and quantities of different chemicals such as zinc and sulphur. She told me [Chopra] that these two chemicals look the same but have different effects so it would help to be able to read and tell them apart. She normally tries to remember which bag contains each chemical after asking a shopkeeper. She said that it would also be useful for her to: write her income and expenditure; budget and record loan payments in a book; write in and read her passbook for her women's organization saving and credit account; and open a bank account" (Chopra 2011: 636). Chopra does not say whether Laila specifies the language in which she would like to be able to do the various tasks. Perhaps such a designation is beside the point. In view of the multilingual and multiscript messages used for advertising just about anything except schools in northern India (see chapter 3 as well as Bhatia 2007 and Vaish 2008), one can easily imagine that Laila would encounter Hindi and English, on the one hand, and Devanagari and roman script, on the other, in the tasks she describes. The significance of the example is that Laila considers literacy to be useful from the point of view of the tasks she needs to accomplish. Neither does she see the institutional domain with its textbooks and exams as useful, nor does she participate in the ways in which people evaluate Hindi and English when they reflect on language-medium schooling.

Some people I knew in the field saw the importance of language in a way similar to Laila. In other words, they saw language to be salient less through the school system, its medium divide, and the "complex" emergent from it, and more through the tasks that one might accomplish with it. A recorded conversation I had with a chaukidar, a gate guard, at Delhi University, shows that someone who is by no means middle-class claims some of the same uses of English as those who lampoon the efforts of people in the chaukidar's class position. Ramdas Singh made approximately Rs 1,500 a month (approximately $40.00 (U.S.)) in 2004 when the interview was conducted. Part of the reason that the chaukidar took an interest in me was that he had moved to Delhi from Bhabua in Bihar, just over the Uttar Pradesh border from Varanasi. Another reason was that I enjoyed playing cards with him at night. My insomnia complemented his loneliness. He had a young boy and girl, both in a Hindi-medium primary school supported by the Delhi government, for which tuition fees were minimal. Mr. Singh's wages were very low for an extremely costly city, and the need to support two children made his life precarious indeed. His wife worked as a servant in a house, but her wages were much lower than his. He described his neighborhood as a *jhuggī jhopṛī*, that is, a neighborhood usually constructed by the residents that can be at risk of demolition given its typical development on land not owned by the residents.

Mr. Singh begins the excerpt by responding to my question about whether English is important in India.

Singh: *bhārat mẽ angrezī bhī zarūrī hai sar. aisā bāt nahī̃ hai binā angrezī ke kām cal jāegā. har maśīn kā nām angrezī mẽ hī hai sar. angrezī to jānā zarūrī hai har ādmī ko.*
English is also necessary in India Sir. One can't do work without it. Every machine's name is in English Sir. It's necessary for everyone to know English.

CL: *aur matlab naukrī ke liye?*
And meaning for a job?

Singh: *naukrī ke liye kuch bhī kām ke liye angrezī to zarūrī hai sar.*
For a job, for any type of job, English is necessary.

CL: *matlab bacpan se angrezī paṛhnā cāhiye?*
Meaning one should study English from childhood?

Singh: *cāhiye sar.*
One should.

CL: *sac?*
True?

Singh: *angrezī aur hindī donõ viśayat zarūrī hai ādmī ke liye.*
It is necessary for one to study English and Hindi.

CL: *lekin āmtaur pe bhāratīya logõ ko angrezī ātī hai?*
But usually do Indian people know English?

Singh: *hã karīb karīb sab ādmī ko thoṛā bahut zarūr ātā hai. aisā bāt to nahī̃ hai bhāratīya log maitrik tak takrīban ājkal sādhāraṇ paṛhāī hãi ek se gyārahavī tak. to angrezī samajh lete hãi. par utnā smārṭ bol nahī̃ sakte ham log lekin samajh lete hãi kī kyā bol rahe hãi. ham ko bolne to nahī̃ āegā lekin kuch kaha sakte ... samajh lenge kī kitnā bol sakte hãi, śāyad* eat foods water. *itnā to, ham log zarūr samajh lete hãi utnā to. īngliś ham log ke ṭāim yā mazbūt nahī̃ hãi.*
Yes, certainly they know some. It's not the case that Indians have gotten to the tenth level as they do today and from first to the eleventh. So they know English. We can't speak as well but we can understand what someone is saying. So we won't be able to speak but we can say a little ... will understand what little we can say, perhaps eat foods water. This much, certainly we can understand that much. We don't have time or strength for English.

Mr. Singh begins by voicing the pervasive notion that English is necessary in India in order to secure employment. His use of "machine" is indexical of a division between employment that is strictly manual, such as sharecropping or being a chaukidar, and employment that is mechanized or involves computers. English is associated with the latter because, in Mr. Singh's description, English is likely to be used to name such machines themselves. He ends his first turn at talk by making the more general assertion that English is necessary for everyone to know. He emphasizes that "for any work" (*kuch bhī kām ke liye*) one must know English. Mr. Singh qualifies matters in a manner typical of reflections on English presented throughout this book by including the importance of Hindi with the claim that English should be known for a job.

When he turns to a discussion of what English people do know, however, he turns away from a perspective that renders English primarily through the lens of the need for employment. Rather, he situates the knowledge of English in generational terms mediated by schooling. He contrasts Indians of the present and their relatively extensive schooling to "we," and contrasts the students of the present and their ability to speak to his own generation's more limited speaking and understanding. In other moments of our conversations, Mr. Singh asserted that he would see to it that his children would stay in school much longer than he had been able to. One might fault Mr. Singh for erasing the finer distinctions that people make about the manner in which English is spoken and the kind of school out of which types of speakers come, but Mr. Singh's lack of attention to such matters, I would argue, indexes him as someone of the working class for whom reflections on language medium are not salient.

Situating Mr. Singh outside of the middle class and its concern with language-medium distinctions in schools should not imply that Mr. Singh does not find value in English. Whereas Mr. Singh sometimes uses lexical items that could be understood as Hindi and English, such as *maśīn* (machine), *sar* (sir), and *smārṭ* (smart), he offers the lexical items eat, foods, and water in such a way that he is claiming that they are English and that he knows them. One might understand the lexical items he provides in English—eat, foods, water—to correspond to what one might call the necessities of life, the basics. Thus, one might understand the lexical items he provides in English to be indexical of the satisfaction of basic needs. Such basic needs stand in contrast to the world of machines and extended schooling mentioned earlier. Whereas Mr. Singh did not enjoy an extended stay in the world of schooling, he will make sure that his children are able to, and whereas Mr. Singh does not control English like others might, he knows a little and that little bit matters.

A final example of someone who sees value in English in ways not likely to be recognized in reflections on language-medium schooling in northern India is my landlady's servant Ravidas. He and I would go around the back of the house and smoke during breaks when members of the household were napping or were out. During one of our conversations, Ravidas explained that knowing "a little bit of English" (*thoṛī sī angrezī*) could prevent "shame" or "shyness" (*śarm*), especially in a place "not already known" (*jān pahacān kā nahī̃*). When I asked whether this is because a person wants for others to know that he or she can speak English, Ravidas replied negatively. He explained that if one sees some item that one needs to purchase, or that if one sees some sign that leads one to one's destination, the words will often be printed in English. He argued that one comes to know the names of things and places in the world in which one regularly lives and moves, but to go outside of that world can be daunting precisely because of the unknown that could be written there. When I gave him a look of confusion, he explained that it can be humiliating to have to ask what something is called when one suspects that it is written somewhere within sight.

The three examples of Laila, Mr. Singh, and Ravidas are different, to be sure. Laila's perspective most resembles Ravidas's, but she does not make explicit what language might be involved. Her desire to read what others have written resembles Ravidas's desire to read public signage in that both have to do with an emergent lack of knowledge and equality when confronted with others. Mr. Singh, on the other hand, offers snippets of English that he knows, but argues that he will keep his children in school for as long as possible, ostensibly toward a better form of labor than that available to him. The three perspectives and the kinds of value that emerge from them are not coordinated as are reflections on language-medium schooling. Indeed, the three people argue for the importance of English in ways likely to be decried in reflections on language-medium schooling. A concern with language-medium schooling and the abilities and routines that it presupposes seem out of reach to the class positions from which the three cases presented herein speak. Furthermore, the working-class dispositions to language do not seem to mimic a defensive stance that serves as a coping mechanism, as safetalk would have it. Rather, the three people whose reflections on language are offered here have very clear notions about how English can be valuable. One might even imagine that such uses of English might be aided by the routines of the English class in the Hindi-medium school. What is certain is that such ideas about English are hidden in reflections on language-medium schooling in India as well as by the notion of safetalk.

Conclusion

Safetalk is one of the most useful notions proposed to account for classroom dynamics in schools in parts of the world where teachers and students who have little access to or practice with former colonial languages must engage in them. The notion of safetalk argues that repetition, chorusing, and little elaboration on the lesson by teachers and students are face-saving techniques to deal with a difficult situation. When applied as an analytical tool to English and Hindi classes in the English-medium Seacrest School and the Hindi-medium Saraswati School, safetalk can be said to exist generally. Safetalk can also be used to discover that there are some practices in the English class in the Hindi-medium school that make the class there different from the others.

This chapter has also asked questions about what happens to the notion of safetalk when it is considered alongside ideologies circulating outside of the classrooms where it might be found. Safetalk joins discourse about less legitimate forms of English in schools in foregrounding English class at the Hindi-medium school. Whereas safetalk takes a sympathetic stance to teachers and students engaged in a situation in which they are particularly disadvantaged, reflections on language-medium schooling criticize and even make fun of the routines of schools, in the case of English-medium schools seen to have little prestige or to be lacking in board affiliation, and of classrooms, in the case of English classes in Hindi-medium schools.

People who occupy class positions below those for which reflections on language-medium schools are salient reflect on languages in ways that are missed by safetalk and reflections on language-medium schools. They attribute the value of Hindi and English, on the one hand, and literacy and speech, on the other hand, to accomplish specific tasks such as the identification of useful objects, the avoidance of embarrassment, and provision for their children's basic needs. These kinds of practices are likely to go unnoticed in reflections on classrooms and schools that assume that the purpose of schooling is to interact in a (specific) language toward the mastery of lessons from the textbook or the preparation for the successful completion of exams. The consideration of discursive activity from outside of classrooms is crucial for locating the fault lines of relationships between languages and schools and their relationship to class distinctions. But, one must remember that those fault lines presuppose a class-marked milieu, and might not correspond to others. This is especially evident in the arguments for language value considered in this chapter that cannot be explained with the notion of safetalk or with reflections on language-medium schooling.

Notes

1. Chick has argued that safetalk is not indicative of Zulu interactional styles, but rather provides "a means of avoiding the oppressive and demeaning effects of apartheid ideology and structures" (1996: 29). Teachers and students are "*colluding* in preserving their dignity by hiding the fact that little or no learning is taking place" (1996: 24).
2. Arthur adds, "it is the combination of routinized teacher-dominated performances of teaching and learning with the internalized discourse rules of English-medium instruction that most powerfully inhibits attempts by teachers and pupils to pursue more challenging and culturally congruent learning. Pupils are, in effect, prevented from meaningful and critical engagement with the curriculum" (2001: 73).
3. She also notes that Mehan's work identified the basic I (initiation), R (response), and E (evaluation) sequence, but also the T (topically) R (related) S (set) in which teachers could extend the basic pattern and investigate more broadly the basis of students' knowledge (Cazden 2001: 32). Cazden identifies "nontraditional" methods as diverging from the IRE sequence, and advocates for a mixture of the traditional and the nontraditional.
4. One might argue that the teacher is improving on the classroom routine as the lesson progresses.

Conclusion

Two languages—Hindi and English—have come to stand as options in the educational system of Hindi-speaking northern India. Hindi- and English-medium schools call into play differences in massive test-taking regimes, the price of school attendance, and feelings about what it means to live in a nation. The institutional distinction has grown in importance in the era of economic liberalization in India because educational pursuits and credentials are linked to future employment plans for more people than ever before. One might describe education through the rubric of language-medium schooling as a pursuit of—but also a sign of—India's new middle classes. The name for the group throughout the book has been plural—new middle classes—because many people that can be considered middle-class in Varanasi are involved in educational endeavors bifurcated by language. While it is true that English often serves as a symbol of the new middle classes in India, people in Varanasi often conceptualize English by invoking Hindi, and many people who can be considered middle-class were educated in Hindi-medium schools.

People seek English to allow them to participate in economic endeavors brought by liberalization in India as well as in other parts of the world. Particularly prominent in reflections on globalization in India are call centers because they require orientation to and competency in language practices of distant places. This book describes the ways in which processes of globalization are salient in a small city in a part of India despite the local lack of employment niches such as call centers and other job opportunities in India's massive information technology sector. People who plan to move from Varanasi to cities with more advanced technological infrastructures are not the only ones for whom English is relevant. In Varanasi, what English is cannot be understood without considering what Hindi is—and is not. That the two languages play a prominent role in the ways that people conceptualize and reflect on relationships between the global and the local, the international and the national, the urban and the rural, and the center and the periphery is made evident by uses of terms like *mātrabhāṣā* (mother tongue), *rāṣṭrabhāṣā* (national language), and *antarrāṣṭrabhāṣā* (international language). These terms are part of everyday parlance.

Hindi and English, via language-medium schooling, are intertwined, albeit unevenly, in pursuits of class reproduction because schools unable to offer exams are excluded in discursive reflection on medium distinctions. Thus, those schools for which language medium is an issue worthy of reflection are relevant to aspirations of class mobility. Schools run by volunteers or NGOs are not able to provide a seat in board examination. People do not imagine, for example, that instruction in English is a possibility in such schools. That instruction occurs in Hindi is a foregone conclusion. The tension animating discussions of language-medium schooling is missing in volunteer and NGO schools.

The school system provides an especially important means by which people imagine the relationship between Hindi and English. The school system takes its part in providing a vehicle for language ideology in explicit comments that people make about students of Hindi- and English-medium schools. These reflections use the notion of mother tongue to differentiate Hindi- and English-medium schools. In so doing, people exclude many language varieties that serve as candidates for the mother tongue outside of school contexts. Schools also provide the language-medium division substance with practices that are not embodied in overt reflection. Such aspects of schooling as the charging of fees and the affiliation with school boards do not correspond directly to distinctions between Hindi- and English-medium schools, but are understood to. Such alignments of language medium and school practices are crucial to consider because they rest on the exclusion of schools such as fees-taking Hindi-medium schools, and they support the distinction between school types by providing a political-economic contrast of a different semiotic nature from overt reflection on language.

Many people who talk about the issue of language medium reproduce the notion that one belongs to one or the other medium and that the distinction between Hindi- and English-medium schools divides the world. At the same time, their talk introduces cracks in the picture. They describe the complex that pits students of English-medium background above those of Hindi-medium background at the same time that they give evidence that they were able to escape it, or at least overcome it. Their transcendence, however, is not transformative because they cast themselves as exceptions or cast their detractors as even more peripheral than themselves. That is to say, they maintain the logic of the complex and the unequal relationship between Hindi- and English-medium schools that the complex rests on.

It is true that within Varanasi, reflections on the language medium of a school tend to reproduce the dichotomizing logic that the difference between the global and the local parallels the spatial difference between there and here. Hindi-medium schools can index the national while English-medium schools can index the international, just as Hindi-medium schools can index the local, even the peripheral, while English-medium schools can index an elsewhere that is central. These different possibilities do not exhaust the ways in which the value of schools in Varanasi can be configured. Several markets exist in India such that the indexical values of schools in overt discursive activity in Varanasi hardly reflect the value of schools when seen from a wider view. The salience of the division between Hindi and English as well as between Hindi- and English-medium schools fades as one considers discursive reflections of people who have chosen and paid for their children to be schooled elsewhere. What seems so salient to residents of Varanasi who contemplate the value of their own schooling experiences in the city fades as other, more encompassing market spheres are considered.

A specific sphere of communication—advertising for schools—exhibits in a particularly clear manner the ways in which the language-medium divide can render Varanasi a peripheral place. Within the city, language and script combinations reinforce the distinction between government Hindi-medium schools and expensive private English-medium schools. When one considers advertising for schools from afar, via the newspaper, however, only the English-medium school rendered in English in roman script can be found. Only a few schools in Varanasi—the most expensive—are reflected in the mirror of the newspaper. And no local schools are actually found in the newspaper. Most schools in the city advertise via signboards that use lexical and script combinations that cannot be found in school advertising in the newspaper.

Reflections on lexical and script combinations bolster the distinction between Hindi-medium status and government affiliation, on the one hand, and English-medium status and private ownership, on the other hand. Indeed, only one person I met during fieldwork provided a vision of schooling that compromised the strict division between Hindi- and English-medium schools rather than claiming to be an exception or unveiling the lower status of a would-be superior person. In order to understand how she accomplishes the creation of an alter vision of schooling, one must consider the way in which she deploys voices and the ways in which such voices resonate or fail to resonate with each other. The orchestration of voices exceeds the teacher's own present speaking self. Indeed, it constructs a set of actors or characters involved in a complex set of relationships that depend on the temporal frame in play at specific moments of her narration. What results is the performance of a claim that the strict division between Hindi- and English-medium schools could be otherwise, even if this possibility must be drawn from the past. The teacher who deploys such voices does not work at claiming herself to be an exception, leaving the dichotomy between Hindi- and English-medium schools intact, but rather introduces the possibility that the language-medium divide might once have been less significant. The distinction between Hindi- and English-medium schools is a pervasive aspect of language ideology among those who send their children to schools in Varanasi, of course, and the alter voices of the veteran biology teacher are suggestive rather than utopian. Indeed, their particularity might be taken as an index of the robust quality of the language-medium divide as well as an index that the divide has grown more robust during the period of India's economic liberalization. Such is the time period that divides the biology teacher's student days and the ethnographic present of my interview with her.

As one enters the classroom, one encounters a world wherein discursive reflections on schooling outside cannot account for experiences within. Scholars such as Vaidehi Ramanathan and Viniti Vaish who have studied classrooms in India have found this to be true of all grade levels in various locations and types of schools in Gujarat and Delhi. Of special concern is interaction in English class because the language requires experiences and practices inaccessible to most people in postcolonial societies. The concept of "safetalk" offers a means to explain a kind of routine in which the teacher and students, lacking an ability to interact with each other, much less with the text, save face. This is accomplished by minimizing interaction in English by such methods as having the students chorus what the teacher says, or offering most of the lesson in a language with which the teacher and students are familiar. Understood as safetalk, these strategies make completion of the lesson possible. The English class in the Hindi-medium school most prominently exhibits features of safetalk.

This is unsurprising given that the English class in the Hindi-medium school requires the use of the former colonial language in a school differentiated from it as a type in postcolonial India. While the language-medium divide sets the stage for the description of classroom routines in English in Hindi-medium schools as safetalk, many people use the routines of schooling itself to render English in schools as something often needing qualification. By ridiculing the English in Hindi-medium schools and in English-medium schools described as new, rural, or unaffiliated to a board, people represent practices and competence there as so confined as to be useless to anyone but proud relatives.

This book argues that safetalk might not account fully for what teachers and students might be said to accomplish in their safetalk interactions. Narratives from people who did not attend English-medium schools of any repute use the very same notion of movement, *ghūmnā* (to wander or roam), and a job (*naukarī*), to claim that the ability, verbal or literate, to produce or recognize English words, however limited, is useful. Sometimes the value of recognizing written or verbal tokens is grounded in the preservation of dignity. But the person arguing for the value of written or verbal tokens is not colluding with others to preserve dignity. That person is demonstrating knowledge. Such notions of language value do not emerge from the point of view of safetalk nor from the point of view of people when they are reflecting on schools and the language-medium divide.

From the point of view of people whose lives are involved in the formation of the middle classes in India, Hindi and English are languages, but they are also institutions. The differences between Hindi- and English-medium schools are so robust because they involve and actively shape notions like the mother tongue, the national, the international, the rural, the urban, the local, and the global. The particular ways in which Hindi- and English-medium schools emerge in practice and reflection are complex, rooted in some practices that are not linguistic, and partially dependent on the person who is attributing value to them. People, in turn, have more or less ability to attribute value to Hindi- and English-medium schools dependent on the communicative genre in which they are engaged. Few involved in language-medium schooling see the medium divide as anything but inevitable. And finally, the rootedness of the language-medium divide in social class is made evident by the ways in which working-class perspectives on language fail to attain value, much less salience.

Three Concluding Reflections

Three themes stand out as especially important in this discussion of schooling and language in northern India.

The Postcolonial Nation and the Dilemmas of Language Planning

The case of schooling and language in India shows that postcolonial societies can bear burdens that so-called developed societies are not believed to bear. The dilemmas of language planning, thus, are not equivalent among nations. The postcolonial nation is susceptible to the claim that development is required, whether it be in the educational or linguistic sphere. Those nations that are described as developing are susceptible to the charge that languages—particularly ones with global renown—are missing or flawed within their borders. The English spoken by or associated with Indians, for example, can emerge as a metonym of the condition of the nation. It is possible to imagine the English as spoken by Indians as somehow qualified in a manner that does not apply to the English spoken in the United States and other nations in what is called the developed world. Such criticisms can come from angry customers abroad connected via telephone, but often such criticisms are launched by citizens who express embarrassment about their own nation and educational system. People can target postcolonial nations, focusing on emblems of developmental progress, in order to bemoan their inadequacies or to call for change. Discourse about education and language is postcolonial societies often reifies the state and its activities, treating it as culpable and lazy. Processes of globalization do not solve such dilemmas, but sometimes provide them new possibilities.

The nation, of course, is not the only locus relevant to such dilemmas. Many people in Varanasi know that their city provides a more restricted range of schools in terms of prestige than more metropolitan locales, though many try to access some of that prestige through English locally. At the same time, many feel that their city occupies an especially important place in the development of Hindi. They find both English and Hindi in schools, but they find that those languages define types of schools too.

While some people do see the Indian state's dilemma to be its inability to foster an English on par with English elsewhere, it would seem that just as pressing is the way in which language is institutionalized in most of its cities, in the vast Hindi-speaking region of the north, at least. What people see in English depends on what they see in Hindi, and vice versa. Most of what they see in both languages is underpinned by schooling, locked as it is in a dichotomy. It is true that the state in India, via the educational system, has sought to promote several languages rather than one. But it would seem that for most people involved in the education system, contrasting qualities resting on the difference between the national and the international set the parameters of language value. Language planning efforts, such as the three-language formula, that do not address the ways in which people construct schools by way of language distinctions are bound to fail to attain salience. This is especially so given that schools and languages are tied to ideas about economic mobility and national belonging in the period of economic liberalization.

The Contradictions of the Mother Tongue

One of the most obvious ways in which Hindi, and not just English, matters to people who are middle-class in Varanasi is through the notion of the mother tongue. On the one hand, schooling focuses attention on Hindi specifically because Hindi defines a type of school as the alternative to English. One the other hand, many people in Varanasi see Hindi as their mother tongue (*mātrabhāṣā*) and national language (*rāṣṭrabhāṣā*) generally, deserving of love and respect.

Which language-medium school one attended does not always predict one's language abilities. People who attended Hindi-medium schools and developed the ability to speak English, and now work in jobs that require ability in English, wrestle with the notion of Hindi as the mother tongue. They stress that the mother tongue should be a source of pride at the same time that they express awareness that the mother tongue—in the face of English—can be a source of inadequacy and shame. This is especially so in the realm of schooling.

One might argue that the ways in which languages and schools have been inflected by colonization and globalization are reminiscent of Partha Chatterjee's (1994) arguments about the ways that colonial subjects managed to engage with notions of colonial development without being completely interpellated by them. Chatterjee famously argued that Indian life was split between an outer world of masculine political maneuverability and an inner world of feminine tradition maintenance. Likewise, in the ethnographic and interview material presented herein, people speak of English as a useful language needed for physical and economic mobility, and of Hindi as a precious language deserving of adoration.

This study acknowledges the dualistic manner in which languages and institutions have emerged. But it also points out that the relationship between Hindi and English is not straightforward—rendered, for example, as appropriate for an inner sphere and an outer sphere, respectively—and is often tied to the particular domains of activity in which it emerges. First, the cultural logics that underpin Hindi and English are several. Although their values are relational, even oppositional, they can vary radically depending on who is reflecting on them. Second, the potential for variation itself depends on the domain in which the languages—via schooling—are presented. Evidence of the prominence of English, for example, transcends individual reflections by its use in especially prominent educational institutions and in newspaper advertising from afar. And third, though they might be very few in number, there are some people who have the ability to question the very basis on which the language-medium distinction exists. Mrs. Khatri, the biology teacher, is especially skeptical about *śuddh* Hindi, which, for so many people, represents the mother tongue. It is important to examine the particular ways by which the language-medium divide is manifested in the world because its deployment, just like its composition, is uneven and unequal. In sum, the mother tongue is an ambivalent notion for those people whose aspirations have allowed them to see its limitations in education.

Language, Education, and the New Middle Classes

A final notion woven throughout the book is that language-medium schooling is connected to class dispositions in Varanasi, but that there is no one ideological basis that defines the connection. Institutional differences between schools able to offer seats in board exams and schools unable to offer such seats correspond to the differences between schools among which language-medium distinctions matter and schools among which they do not. While it is true that Hindi-medium schools are generally cheaper and do not prepare one for the most prestigious lines of study or most lucrative occupations, this does not mean that Hindi-medium education places one outside of what can be considered a middle-class status. There are many employment opportunities such as those for Mr. Sharma's sons, described in the introduction, for which English-medium education is ultimately unnecessary. Only if Mr. Sharma's youngest son continues in commerce with a focus on computers will he need an English-medium education. If he returns home to work with his father, his Hindi-medium education will suit his middle-class status perfectly well.

One cannot simply associate English-medium schooling with upward mobility in contrast to a more modest set of ambitions tied to Hindi-medium education. English entails risks as the ideological underpinnings of English are several. In Varanasi's schools, what is English-medium derives much of its prestige and associations with elsewhere through its opposition to Hindi-medium schools. But the elsewhere invoked by English-medium education is fractured by ideological difference. The Bankwalla, described in chapter 2, does not see his daughter's school as valuable because it is not Hindi-medium, but rather because it offers her an English that he sees as unavailable in Varanasi. This marks the Bankwalla as having a class disposition that is different, but also recognized as higher, in his neighborhood. It is a class level tied to a language ideology different from the one according to which most others in the neighborhood operate.

Middle-class status is not just complicated by language ideological difference, but it is also reproduced as seemingly unified. The notion of English-medium schooling leads many people to decry the English taught at Hindi-medium schools as deficient—even laughable. Such commentary assumes that English should be taught in a certain way in a certain kind of school. Passed over in such commentary are the uses of English that people like Mr. Singh, described in chapter 5, claim as valuable. While it is true that Mr. Singh is working-class and socioeconomically distant from someone who could be considered middle-class, he asserts that English is important—in his own life. The ways in which he describes English to be useful—the ability to recognize and use particular words and proper names—is exactly what seems to be the purpose of the English class in the Hindi-medium school. Sometimes people bolster the status of their own English-medium education and their status as middle-class by decrying or mocking the kind of English that Mr. Singh claims for himself. While language-medium schooling assumes the participation of students in class-inflected institutions, the institutional divide marked by language-medium difference emerges as an unfinished endeavor when one begins to examine what it makes possible and what it hides.

References

Advani, Shalini. 2009. *Schooling the National Imagination: Education, English, and the Indian Modern.* New Delhi: Oxford University Press.

Aggarwal, Kailash. 1988. "English and India's Three-language Formula: An Empirical Perspective." *World Englishes* 7 (3): 289–298.

———. 1997. "What's Indian about Indian Plurilingualism?" *Language Problems and Language Planning* 21 (1): 35–50.

Agha, Asif. 1998. "Form and Function in Urdu-Hindi Verb Inflection." In *The Yearbook of South Asian Languages and Linguistics,* ed. Rajendra Singh, 105–133. New Delhi: Sage.

———. 2005. "Voice, Footing, Enregisterment." *Journal of Linguistic Anthropology* 15 (1): 38–59.

———. 2007. *Language and Social Relations.* Cambridge: Cambridge University Press.

Agnihotri, R.K., and A.L. Khanna. 1997. *Problematizing English in India.* New Delhi: Sage Publications.

Ahearn, Laura. 2001. *Invitations to Love: Literacy, Love Letters, & Social Change in Nepal.* Ann Arbor: University of Michigan Press.

Ahmad, Rizwan. 2011. "Urdu in Devanagari: Shifting Orthographic Practices and Muslim Identity in Delhi." *Language in Society* 40: 259–284.

Amin, Shahid. 1989. "Editor's Introduction." In *A Glossary of North Indian Peasant Life,* by William Crooke, xviii–xlii. Delhi: Oxford University Press.

Anderson, Benedict. 1983. *Imagined Communities: Reflections on the Origin and Spread of Nationalism.* London: Verso.

Annamalai, E. 1991. "Satan and Saraswati: The Double Face of English in India." *South Asian Language Review* 1 (1): 33–43.

———. 2001. *Managing Multilingualism in India: Political and Linguistic Manifestations.* New Delhi: Sage.

———. 2004. "Medium of Power: The Question of English in Education in India." In *Medium of Instruction Policies: Which Agenda? Whose Agenda?,* ed.

James Tollefson and Amy Tsui, 177–194. Mahwah, NJ: Lawrence Erlbaum Associates.

———. 2005. "Nation-building in a Globalised World: Language Choice and Education in India." In *Decolonisation, Globalisation: Language-in-Education Policy and Practice,* ed. Angel Lin and Peter Martin, 20–37. Clevedon: Multilingual Matters.

Apte, Mahadev. 1976a. "Multilingualism in India and Its Socio-Political Implications: An Overview." In *Language and Politics,* ed. William O'Barr and Jean O'Barr, 141–164. The Hague: Mouton.

———. 1976b. "Language Controversies in the Indian Parliament (Lok Sabha): 1952-1960." In *Language and Politics,* ed. William O'Barr and Jean O'Barr, 213–234. The Hague: Mouton.

Arthur, Jo. 2001. "Codeswitching and Collusion: Classroom Interaction in Botswana Primary Schools." In *Voices of Authority: Education and Linguistic Difference,* ed. Monica Heller and Marilyn Martin-Jones, 57–75. Westport, CT: Ablex Publishing.

Axel, Brian. 2002. "Fantastic Community." In *From the Margins: Historical Anthropology and Its Futures,* ed. Brian Axel, 233–266. Durham: Duke University Press.

Bakhtin, M.M. 1981. "Discourse and the Novel." In *The Dialogic Imagination—Four Essays,* ed. M. Holquist, trans. C. Emerson and M. Holquist, 259–422. Austin: University of Texas Press.

———. 1984. *Problems of Dostoevsky's Poetics,* ed. and trans. C. Emerson. Minneapolis: University of Minnesota Press.

———. 1986. *Speech Genres & Other Late Essays,* ed. C. Emerson and M. Holquist, trans. V. McGee. Austin: University of Texas Press.

Baral, Kailash. 2006. "Postcoloniality, Critical Pedagogy, and English Studies in India." *Pedagogy* 6 (3): 475–491.

Baruah, Sanjib. 1999. *India against Itself: Assam and the Politics of Nationality.* Philadelphia: University of Pennsylvania Press.

Barz, R.K., and J. Siegel, eds. 1988. *Language Transplanted: The Development of Overseas Hindi.* Wiesbaden: Otto Harrassowitz.

Basu, Amrita. 1996. "Mass Movement or Elite Conspiracy? The Puzzle of Hindu Nationalism." In *Contesting the Nation: Religion, Community, and the Politics of Democracy in India,* ed. David Ludden, 55–80. Philadelphia: University of Pennsylvania Press.

Baviskar, Amita, and Raka Ray. 2011. "Introduction." In *Elite and Everyman: The Cultural Politics of the Indian Middle Classes,* ed. Amita Baviskar and Raka Ray, 1–26. New Delhi: Routledge.

Benei, Véronique. 2008. *Schooling Passions: Nation, History, and Language in Contemporary Western India.* Stanford: Stanford University Press.

Ben-Rafael, Eliezer, Elana Shohamy, and Monica Barni. 2010. "Introduction: An Approach to an 'Ordered Disorder'." In *Linguistic Landscape in the City,* ed. Elana Shohamy, Eliezer Ben-Rafael, and Monica Barni, xi–xxviii. Clevedon: Multilingual Matters.

Bernstein, Basil. 1971. *Class, Codes, and Control. Theoretical Studies Towards a Sociology of Language.* Vol. 1. London: Routledge and Kegan Paul.

Bhatia, Tej. 2007. *Advertising and Marketing in Rural India: Language, Culture, and Communication.* Delhi: Macmillan Publishers India.

Blommaert, Jan. 2006. "Language Ideology." In *Encyclopedia of Language and Linguistics,* ed. K. Brown. Vol. 6, 510–522. New York: Elsevier.

———. 2007. "Sociolinguistic Scales." *Intercultural Pragmatics* 4: 1–19.

———. 2010. *The Sociolinguistics of Globalization.* Cambridge: Cambridge University Press.

Blommaert, Jan, James Collins, and Stef Slembrouck. 2005. "Spaces of Multilingualism." *Language and Communication* 25: 197–216.

Board of High School and Intermediate Education Uttar Pradesh, n.d. "About Us." http://upmsp.nic.in/aboutus.htm.

Bourdieu, Pierre. 1977. "The Economics of Linguistic Exchanges." *Social Science Information* 16 (6): 645–668.

———. 1986. "The Forms of Capital." In *Handbook of Theory and Research for the Sociology of Education,* ed. John Richardson, 241–258. Westport, CT: Greenwood Press.

———. 1991. *Language and Symbolic Power,* ed. John Thompson, trans. Gino Raymond and Matthew Adamson. Cambridge, MA: Harvard University Press.

Brass, Paul. 1990. *The New Cambridge History of India. Part 1: The Politics of India Since Independence.* Vol. 4. Cambridge: Cambridge University Press.

Bucholtz, Mary, and Kira Hall. 2004. "Language and Identity." In *A Companion to Linguistic Anthropology,* ed. Alessandro Duranti, 369–394. Malden, MA: Blackwell.

Cazden, Courtney. 2001. *Classroom Discourse: The Language of Teaching and Learning.* Portsmouth: Heinemann.

Chakravarty, Rangan, and Nandini Gooptu. 2000. "Imagi-nation: The Media, Nation and Politics in Contemporary India." In *Cultural Encounters: Representing "Otherness,"* ed. Elizabeth Hallam and Brian Street, 89–107. London: Routledge.

Chand, Vineeta. 2011. "Elite Positionings towards Hindi: Language Policies, Political Stances and Language Competence in India." *Journal of Sociolinguistics* 15 (1): 6–35.

Chatterjee, Partha. 1994. *The Nation and Its Fragments: Colonial and Postcolonial Histories.* Delhi: Oxford University Press.

———. 1997. *A Possible India: Essays in Political Criticism.* New Delhi: Oxford University Press.

Chatterjee, Upamanyu. 1988. *English, August: An Indian Story.* New Delhi: Rupa and Co.

———. 2000. *The Mammaries of the Welfare State.* New Delhi: Viking.

Chaturvedi, M.G., and B.V. Mohale. 1976. *Position of Languages in School Curriculum in India.* Delhi: National Council on Educational Research and Training.

Chick, J. Keith. 1996. "Safe-talk: Collusion in Apartheid Education." In *Society and the Language Classroom,* ed. Hywel Coleman, 21–39. Cambridge: Cambridge University Press.

Chopra, Priti. 2011. "(Un)veiling Desire: Re-defining Relationships between Gendered Adult Education Subjects and Adult Education Programmes." *International Journal of Educational Development* 31: 634–642.

Chopra, Surabhi. 2011. "The 'Right of Children to Free and Compulsory Education Act, 2009.'" In *PROBE Revisited: A Report on Elementary Education in India,* by Anuradha De, Reetika Khera, Meera Samson, and A.K. Shiva Kumar, 17–19. Delhi: Oxford University Press.

Cohen, Lawrence. 1998. *No Aging in India: Alzheimer's, the Bad Family, and Other Modern Things.* Berkeley: University of California Press.

Cohn, Bernard. 1985. "The Command of Language and the Language of Command." In *Subaltern Studies IV: Writings on South Asian History and Society,* ed. Ranajit Guha, 276–329. Delhi: Oxford University Press.

Collins, James. 2012. "Migration, Sociolinguistic Scale, and Educational Reproduction." *Anthropology and Education Quarterly* 43 (2): 192–213.

Collins, James, and Richard Blot. 2003. *Literacy and Literacies: Texts, Power, and Identity.* Cambridge: Cambridge University Press.

Dalmia, Vasudha. 1997. *The Nationalization of Hindu Traditions: Bharatendu Harischandra and 19th-Century Banaras.* Delhi: Oxford University Press.

——. 2003. "The Locations of Hindi." *Economic and Political Weekly* April 5: 1377–1384.

Das Gupta, Jyotirindra. 1970. *Language Conflict and National Development: Group Politics and National Language Policy in India.* Berkeley: University of California Press.

——. 1976. "Practice and Theory of Language Planning: The Indian Policy Process." In *Language and Politics,* ed. William O'Barr and Jean O'Barr, 195–212. The Hague: Mouton.

Dasgupta, Probal. 1993. *The Otherness of English: India's Auntie Tongue Syndrome.* New Delhi: Sage Publications.

Daswani, C.J. 1989. "Aspects of Modernization of Indian Languages." In *Language Adaptation,* ed. Florian Coulmas, 79–89. Cambridge: Cambridge University Press.

De, Anuradha, Reetika Khera, Meera Samson, and A.K. Shiva Kumar. 2011. *PROBE Revisited: A Report on Elementary Education in India.* Delhi: Oxford University Press.

Demerath, Peter. 1999. "The Cultural Production of Educational Utility in Pere Village, Papua New Guinea." *Comparative Education Review* 43 (2): 162–192.

——. 2000. "The Social Costs of Acting 'Extra': Students' Moral Judgments of Self, Social Relations and Academic Success in Papua New Guinea." *American Journal of Education* 108: 196–235.

Deshpande, Satish. 2003. *Contemporary India: A Sociological View.* Delhi: Viking.

Doerr, Neriko Musha. 2009. *Meaningful Inconsistencies: Bicultural Nationhood, The Free Market, and Schooling in Aotearoa/New Zealand.* New York: Berghahn Books.

Dua, Hans. 1994a. *The Hegemony of English.* Jaipur: Yashoda.

——. 1994b. "Hindi Language Spread Policy and Its Implementation: Achievements and Prospects." *International Journal of the Sociology of Language* 107: 115–143.

Eckert, Penelope. 1989. *Jocks and Burnouts: Social Categories and Identity in the High School.* New York: Teachers College Press.

Eisenlohr, Patrick. 2004. "Register Levels of Ethno-national Purity: The Ethnici-

zation of Language and Community in Mauritius." *Language in Society* 33 (1): 59–80.
———. 2006. *Little India: Diaspora, Time, and Ethnolinguistic Belonging in Mauritius.* Berkeley: University of California Press.
Errington, J. Joseph. 1998. *Shifting Languages: Interaction and Identity in Javanese Indonesia.* Cambridge: Cambridge University Press.
———. 1999. "Ideology." *Journal of Linguistic Anthropology* 9 (1–2): 115–117.
———. 2001. "Colonial Linguistics." *Annual Review of Anthropology* 30: 19–39.
Faust, David, and Richa Nagar. 2001. "Politics of Development in Postcolonial India: English-medium Education and Social Fracturing." *Economic and Political Weekly* 36 (30): 2878–2883.
Fenigsen, Janina. 1999. "'A Broke-Up Mirror': Representing Bajan in Print." *Cultural Anthropology* 14 (1): 61–87.
Ferguson, Charles. 1959. "Diglossia." *Word* 15: 325–340.
Fernandes, Leela. 2000a. "Nationalizing 'the Global': Media Images, Cultural Politics, and the Middle Class in India." *Media, Culture, and Society* 22: 611–628.
———. 2000b. "Restructuring the New Middle Class in Liberalizing India." *Comparative Studies of South Asia, Africa, and the Middle East* 20: 88–112.
———. 2001. "Rethinking Globalization: Gender and the Nation in India." In *Feminist Locations: Global and Local, Theory and Practice,* ed. Marianne DeKoven, 147–167. New Brunswick: Rutgers University Press.
———. 2006. *India's New Middle Class: Democratic Politics in an Era of Economic Reform.* Minneapolis: University of Minnesota Press.
Fishman, Joshua. 1967. "Bilingualism with and Without Diglossia: Diglossia with and Without Bilingualism." *Journal of Social Issues* 23: 29–38.
Foley, Douglas. 2010. *Learning Capitalist Culture: Deep in the Heart of Tejas.* 2nd ed. Philadelphia: University of Pennsylvania Press.
Fox, Richard. 1990. "Hindu Nationalism in the Making, or the Rise of the Hindian." In *Nationalist Ideologies and the Production of National Cultures,* ed. Richard Fox, 63–80. American Ethnological Society Monograph Series 2. Washington, DC: American Anthropological Association.
Friedrich, Paul. 1989. "Language, Ideology, and Political Economy." *American Anthropologist* 91 (2): 295–312.
Gal, Susan, and Judith Irvine. 1995. "The Boundaries of Languages and Disciplines: How Ideologies Construct Differences." *Social Research* 62 (4): 967–1001.
Gambhir, S. 1981. *The East Indian Speech Community in Guyana: A Sociolinguistic Study with Special Reference to Koinė Formation.* Ph.D. diss., University of Pennsylvania.
Ganguly-Scrase, Ruchira, and Timothy Scrase. 2009. *Globalisation and the Middle Classes in India: The Social and Cultural Impact of Neoliberal Reforms.* London: Routledge.
Ghosh, Avik. 2004. "Alternative Schools and Education Guarantee Scheme." In *Gender and Social Equity in Primary Education: Hierarchies of Access,* ed. Vimala Ramachandran, 120–142. New Delhi: Sage.
Goffman, Erving. 1981. "Footing." In *Forms of Talk,* ed. Erving Goffman, 124–159. Philadelphia: University of Pennsylvania Press.

Gold, Ann. 2002. "New Light in the House: Schooling and Girls in Rural North India." In *Everyday Life in South Asia,* ed. Diane Mines and Sarah Lamb, 86–99. Bloomington: Indiana University Press.

Gray, Edward. 1999. *New World Babel: Languages and Nations in Early America.* Princeton: Princeton University Press.

Grierson, G.A. [1903–1928] 1967. *Linguistic Survey of India.* Vol. 5, pt. 2, *Bihari and Oriya Languages* and Vol. 6, *Eastern Hindi.* Delhi: Motilal Banarsidass.

Guichard, Sylvie. 2010. *The Construction of History and Nationalism in India: Textbooks, Controversies and Politics.* New York: Routledge.

Gumperz, John. 1958. "Dialect Differences and Social Stratification in a North Indian Village." *American Anthropologist* 60 (4): 668–681.

———. 1961. "Speech Variation and the Study of Indian Civilization." *American Anthropologist* 63 (5, pt. 1): 976-988.

———. 1964. "Linguistic and Social Interaction in Two Communities." *American Anthropologist* 66 (6, pt. 2): 137–153.

Gupta, Akhil. 1995. "Blurred Boundaries: The Discourse of Corruption, the Culture of Politics, and the Imagined State." *American Ethnologist* 22 (2): 375–402.

———. 1998. *Postcolonial Developments: Agriculture in the Making of Modern India.* Durham: Duke University Press.

Gupta, Akhil, and James Ferguson. 1997. "Culture, Power, Place: Ethnography at the End of an Era." In *Culture, Power, Place: Explorations in Critical Anthropology,* ed. Akhil Gupta and James Ferguson, 1–29. Durham: Duke University Press.

Gupta, Akhil, and Aradhana Sharma. 2006. "Globalization and Postcolonial States." *Current Anthropology* 47 (2): 277–307.

Gupta, Dipankar. 2010. *The Caged Phoenix: Can India Fly?* Stanford: Stanford University Press.

Gupta, R.S., Anvita Abbi, and Kailash Aggarwal, eds. 1995. *Language and the State: Perspectives on the Eighth Schedule.* New Delhi: Creative Books.

Haeri, Niloofar. 1997. "The Reproduction of Symbolic Capital: Language, State, and Class in Egypt." *Current Anthropology* 38 (5): 795–816.

Hall, Kathleen. 2002. *Lives in Translation: Sikh Youth as British Citizens.* Philadelphia: University of Pennsylvania Press.

Hall, Kira. 2002. "'Unnatural' Gender in Hindi." In *Gender Across Languages: The Linguistic Representation of Women and Men,* ed. Marlis Hellinger and Hadumod Bussman, 133–162. Amsterdam: John Benjamins.

———. 2009. "Boys' Talk: Hindi, Moustaches and Masculinity in New Delhi." In *Gender and Spoken Interaction,* ed. Pia Pichler and Eva Eppler, 139–162. Basingstoke: Palgrave Macmillan.

Hanks, William. 1987. "Discourse Genres in a Theory of Practice." *American Ethnologist* 14: 668–692.

———. 1996. *Language and Communicative Practices.* Boulder, CO: Westview.

———. 2005. "Explorations in the Deictic Field." *Current Anthropology* 46 (2): 191–220.

Hansen, Thomas. 1999. *The Saffron Wave: Democracy and Hindu Nationalism in Modern India.* Princeton: Princeton University Press.

———. 2001. *Wages of Violence: Naming and Identity in Postcolonial Bombay.* Princeton: Princeton University Press.

Hansen, Thomas, and Finn Stepputat. 2001. "Introduction: States of Imagination." In *States of Imagination: Ethnographic Explorations of the Postcolonial State,* ed. Thomas Hansen and Finn Stepputat, 1–40. Durham: Duke University Press.

Heath, Shirley Brice. 1981. "English in Our Language Heritage." In *Language in the USA,* ed. Charles A. Ferguson and Shirley Brice Heath, 6–20. Cambridge: Cambridge University Press.

Heller, Monica. 1995. "Language Choice, Social Institutions, and Symbolic Domination." *Language in Society* 24 (3): 373–405.

———. 1999. *Linguistic Minorities and Modernity: A Sociolinguistic Ethnography.* London: Longman.

Heller, Monica, and Marilyn Martin-Jones. 2001. "Introduction: Symbolic Domination, Education, and Linguistic Difference." In *Voices of Authority: Education and Linguistic Difference,* ed. Monica Heller and Marilyn Martin-Jones, 1–28. Westport, CT: Ablex Publishing.

Hill, Jane. 1998. "Language, Race, and White Public Space." *American Anthropologist* 100 (3): 680–689.

Holland, Dorothy, and Jean Lave, eds. 2001. *History in Person.* Santa Fe: School of American Research Press.

Hornberger, Nancy, and J. Keith Chick. 2001. "Co-Constructing School Safetime: Safetalk Practices in Peruvian and South African Classrooms." In *Voices of Authority: Education and Linguistic Difference,* ed. Monica Heller and Marilyn Martin-Jones, 31–55. Westport, CT: Ablex Publishing.

Huberman, Jenny. 2005. "'Consuming Children': Reading the Impacts of Tourism in the City of Banaras." *Childhood: A Journal of Global Child Research* 12 (2): 161–176.

———. 2012. *Ambivalent Encounters: Childhood, Tourism, and Social Change in Banaras, India.* New Brunswick: Rutgers University Press.

Ilaih, Kancha. 1996. "Productive Labour, Consciousness and History: The Dalitbahujan Alternative." In *Subaltern Studies IX: Writings on South Asian History and Society,* ed. Shahid Amin and Dipesh Chakrabarty, 165–200. Delhi: Oxford University Press.

Irvine, Judith. 1989. "When Talk Isn't Cheap: Language and Political Economy." *American Ethnologist* 16: 248–267.

———. 1996. "Shadow Conversations: The Indeterminacy of Participant Roles." In *Natural Histories of Discourse,* ed. Michael Silverstein and Greg Urban, 131–159. Chicago: University of Chicago Press.

Irvine, Judith, and Susan Gal. 2000. "Language Ideology and Linguistic Differentiation." In *Regimes of Language: Ideologies, Polities, and Identities,* ed. Paul Kroskrity, 35–84. Santa Fe: School of American Research Press.

Jacquemet, Marco. 2005. "Transidiomatic Practices: Language and Power in the Age of Globalization." *Language and Communication* 25: 257–277.

Jaffe, Alexandra. 1993. "Obligation, Error and Authenticity: Competing Cultural Principles in the Teaching of Corsican." *Journal of Linguistic Anthropology* 3 (1): 99–114.

———. 1996. "The Second Annual Corsican Spelling Contest: Orthography and Ideology." *American Ethnologist* 23 (4): 816–835.

———. 1999. *Ideologies in Action: Language Politics on Corsica.* Berlin: Mouton de Gruyter.

——. 2000. "Introduction: Non-standard Orthography and Non-standard Speech." *Journal of Sociolinguistics* 4 (4): 497–513.

——. 2009. "Introduction: The Sociolinguistics of Stance." In *Stance: Sociolinguistic Perspectives*, ed. Alexandra Jaffe, 3–28. Oxford: Oxford University Press.

Jayaram, N. 1993. "The Language Question in Higher Education: Trends and Issues." *Higher Education* 26 (July): 93–114.

Jeffery, Patricia. 2005. "Introduction: Hearts, Minds, and Pockets." In *Educational Regimes in Contemporary India*, ed. Radhika Chopra and Patricia Jeffery, 13–38. New Delhi: Sage Publications.

Jeffery, Roger, Patricia Jeffery, and Craig Jeffrey. 2005. "Social Inequalities and the Privatisation of Secondary Schooling in North India." In *Educational Regimes in Contemporary India*, ed. Radhika Chopra and Patricia Jeffery, 41–61. New Delhi: Sage Publications.

Jeffrey, Craig. 2010. *Timepass: Youth, Class, and the Politics of Waiting in India.* Stanford: Stanford University Press.

Jeffrey, Craig, Patricia Jeffery, and Roger Jeffery. 2008. *Degrees Without Freedom? Education, Masculinities, and Unemployment in North India.* Stanford: Stanford University Press.

Joshi, Svati, ed. 1994. *Rethinking English: Essays in Literature Language, History.* Delhi: Oxford University Press.

Kachru, Braj. 1992. "Meaning in Deviation: Toward Understanding Non-Native English Texts." In *The Other Tongue: English across Culture*, ed. Braj Kachru, 301–326. Urbana: University of Illinois Press.

——. 1996. "South Asian English: Toward an Identity in Diaspora." In *South Asian English: Structure, Use, and Users*, ed. Robert Baumgardner, 9–28. Urbana: University of Illinois Press.

Kaplan, Sam. 2006. *The Pedagogical State: Education and the Politics of National Culture in Post-1980 Turkey.* Stanford: Stanford University Press.

Katz, Cindi. 2004. *Growing Up Global: Economic Restructuring and Children's Everyday Lives.* Minneapolis: University of Minnesota Press.

Kaviraj, Sudipta. 1992a. "The Imaginary Institution of India." In *Subaltern Studies VII: Writings on South Asian History and Society*, ed. Partha Chatterjee and Gyanendra Pandey, 1–39. Delhi: Oxford University Press.

——. 1992b. "Writing, Speaking, Being: Language and the Historical Formation of Identities in India." In *Nationalstaat und Sprachkonflikt in Süd- und Südostasien*, ed. Dagmar Hellman-Rajanayagam and Dietmar Rothermund, 25–65. Stuttgart: Steiner.

Keane, Webb. 1997. "Knowing One's Place: National Language and the Idea of the Local in Eastern Indonesia." *Cultural Anthropology* 12 (1): 37–63.

——. 2001. "Voice." In *Key Terms in Language and Culture*, ed. Alessandro Duranti, 268–271. Malden, MA: Blackwell.

Khilnani, Sunil. 1999. *The Idea of India.* New York: Farrar, Straus and Giroux.

Khubchandani, Lachman. 1979. "A Demographic Typology for Hindi, Urdu, Punjabi Speakers in South Asia." In *Language and Society: Anthropological Issues*, ed. William McCormack and Stephen Wurm, 183–194. The Hague: Mouton.

——. 1983. *Plural Languages, Plural Cultures: Communication, Identity, and Sociopolitical Change in Contemporary India.* Honolulu: University of Hawai'i Press.

——. 1984. "Sociolinguistics in India: The Decade Past, the Decade to Come." *International Journal of the Sociology of Language* 45: 47–64.

——. 1994. "English as a Contact Language." In *Second Language Acquisition: Socio-cultural and Linguistic Aspects of English in India,* ed. R.K. Agnihotri and A.L. Khanna, 77–91. New Delhi: Sage Publications.

——. 2003. "Defining Mother Tongue Education in Plurilingual Contexts." *Language Policy* 2: 239–254.

King, Christopher. 1994. *One Language, Two Scripts: The Hindi Movement in Nineteenth Century North India.* Delhi: Oxford University Press.

——. 2001. "The Poisonous Potency of Script: Hindi and Urdu." *International Journal of the Sociology of Language* 150: 43–59.

King, Robert. 1997. *Nehru and the Language Politics of India.* Delhi: Oxford University Press.

Klenk, Rebecca. 2003. "'Difficult Work': Becoming Developed." In *Regional Modernities: The Cultural Politics of Development in India,* ed. K. Sivaramakrishnan and Arun Agrawal, 99–121. Stanford: Stanford University Press.

Koven, Michèle. 1998. "Two Languages in the Self/The Self in Two Languages: French-Portuguese Bilinguals' Verbal Enactments and Experiences of Self in Narrative Discourse." *Ethos* 26 (4): 410–455.

——. 2002. "An Analysis of Speaker Role Inhabitance in Narratives of Personal Experience." *Journal of Pragmatics* 34: 167–217.

——. 2004. "Getting 'Emotional' in Two Languages: Bilinguals' Verbal Performance of Affect in Narratives of Personal Experience." *Text* 24 (4): 471–515.

Krishnamurti, Bh. 1979. "Problems of Language Standardization in India." In *Language and Society: Anthropological Issues,* ed. William McCormack and Stephen Wurm, 673–692. The Hague: Mouton.

Krishnaswamy, N., and Archana S. Burde. 1998. *The Politics of Indians' English: Linguistic Colonialism and the Expanding English Empire.* Delhi: Oxford University Press.

Kroskrity, Paul. 2001. "Identity." In *Key Terms in Language and Culture,* ed. Alessandro Duranti, 106–109. Malden, MA: Blackwell.

——. 2004. "Language Ideologies." In *A Companion to Linguistic Anthropology,* ed. Alessandro Duranti, 496–517. Malden, MA: Blackwell Publishing.

Kumar, Amitava. *Home Products.* New Delhi: Picador.

Kumar, Krishna. 1988. "Origin of India's 'Textbook Culture.'" *Comparative Education Review* 32 (4): 452–464.

——. 1989. *Social Character of Learning.* New Delhi: Sage.

——. 1990. "Quest for Self-Identity: Cultural Consciousness and Education in Hindi Region, 1880-1950." *Economic and Political Weekly,* June 9: 1247–1255.

——. 1991a. "Slowing Down." *Economic and Political Weekly,* March 30: 815–816.

——. 1991b. *Political Agenda of Education: A Study of Colonialist and Nationalist Ideas.* Delhi: Sage.

——. 1991c. "Foul Contract." *Seminar* 377: 43–46.

——. 1993. "Hindu Revivalism and Education in North-Central India." In *Fundamentalisms and Society: Reclaiming the Sciences, the Family, and Education,* ed. Martin Marty and R. Scott Appleby, 536–557. Chicago: University of Chicago Press.

——. 1996. *Learning from Conflict.* Hyderabad: Orient Longman.

———. 1998. "Education and Society in Post-Independence India: Looking towards the Future." *Economic and Political Weekly,* June 6: 1391–1396.
Kumar, Nita. 1988. *The Artisans of Banaras: Popular Culture and Identity 1880-1986.* Princeton: Princeton University Press.
———. 1992. *Friends, Brothers, and Informants: Fieldwork Memoirs of Banaras.* Berkeley: University of California Press.
———. 1994. "Oranges for the Girls, or, the Half-Known Story of the Education of Girls in Twentieth-Century Banaras." In *Women as Subjects: South Asian Histories,* ed. Nita Kumar, 211–231. Calcutta: Stree.
———. 1998. "Lessons from Contemporary Schools." *Sociological Bulletin* 47 (1): 33–49.
———. 2000. *Lessons from Schools: The History of Education in Banaras.* New Delhi: Sage.
———. 2001. "Children and the Partition." In *The Partitions of Memory: The Afterlife of the Division of India,* ed. Suvir Kaul, 269–301. Bloomington: Indiana University Press.
———. 2007. *The Politics of Gender, Community, and Modernity: Essays on Education in India.* Delhi: Oxford University Press.
———. 2011. "The Middle-class Child: Ruminations on Failure." In *Elite and Everyman: The Cultural Politics of the Indian Middle Classes,* ed. Amita Baviskar and Raka Ray, 220–245. New Delhi: Routledge.
Kumar, Ravi. 2009. "State, Inequality, and Politics of Capital: The Neoliberal Scourge in Education." In *The Developing World and State Education: Neoliberal Depredation and Egalitarian Alternatives,* ed. Dave Hill and Ellen Rosskam, 140–161. New York: Routledge.
Kurzon, Dennis. 2004. *Where East Looks West: Success in English in Goa and on the Konkan Coast.* Clevedon: Multilingual Matters.
LaDousa, Chaise. 2004. "In the Mouth but Not on the Map: Visions of Language and Their Enactment in the Hindi Belt." *Journal of Pragmatics* 36 (4): 633–661.
———. 2007. "Liberalisation, Privatisation, Modernisation and Schooling in India: An Interview with Krishna Kumar." *Globalisation, Societies and Education* 5 (2): 137–152.
Lee, Benjamin. 1997. *Talking Heads: Language, Metalanguage, and the Semiotics of Subjectivity.* Durham: Duke University Press.
Lelyveld, David. 1993. "The Fate of Hindustani: Colonial Knowledge and the Project of a National Language." In *Orientalism and the Postcolonial Predicament: Perspectives on South Asia,* ed. Carol Breckenridge and Peter van der Veer, 198–214. Philadelphia: University of Pennsylvania Press.
Levinson, Bradley, and Dorothy Holland. 1996. "The Cultural Production of the Educated Person: An Introduction." In *The Cultural Production of the Educated Person: Critical Ethnographies of Schooling and Local Practice,* ed. Bradley Levinson, Douglas Foley, and Dorothy Holland, 1–56. Albany: State University of New York Press.
Majumdar, Manabi, and Jos Mooij. 2011. *Education and Inequality in India: A Classroom View.* New York: Routledge.
Mankekar, Purnima. 1999. *Screening Culture, Viewing Politics: An Ethnography of Television, Womanhood, and Nation in Postcolonial India.* Durham: Duke University Press.

Marriott, McKim. 1976. "Hindu Transactions: Diversity without Dualism." In *Transaction and Meaning: Directions in the Anthropology of Exchange and Symbolic Behavior*, ed. Bruce Kapferer, 109–142. Philadelphia: ISHI.

Martin, Peter. 2005. "'Safe' Language Practices in Two Rural Schools in Malaysia: Tensions between Policy and Practice." In *Decolonisation, Globalisation: Language-in-Education Policy and Practice*, ed. Angel Lin and Peter Martin, 74–97. Clevedon: Multilingual Matters.

Masica, Colin. 1991. *The Indo-Aryan Languages*. Cambridge: Cambridge University Press.

Mazzarella, William. 2005. "Middle Class." In *Keywords in South Asian Studies (An Online Encyclopedia Published by the School of Oriental and African Studies, University of London)*, ed. Rachel Dwyer. http://www.soas.ac.uk/centres/centreinfo.cfm?navid=912.

McKean, Lise. 1996. *Divine Enterprise: Gurus and the Hindu Nationalist Movement*. Chicago: University of Chicago Press.

Mehan, Hugh. 1979. *Learning Lessons: Social Organization in the Classroom*. Cambridge: Harvard University Press.

Mendoza-Denton, Norma. 2002. "Language and Identity." In *The Handbook of Language Variation and Change*, ed. J.K. Chambers, Peter Trudgill, and Natalie Schilling-Estes, 475–499. Malden, MA: Blackwell Publishing.

Mertz, Elizabeth. 1985. "Beyond Symbolic Anthropology: Introducing Semiotic Mediation." In *Semiotic Mediation*, ed. Elizabeth Mertz and Richard Parmentier, 1–19. Orlando: Academic Press.

———. 1998. "Linguistic Ideology and Praxis in U.S. Law School Classrooms." In *Language Ideologies: Practice and Theory*, ed. Bambi Schieffelin, Kathryn Woolard, and Paul Kroskrity, 149–162. Oxford: Oxford University Press.

Mesthrie, Rajend. 1991. *Language in Indenture: A Sociolinguistic History of Bhojpuri-Hindi in South Africa*. Johannesburg: Witwatersrand University Press.

Mitchell, Lisa. 2009. *Language, Emotion, and Politics in South India: The Making of a Mother Tongue*. Bloomington: Indiana University Press.

Mohan, Peggy. 1978. *Trinidad Bhojpuri: A Morphological Study*. Ph.D. diss., University of Michigan.

Mukherjee, Alok. 2009. *This Gift of English: English Education and the Formation of Alternative Hegemonies in India*. New Delhi: Orient BlackSwan.

Mukhopadyay, Carol, and Susan Seymour, eds. 1994. *Women, Education, and Family Structure in India*. Boulder: Westview.

Nadkarni, M.V. 1994. "English in Mother Tongue Medium Education." In *Second Language Acquisition: Socio-cultural and Linguistic Aspects of English in India*, ed. R.K. Agnihotri and A.L. Khanna, 130–142. New Delhi: Sage Publications.

Naik, J.P., and Syed Nurullah. [1945] 1974. *A Students' History of Education in India (1800-1973)*. 6th rev. ed. New Delhi: Macmillan India Ltd.

Narayan, Kirin. 1993. "Banana Republics and V.I. Degrees: Rethinking Indian Folklore in a Postcolonial World." *Asian Folklore Studies* 52: 177–204.

National Council for Educational Research and Training. 2005. *National Curriculum Framework*. New Delhi: NCERT.

National Policy on Education. 1968. *Education and National Development: Report of the Education Commission 1964-1966*. New Delhi: NCERT.

Orsini, Francesca. 2002. *The Hindi Public Sphere 1920-1940: Language and Literature in the Age of Nationalism.* Delhi: Oxford University Press.

Pandit, P.B. 1977. *Language in a Plural Society: The Case of India.* New Delhi: Amrik Singh.

———. 1979. "Perspectives on Sociolinguistics in India." In *Language and Society: Anthropological Issues,* ed. William McCormack and Stephen Wurm, 171–182. The Hague: Mouton.

Parmentier, Richard. 1994. *Signs in Society: Studies in Semiotic Anthropology.* Bloomington: Indiana University Press.

Parry, Jonathan. 1994. *Death in Banaras.* Cambridge: Cambridge University Press.

Patel, Reena. 2010. *Working the Night Shift: Women in India's Call Center Industry.* Stanford: Stanford University Press.

Pattanayak, Debi Prasanna. 1981. *Multilingualism and Mother Tongue Education.* Delhi: Oxford University Press.

———. 1985. "Diversity in Communication and Languages; Predicament of a Monolingual State: India, a Case Study." In *Language of Inequality,* ed. Nessa Wolfson and Joan Manes, 399–407. The Hague: Mouton.

Pérez-Milans. 2012. "Beyond 'Safe-talk': Institutionalization and Agency in China's English Language Education." *Linguistics and Education* 23 (1): 62–76.

Philips, Susan U. 1998. "Language Ideologies in Institutions of Power: A Commentary." In *Language Ideologies: Practice and Theory,* ed. Bambi Schieffelin, Kathryn Woolard, and Paul Kroskrity, 211–225. Oxford: Oxford University Press.

Pinney, Christopher. 2001. "Introduction: Public, Popular, and Other Cultures." In *Pleasure and the Nation: The History, Politics and Consumption of Public Culture in India,* ed. Rachel Dwyer and Christopher Pinney, 1–34. Delhi: Oxford University Press.

Pollock, Mica, and Bradley Levinson. 2011. "Introduction." In *A Companion to the Anthropology of Education,* ed. Bradley Levinson and Mica Pollock, 1–8. Malden, MA: Wiley-Blackwell.

Prasad, H.Y. Sharada. 1986. "Coming Home." *Seminar* 321: 23–26.

PROBE (Public Report on Basic Education in India) Team. 1999. *Public Report on Basic Education in India.* New Delhi: Oxford University Press.

Raheja, Gloria. 1996. "Caste, Colonialism, and the Speech of the Colonized: Entextualization and Disciplinary Control in India." *American Ethnologist* 23 (3): 494–513.

———. 1999. "The Illusion of Consent: Language, Caste, and Colonial Rule in India." In *Colonial Subjects: Essays on the Practical History of Anthropology,* ed. Peter Pels and Oscar Salemink, 117–152. Ann Arbor: University of Michigan Press.

Rahman, Tariq. 2011. *From Hindi to Urdu: A Social and Political History.* Karachi: Oxford University Press.

Rai, Alok. 2001. *Hindi Nationalism.* Delhi: Orient Longman.

Rai, Amrit. 1984. *A House Divided: The Origin and Development of Hindi/Hindavi.* Delhi: Oxford University Press.

Rajagopal, Arvind. 2001. *Politics after Television: Hindu Nationalism and the Reshaping of the Public in India.* Cambridge: Cambridge University Press.

Rajan, Rajeswari. 1992. "Fixing English: Nation, Language, Subject." In *The Lie of the Land: English Literary Studies in India,* ed. Rajeswari Rajan, 7–28. Delhi: Oxford University Press.

Ramachandran, Vimala. 2004. "Introduction." In *Gender and Social Equity in Primary Education: Hierarchies of Access,* ed. Vimala Ramachandran, 19–31. New Delhi: Sage.

Ramanathan, Vaidehi. 1999. "English Is Here to Stay: A Critical Look at Institutional and Educational Practices in India." *Teachers of English to Speakers of Other Languages Quarterly* 33 (2): 211–231.

———. 2005a. *The English-Vernacular Divide: Postcolonial Language Politics and Practice.* Clevedon: Multilingual Matters.

———. 2005b. "Ambiguities about English: Ideologies and Critical Practice in Vernacular-medium College Classrooms in Gujarat, India." *Journal of Language, Identity, and Education* 4: 45–65.

Ramaswamy, Sumathi. 1997. *Passions of the Tongue: Language Devotion in Tamil India, 1891-1970.* Berkeley: University of California Press.

Rubdy, Rani. 2008. "English in India: The Privilege and Privileging of Social Class." In *Language as Commodity: Global Structures, Local Marketplaces,* ed. Peter Tan and Rani Rubdy, 122–145. London: Continuum International Publishing Group.

Rumsey, Alan. 1990. "Wording, Meaning, and Linguistic Ideology." *American Anthropologist* 92 (2): 346–361.

Rutz, Henry, and Erol Balkan. 2009. *Reproducing Class: Education, Neoliberalism, and the Rise of the New Middle Class in Istanbul.* New York: Berghahn Books.

Sadana, Rashmi. 2012. *English Heart, Hindi Heartland: The Political Life of Literature in India.* Berkeley: University of California Press.

Sarangapani, Padma. 2003a. "Childhood and Schooling in an Indian Village." *Childhood* 10 (4): 403–418.

———. 2003b. *Constructing School Knowledge: An Ethnography of Learning in an Indian Village.* New Delhi: Sage.

Schieffelin, Bambi and Rachelle Doucet. 1998. "The 'Real' Haitian Creole: Ideology, Metalinguistics, and Orthographic Choice." In *Language Ideologies: Practice and Theory,* ed. Bambi Schieffelin, Kathryn Woolard, and Paul Kroskrity, 285–316. Oxford: Oxford University Press.

Schiffman, Harold. 1996. *Linguistic Culture and Language Policy.* New York: Routledge.

Sengupta, Parna. 2011. *Pedagogy for Religion: Missionary Education and the Fashioning of Hindus and Muslims in Bengal.* Berkeley: University of California Press.

Seth, Sanjay. 2007. *Subject Lessons: The Western Education of Colonial India.* Durham: Duke University Press.

Seymour, Susan. 1999. *Women, Family, and Child Care in India: A World in Transition.* Cambridge: Cambridge University Press.

———. 2002. "Family and Gender Systems in Transition: A Thirty-Five-Year Perspective." In *Everyday Life in South Asia,* ed. Diane Mines and Sarah Lamb, 100–115. Bloomington: Indiana University Press.

Shapiro, Michael, and Harold Schiffman. 1981. *Language and Society in South Asia.* Delhi: Motilal Banarsidass.

Sharma, Aradhana. 2006. "Crossbreeding Institutions, Breeding Struggle: Women's Empowerment, Neoliberal Governmentality, and State (Re)Formation in India." *Cultural Anthropology* 21 (1): 60–95.

Sheth, D.L. 1990. "No English Please, We're Indian." *Illustrated Weekly of India,* August 19: 34–37.

Shohamy, Elana, and Durk Gorter. 2009. "Introduction." In *Linguistic Landscape: Expanding the Scenery,* ed. Elana Shohamy and Durk Gorter, 1–10. New York: Routledge.

Shukla, Shrilal. [1968] 1992. *Raag Darbari: A Novel,* trans. Gillian Wright. New Delhi: Penguin.

Silverstein, Michael. 1976. "Shifters, Linguistic Categories, and Cultural Description." In *Meaning in Anthropology,* ed. Keith Basso and Henry Selby, 11–55. Albuquerque: University of New Mexico Press.

———. 1979. "Language Structure and Linguistic Ideology." In *Papers from the Parasession on Linguistic Units and Levels,* ed. P. Clyne et al., 193–247. Chicago: Chicago Linguistic Society.

———. 1992. "Metapragmatic Discourse and Metapragmatic Function." In *Reflexive Language: Reported Speech and Metapragmatics,* ed. John Lucy, 33–58. Cambridge: Cambridge University Press.

———. 1996. "Indexical Order and the Dialectics of Sociolinguistic Life." In *SALSA III (Proceedings of the Third Annual Symposium About Language and Society),* ed. Risako Ide, Rebecca Parker, and Yukako Sunaoshi, 266–295. Texas Linguistic Forum. Vol. 36. Austin: University of Texas Linguistics Department.

———. 1998. "Contemporary Transformations of Local Linguistic Communities." *Annual Review of Anthropology* 27: 401–426.

Simon, Beth. 1986. *Bilingualism and Language Maintenance in Banaras.* Ph.D. diss., University of Wisconsin, Madison.

———. 1993. "Language Choice, Religion, and Identity in the Banarsi Community." In *Living Banaras: Hindu Religion in Cultural Context,* ed. Bradley Hertel and Cynthia Ann Humes, 245–268. Albany: State University of New York Press.

———. 1995. "Mangoes." *The Massachusetts Review* 36 (2): 207-214.

———. 2003. "Here We Do Not Speak Bhojpuri: A Semantics of Opposition." In *Emancipating Cultural Pluralism,* ed. Cris E. Toffolo, 147–162. Albany: State of New York Press.

Singh, Khushwant. 1986. "Indish." *Seminar* 321: 36–38.

Skutnabb-Kangas, T., and R. Phillipson. 1989. "'Mother Tongue': The Theoretical and Sociopolitical Construction of a Concept." In *Status and Function of Languages and Language Varieties,* ed. U. Ammon, 450–477. Berlin: Walter de Gruyter.

Sonntag, Selma. 1996. "The Political Saliency of Language in Bihar and Uttar Pradesh." *The Journal of Commonwealth and Comparative Politics* 34 (2): 1–18.

———. 2000. "Ideology and Policy in the Politics of the English Language in North India." In *Ideology, Politics and Language Policies: Focus on English,* ed. Thomas Ricento, 133–150. Amsterdam: John Benjamins.

Southworth, Franklin. 1985. "The Social Context of Language Standardization in India." In *Language of Inequality,* ed. Nessa Wolfson and Joan Manes, 225–239. The Hague: Mouton.

Spitulnik, Debra. 1993. "Anthropology of Mass Media." *Annual Review of Anthropology* 22: 293–315.

———. 1998. "Mediating Unity and Diversity." In *Language Ideologies: Practice and Theory,* ed. Bambi Schieffelin, Kathryn Woolard, and Paul Kroskrity, 163–188. Oxford: Oxford University Press.

Sridhar, S.N. 1987. "Language Variation, Attitudes, and Rivalry: The Spread of Hindi in India." In *Language Spread and Language Policy: Issues, Implications, and Case Studies,* ed. Peter Lowenberg, 300–319. Washington, DC: Georgetown University Press. (Georgetown University Roundtable on Languages and Linguistics 1987).

———. 1991. "Bilingual Education in India." In *Bilingual Education: Focusschrift in Honor of Joshua A. Fishman on the Occasion of His 65th Birthday,* ed. Ofelia Garcia. Vol. 1, 89–101. Amsterdam: John Benjamins.

Srivastava, A.K. 1990. "Multilingualism and School Education in India: Special Features, Problems, and Prospects." In *Multilingualism in India,* ed. D.P. Pattanayak, 37–53. Clevedon: Multilingual Matters.

Srivastava, Sanjay. 1998. *Constructing Post-Colonial India: National Character and the Doon School.* New York: Routledge.

———. 2003. "Schooling, Culture, and Modernity." In *The Oxford Companion to Sociology and Social Anthropology,* ed. Veena Das. Vol. 2. 998–1031. New Delhi: Oxford University Press.

Stambach, Amy. 2000. *Lessons from Mount Kilimanjaro: Schooling, Community, and Gender in East Africa.* New York: Routledge.

Suraiya, Jug. 1990. "The Chips Are Down for Post-Modern Hindi." *Times of India,* 19 June.

Swigart, Leigh. 2000. "The Limits of Legitimacy: Language Ideology and Shift in Contemporary Senegal." *Journal of Linguistic Anthropology* 10 (1): 90–130.

Thapar, Romesh. 1986. "The Problem." *Seminar* 321: 2–3.

Trautmann, Thomas. 1997. *Aryans and British India.* Berkeley: University of California Press.

Trawick, Margaret. 1988. "Spirits and Voices in Tamil Songs." *American Ethnologist* 15 (2): 193–215.

Urban, Greg. 1989. "The 'I' of Discourse." In *Semiotics, Self, and Society,* ed. Benjamin Lee and Greg Urban, 27–51. Berlin: Mouton de Gruyter.

Urciuoli, Bonnie. 1991. "The Political Topography of Spanish and English: The View from a Puerto Rican Neighborhood." *American Ethnologist* 18 (2): 295–310.

———. 1995. "Language and Borders." *Annual Review of Anthropology* 24: 525–546.

———. 1996. *Exposing Prejudice: Puerto Rican Experiences of Language, Race, and Class.* Boulder: Westview.

Urla, Jaqueline. 1993. "Cultural Politics in an Age of Statistics: Numbers, Nations, and the Making of Basque Identity." *American Ethnologist* 20 (4): 818–843.

Vaish, Viniti. 2008. *Biliteracy and Globalization: English Language Education in India.* Clevedon: Multilingual Matters.

Verma, M. 1994. "English in Indian Education." In *Second Language Acquisition: Socio-cultural and Linguistic Aspects of English in India,* ed. R.K. Agnihotri and A.L. Khanna, 105–129. New Delhi: Sage Publications.

Viswanathan, Gauri. 1989. *Masks of Conquest: Literary Study and British Rule in India.* New York: Columbia University Press.

———. 1992. "English in a Literate Society." In *The Lie of the Land: English Literary Studies in India,* ed. Rajeswari Rajan, 29–41. Delhi: Oxford University Press.

———. 2007. "Literacy and Conversion in the Discourse of Hindu Nationalism." In *The Crisis of Secularism in India,* ed. Anuradha Needham and Rajeswari Sunder Rajan, 333–355. Durham: Duke University Press.

Wadley, Susan. 1994. *Struggling with Destiny in Karimpur, 1925-1984.* Berkeley: University of California Press.

Washbrook, David. 1991. "'To Each a Language of His Own': Language, Culture, and Society in Colonial India." In *Language, History, and Class,* ed. Penelope Corfield, 179–203. Oxford: Basil Blackwell.

Weber, Jean Jacques. 2008. "Safetalk Revisited, or: Language and Ideology in Luxembourgish Educational Policy." *Language and Education* 22 (2): 155–169.

Wilce, James. 1998a. "The Kalimah in the Kaleidophone: Ranges of Multivocality in Bangladeshi Muslim's Discourses." *Ethos* 26 (2): 229–257.

———. 1998b. *Eloquence in Trouble: The Poetics and Politics of Complaint in Rural Bangladesh.* Oxford: Oxford University Press.

Willis, Paul. 1977. *Learning to Labor: How Working Class Kids Get Working Class Jobs.* New York: Columbia University Press.

———. 2003. "Cultural Production and Theories of Reproduction." In *Culture: Critical Concepts in Sociology,* ed. Chris Jenks, 178–202. London: Routledge.

Woolard, Kathryn. 1985. "Language Variation and Cultural Hegemony: Toward an Integration of Sociolinguistic and Social Theory." *American Ethnologist* 12 (4): 738–748.

———. 1989. "Sentences in the Language Prison: The Rhetorical Structuring of an American Language Policy Debate." *American Ethnologist* 16 (2): 268–278.

———. 1998. "Introduction: Language Ideology as a Field of Inquiry." In *Language Ideologies: Practice and Theory,* ed. B. Schieffelin, K. Woolard, and P. Kroskrity, 3–50. New York: Oxford University Press.

———. 1999. "Simultaneity and Bivalency as Strategies in Bilingualism." *Journal of Linguistic Anthropology* 8: 3–29.

Woolard, Kathryn, and Bambi Schieffelin. 1994. "Language Ideology." *Annual Review of Anthropology* 23: 55–82.

Wortham, Stanton. 2003a. "Accomplishing Identity in Participant-Denoting Discourse." *Journal of Linguistic Anthropology* 13 (2): 189–210.

———. 2003b. "Linguistic Anthropology of Education: An Introduction." In *Linguistic Anthropology of Education,* ed. Stanton Wortham and Betsy Rymes, 1–29. Westport, CT: Praeger.

Zurbuchen, Mary. 1992. "Wiping Out English." *Seminar* 391: 47–54.

Index

Figure 16. Students head home after school.